DEBRETT'S
CORRECT FORM

Other Debrett's titles

Debrett's New Guide to Etiquette and Modern Manners
(John Morgan)
Debrett's Wedding Guide (Jacqueline Llewelyn-Bowen)
*Debrett's Guide to Tracing Your Family Tree
(Noel Currer-Briggs and Royston Gambier)

*Published September 1999

DEBRETT'S
CORRECT FORM

HEADLINE

Copyright © 1999 Debrett's Peerage Limited
Debrett Trade Mark copyright © 1999 Debrett's Peerage Limited

The right of Debrett's to be identified as the Author of
the Work has been asserted by them in accordance with
the Copyright, Designs and Patents Act 1988.

First published in 1999
by HEADLINE BOOK PUBLISHING

10 9 8 7 6 5 4 3 2 1

British Library Cataloguing in Publication Data

Debrett's correct form
1. Forms of address 2. Etiquette
I. Debrett's Peerage (Firm) II. Correct form
395.4

ISBN 0 7472 2330 0

Typeset by Avon Dataset Ltd, Bidford-on-Avon, Warks

Printed and bound in Great Britain by
Mackays of Chatham PLC, Chatham, Kent

HEADLINE BOOK PUBLISHING
A division of Hodder Headline PLC
338 Euston Road
London NW1 3BH

CONTENTS

ACKNOWLEDGEMENTS

This book is a revision and rewrite of the original *Correct Form* by Patrick Montague-Smith (1920–86), first published in 1970. For nearly thirty years this book has been the seminal work on the wide range of forms of address used in the UK, and we hope this new version does justice to his original.

Our thanks to:
Lt Kennelly of the Royal Marines; Col (Retd) J W S Trelawny of the Guards' Division; Maj (Retd) D M Wilson of the QARANC Association; Mrs Debbie Branton of QARNNS; Sq Ldr D E M Stewart, RAF, of RAF Cranwell; Sq Ldr Pippa Ward of PMRAFNS; George Griffin, Esq, PR Office, The Army; Mrs J Young, Royal College of Surgeons; Miss Jenny Kaye at the Department of Health; Mr Tim Noakes, ACPO; Ms Gillian Pole, British Airline Pilots' Association; Ms Alison Miles, Vice-Chancellor's Office, University of Oxford; Geoffrey Skelsey, Esq, Vice-Chancellor's Office, University of Cambridge; Ms Penelope Lisles, Australian High Commission; Miss Morris, FCO Protocol Department; Ms Anne Stewart, Canadian High Commission; Miss A G V Piper, Association of Lord-Lieutenants; Ms Jackie Lindsay, Privy Council Office; Ms Laura Gilbert, Chamber of Shipping; D C White, National Secretary, NUMAST; Ms Sylvia Jakeman; Hacketts Ltd; The Wren Press; Malachi Smyth, Esq; Daniel Hall, Esq; Miss Fiona Robertson; Miss Emma Humphreys; Mr and Mrs David Roberts; Miss Janet Collins; Charles Kidd, Esq; David Williamson, Esq; Rolf Kurt, Esq; John Wheatley, Esq; Nick Jotischky, Esq; Alistair Graham, Esq; Miss Jessica Hailstone.

INTRODUCTION

by Celestria Noel

We all get computer-generated post every day, often addressed to the oddest versions of our names. Now computers are very clever, but they prefer these things to be standardised – first name, middle initial, last name and not too many characters. They can just about manage gender, though they frequently get it wrong, but more complex styles and titles are apparently beyond them. It is just because so many of us are bombarded on a daily basis with so much junk mail that it is important for real correspondence to be addressed correctly. Picking up a letter from the doormat and finding it right in every particular is a rare pleasure. A business letter properly addressed to the recipient is going to make a far better impression than one that gets the form of address wrong. If you are asking for help or a charitable donation in the form of a 'personalised' letter, it may make all the difference to the appeal going straight into the bin. To get the recipient's name and form of address wrong in a personal letter is plain rude.

But, you moan, this is so complicated: names and titles are impossible to get right. How do you find out what to call people? The answer is to use *Correct Form*, an invaluable tool that has been brought up to date by the *Debrett's* team and is now simpler than ever to use. But, you go on, defensively this time: surely nowadays no one cares about all that? You'd be surprised. Even people who claim to love informality may not take kindly to being addressed incorrectly when it comes to their own style or title. Getting things right shows that you have bothered to take the trouble. Then there is the small matter of accuracy. Minute differences in titles, which may seem too trivial to bother about, can differentiate between two people with very similar names. 'Lady Anne Smith', for example, is the daughter of an Earl and married to Mr James Smith. 'Lady Smith' is the wife of Sir James Smith, 'Anne, Lady Smith' would be the ex-wife or widow of Sir James, while the Rt Hon Lady Smith of Gilmorehill is Elizabeth, the widow of John Smith, the former leader of the Labour Party. An Hon is not the same as a Right Hon and even the most right-on may need to know this.

Indeed, contrary to what many people seem to imagine, there are still rules, which are there to make things clearer, and do in fact do so when properly applied. Mistakes are so commonplace that many titled people are ruefully resigned to being called almost anything; one friend of mine, whose name and title are, admittedly, quite complicated, has made some of the funniest examples she has received into a collage for the wall of her downstairs loo. However, if you want your letter to be taken seriously or your invitation to be correctly worded, which most of us do, then you should take the trouble to look it up. Getting it wrong always looks bad, whomever you are writing to, while when writing to members of the Royal Family or holders of certain offices it becomes essential to get it right; you should wish to do so for your own satisfaction as well as from respect and good manners. Getting letters after a name wrong can be particularly insulting, as these are usually abbreviations of honours or degrees, hard earned and much valued. They should be used correctly and in the correct order. A book like this is invaluable as the subject is complex even for those who are experts.

You may think you are unlikely to come across many titled people in either your business or private life, but titles are far more widespread than you might imagine. You may never meet the Knight of Glin or have tea with the Archbishop of Canterbury, but what of doctors, professors, judges, vicars or holders of military rank? Do not forget that Mr and Mrs are titles, and when should you use Esquire?

And what of Ms? The position of women in society is the thing that has changed most since the late Patrick Montague-Smith compiled his edition of *Correct Form*, which this new edition replaces. We had a female monarch then, as now, but we have also had a woman Prime Minister (in case no one had noticed), a woman Director of Public Prosecutions, a woman Speaker of the House of Commons, a woman head of MI5 and several women Leaders of the House of Lords. Many women use a professional name: perhaps their maiden name or their married name from an earlier marriage; it may be a title, a stage name or a pen name. Some anomalous-sounding situations can now exist, partly because while women take their husband's title men do not take their wife's. Far more women use two names: for instance, a business name and a married name. Others insist on the use of their professional name at all times and never use their husband's name. This can cause confusion over children's last names, and many a doughty feminist submits to being called Mrs So-and-So by her child's teacher.

In many ways the whole matter of how to address people is more complicated nowadays than it was when more formal rules were applied universally. One recent correspondent to the *Daily Telegraph* said that when he replied to letters from women signed simply J Smith he had to ring their offices to find out whether or not they were Mrs or Miss. One, a social worker, told him that in her department they did not deal in titles of any sort. Although this may be an extreme example, it is symptomatic of a bigger phenomenon. At one time all married women called themselves by their husband's name. The wife of Mr John Smith was Mrs John Smith. The most famous example of this was the actress Mrs Patrick Campbell, called Mrs Pat by her intimates. Who remembers what her first name was? Now, however, most women are known by their own first names. Indeed, I was asked recently why Princess Michael of Kent uses a man's name. The person asking me genuinely had no grasp of the concept of taking your husband's first name.

Not wishing to be known by a man's name has even spread to nuns. Many used to take a male saint's name as their name in religion, so you had Mother John or Sister Mark. Now they are more often known by their own Christian names – Mother Clare, Sister Frances. To call yourself Mrs Susan Smith rather than Mrs John Smith used to imply that you were divorced. A widow should, technically, continue to call herself Mrs John Smith, to differentiate her status from that of a divorcee. However, more and more women ignore this rule, and it can no longer be taken as an indication that the person is divorced when she is known by her own first name and not that of her husband. It was pointed out to me that the Lord-Lieutenant of Hampshire was gazetted as Mrs Mary Fagan by Downing Street but more correctly referred to in the Court Circular as Mrs Christopher Fagan. I would recommend that the distinction be adhered to on formal social occasions. On a wedding invitation, for instance, the distinction can show that the invitation comes from both parents, who may be either still married or divorced or perhaps specifically from a father and stepmother. In cases such as this correct usage becomes not just desirable but meaningful and significant.

However, usage does change, and this new edition of *Correct Form* takes care to reflect that change. Forms of address are not immutable. In the time of Jane Austen the elder daughter was Miss Bennett and the younger ones Miss Elizabeth, Miss Lydia and so on. A tiny part of the plot of *Pride and Prejudice* turns on this very point. This difference has completely gone out now, though it is still correct in theory. Several other rules are still in force but not always used. The role of this book is to show proper forms of address and their usage, but the world is increasingly informal and sometimes there is no alternative but to ask a person what style he or she prefers. The guidance offered herein is aimed at showing what is correct, but the essence of good manners, based on genuine consideration, is to make people feel comfortable, rather than to wrong-foot them, so if someone habitually uses a form of address which is not technically correct you should abide by their decision (unless, of course, they are making a fraudulent claim to a title or honours). There is also the question of age. Older people may object to being addressed incorrectly or too informally. Nurses have noted that many elderly patients in hospital do not like strangers to automatically address them by their first name. On the other hand some younger holders of courtesy titles are bashful and confused about using them and would consider it pompous to be over-particular on the subject. The professional 'Miss', used by women in the workplace even when married, seems to be on the decline, except in the theatre. Some women may now use Ms, but others prefer just first and last name, especially when their name may also be the name of their business. 'Mr' is still used in horse racing to differentiate between amateur and professional riders, but some jockeys have objected to being addressed by their last names only by the racecourse stewards in disciplinary hearings. Professional sports personalities are referred to by their last names alone when, say, the England team is announced, but socially would be called Mr, Mrs or Miss. Even public schoolboys are less frequently addressed by last name alone, while the practice of men, who know one another well, writing 'My Dear Holmes, My Dear Watson' has almost vanished. On the other hand journalists often refer to a women by her full name in an article when first mentioned and thereafter by last name alone. One woman told me she objected to this on the grounds that it made her sound like the defendant in a courtroom. There are, of course, one or two women universally known by a first name alone: Madonna, for instance.

Another big change since the publication of the last new edition of *Correct Form* has been in the use of the formal style, which is now almost obsolete. When did you last receive a letter in which the sender begged to be, madam, your most humble and obedient servant? A few old-fashioned companies still take a pride in using these forms, and they are still correct, but 'Dear Sir' or 'Dear Madam' and 'Yours faithfully' are accepted almost universally now. There are one or two exceptions, and these are mentioned in the book. However, Dear Sir/

Madam is to be avoided if you wish to make your letter seem at all personal, and I deplore 'Dear Jane Smith'.

You can indicate how you wish to be addressed by giving your name at the top of your letter, and doing so is very helpful. It should ensure that at least the envelope is addressed correctly, but there can still be problems. For instance, the Countess of Gainsborough is fine for the envelope, but a letter should begin 'Dear Lady Gainsborough'. A person may be the Hon Edward Noel and have his name as such on his correspondence card, but on an invitation, say, his name should be given simply as Mr. Even when you have all this right, still the question remains of what you should call people face to face, which is not entirely straightforward either. To make matters worse there is the pronunciation of some unusual surnames. This book contains a comprehensive list, but again this is an area where things are changing and more names are being pronounced as spelled. Compton seems to be gaining ground from Cumpton. Althorp was pronounced as spelled by many commentators at the time of the death of Diana, Princess of Wales, but *Correct Form* still gives the pronunciation as All-trup, as that is what the family use. I have noticed that younger members of the Cecil family pronounce it as spelled rather than Cicil. My mother always says Seamer for Seymour, but Seemore is taking over. Again, it seems to be a generational difference.

At times we must envy the French, who may use Monsieur and Madame almost universally. However, part of the joy of our complex British system of names and titles is the historical aspect. The world would be a duller place without some of our arcane styles and titles, some of which go back to the Middle Ages. While they do still exist, it makes sense to endeavour to use them properly, however difficult. A Duchess may be addressed as Duchess, but a Countess should be called Lady Gainsborough to her face, whereas a foreign Countess may be addressed as 'Countess'. The question of whether or not countries that are republics, such as France, should or actually do still use titles is a thorny one. Sometimes it seems that there are more European titles being bandied around today than there were before the First World War, when most of the countries in question were monarchies. This is curious in the light of the fact that generally we are supposed to be living in a far more egalitarian age. Strictly speaking, such titles should be used sparingly in this country, but caution must be applied if you do not wish to offend. A short guide to the use of foreign titles is included in this book.

Judicious use of *Debrett's Correct Form* should help you issue your invitation and greet your guests correctly, but the next hazard may be where to seat them. Order of precedence has an old-fashioned ring, but in certain areas – civic and diplomatic functions, for instance – fixed rules may apply rather than mere common sense and thoughtfulness, as might prevail at a private gathering. Tables of order of precedence are given here in some detail and are very useful in specific circumstances. Again, as with the order of letters after a name, no one can be expected to hold such information in their heads. There is also a handy section on how to apply for vouchers or tickets to certain social and sporting events. Applications to the Royal Enclosure are one of the now comparatively rare letters always written in the third person, and the wording is quite specific and should be followed.

Luckily, everything you need to know about how to address people can be found between the covers of this book. If those who feed computers with information for mailshots would only keep it to hand, even your next junk-mail offer might be addressed correctly.

GENERAL INSTRUCTIONS

Letter Headings

It avoids confusion if a sender always includes his or her preferred style at the top of a letter above the address, including name and appropriate letters. Replies are often wrongly addressed because the writer has no idea of the appropriate letters to use. Even when the information can be obtained from other sources, doing so takes time and trouble. It also makes clear whether to use Miss, Mrs or Ms Henry Johnson rather than Mrs Catherine Johnson or Mrs C M Johnson. Including Esq or Mr is unnecessary, and can look pretentious, and it is always better to say, for example, John Woodward, MVO, so that the correspondent can easily add the Esq.

This system has many advantages over printing the name under the signature, which only facilitates the deciphering of handwriting, because it is not customary to include a title or letters after the name here.

Beginning a Letter

The writer has to decide whether to use a formal or social form of address. Using the very formal forms of address is unusual, but the writer may occasionally feel this is appropriate. If a letter is written in a more social style, the writer should respond in the same way.

The very formal style of beginning a letter 'Sir' or 'Madam', taking the place of 'Dear Sir' or 'Dear Madam', is rare unless writing to the editor of a newspaper.

The friendly and affectionate style of inserting 'My' before 'Dear' may be adopted if the writer feels that a warmer tone is appropriate. This is not included in the examples to keep them as simple as possible.

The inclusion of both forename and surname is a well-established practice for business purposes and is frequently adopted as half-way between the familiarity of just using the forename and the more formal use of the surname: for example, 'Dear Mary Robinson'. This form is tremendously useful and perfectly acceptable in a business environment where informality is on the increase and avoids spending time enquiring about a woman's preferred style.

Ending a Letter
Formal
Very formal styles of ending letters have become almost obsolete, except for occasional use of the following:

> I remain (or I am), Your Grace, Most Reverend Sir, Right Reverend Sir, Your Excellency, My Lord, My Lord Mayor, Mr Mayor, Mr President, Mr Chairman, Sir, Madam etc.
> Yours faithfully (or Yours truly)

> but it is more usual and simple to say,

> Yours faithfully (or Yours truly)

Always finish a letter the way you start it. If you start Dear Mr Surname, then sign off with your full name. The adverb you use with 'Yours' depends on the level of formality and familiarity of the text of your letter.

The use of 'Yours truly' or 'Yours very truly' has declined in recent years and is now rare.

Social
Yours sincerely (or Yours very sincerely)

Very Formal Forms of Address
This very formal style is now very rarely used and is included mainly for historical interest. Such a formal form of address is still a much simpler version of what was once in vogue, when there was an elaborate scale of 'Most devoted and most obedient', 'Most obedient', 'Most humble and devoted', 'Most humble and obedient' etc. and numerous other complicated styles with 'Most' omitted.

When the ending 'I have the honour to be' or 'remain' is used, the second line of 'My Lord Duke', 'My Lord', 'Sir' or 'Madam' etc. is sometimes omitted:

> I have the honour to be (or to remain),
> . . . (appropriate title),
> Your (Grace's/Lordship's/Ladyship's) obedient servant

Form of Address of Family Members of a Deceased Member of the Peerage before the Funeral

When a peer, peeress in her own right or Baronet dies, it is customary for letters written to members of his (or her) family to be addressed by the titles or styles by which they were previously known until after the funeral has taken place.

Consequently, a letter of sympathy to the eldest son of the late Lord Rugeley, written before his father's funeral, should be addressed to the Hon John Rugeley, even though he has succeeded his father as Lord Rugeley.

For this reason, members of the family are described at the funeral as they were previously known, whereas at a memorial service some days later they are referred to by their new titles and styles.

This custom is followed by courtesy even when the successor to the title is only remotely related to the deceased, and the two families may have had little or no contact with each other.

Official Lists

As a general rule, the form used on an official or similar list should be as for addressing an envelope, except that if the list is in alphabetical order the name can come first. For example:

> Baxter, Admiral Sir George, KCB, DSO
> Baxter, Lady
> Beecher, Edward J, MP
> Beecher, Mrs Edward
> Bilston, The Very Reverend John, KCVO, DD
> Bilston, Mrs John
> Bosham, The Right Hon the Earl of, PC
> Bosham, The Right Hon the Countess of
> Brook, The Right Hon Richard, MP
> Bullion, Colonel P R, MC, JP, DL
> Bullion, Mrs P R
> Burton, the Worshipful the Mayor of

Correspondence with Firms

Whenever possible, correspondence is addressed to an individual member of a firm, either by his or her name or by appointment, such as

The Chairman, The Managing Director, The Secretary or The Manager.

Begin a letter Dear Sir/Madam, although it is always better to find out the name of the person you should be writing to.

Multiple Surnames

Usually, people with double-barrelled names use both names, and those with triple-barrelled names the final name only: for example, the Douglas-Homes use both names, whereas the Twisleton-Wykeham-Fiennes are generally known as Fiennes, and the Montagu Douglas Scotts as Scott.

There are exceptions, and the practice varies according to the individual's wishes. Sometimes the use of all the surnames is restricted to formal occasions, such as wedding announcements and legal documents, and then usually all the surnames are placed on the envelope. If the preferred style is not known, it is not wrong to use all the surnames.

From the eighteenth century onwards a multiple surname was often acquired by Royal Licence. When a member of a family marries an heiress who bears arms, and he (or a descendant) desires to commemorate her surname in addition to his own, it is necessary to have the Sovereign's permission to make the change. In the UK a change of name is not regulated, and your surname is the name by which you are commonly known. However, a deed poll is usually required as legal proof of identity, and this officially records the changed name. A deed poll may be registered in the College of Arms in any appropriate case. In Scotland a change of name and arms is recognised by Lyon Court, and in other cases the Lord Lyon King of Arms issues a certificate of a change of name.

In recent years it has become fashionable in England to dispense with hyphens, a practice that probably originated in Scotland in order to place the emphasis on the final name, though a few families never adopted them. Without a hyphen, it is sometimes difficult to know whether an individual has one surname or two, especially if the signature includes an initial: for example. J Leslie Thomas. Is he Mr John Leslie Thomas or Mr Leslie Thomas who prefers to use his second forename? Should you write to 'Dear Mr Leslie Thomas' or 'Dear Mr Thomas'? If in doubt, use the two names and take careful note of any reply!

There is a distinction between a surname and a family name. In England the latter is often added to the surname to show the identity of a particular family or a branch. For example, should the surname be Smith, and in one branch most or all children are christened Abel, they are known collectively as the 'Abel Smiths'. Due to the fluid system of names in England, it often happens that some members of this family adopt the family name as an additional surname, with the result that their children no longer have this name included as their final first name.

In Wales, as surnames usually evolved from male-line first names, there are a great number of people with such surnames as Jones, Powell, Evans, Davies, Morgan and Price. This has resulted in the frequent use of an additional name for identification purposes. Sometimes this becomes a surname, and sometimes not.

For the same reason, in England and elsewhere those with a common surname, such as Smith or Brown, can acquire an additional name. This sometimes arises by tacking on a second forename, especially if derived from a surname, accelerated by the practice of using this second forename in the signature: for example, John Berkeley Brown is known by the forename of Berkeley, and he signs 'J Berkeley Brown'. People therefore call him and his wife Mr and Mrs Berkeley Brown, instead of Mr and Mrs Brown as they do for his brother Mr George Brown. In course of time his children become known by the double name of Berkeley-Brown.

Divorced women sometimes combine their married name and maiden name in a similar fashion.

Legal Documents

Peers and peeresses (in their own right, and wives and widows of peers) are accorded their full formal styles with their forenames but with no surname:

> The Most Noble Charles John, Duke of Blank
> The Most Noble Anne Frances, Duchess of Blank
> The Most Honourable Charles John, Marquess (of) Blank
> The Most Honourable Anne Frances, Marchioness (of) Blank
> The Right Honourable Charles John, Earl (of), Viscount or
> Baron Blank
> The Right Honourable Anne Frances, Countess (of) Blank,
> Viscountess or Baroness Blank

11

Peers by courtesy and their wives are not accorded the prefix 'Most Honourable' or 'Right Honourable' (unless they are members of the Privy Council). The full description is:

> John Mulgrave Esquire, commonly called Lord John Mulgrave
> Sir John Brandon Knight Bachelor, commonly called Lord Brandon
> Emily Addison Spinster, commonly called the Honourable Emily Addison

but the use of the courtesy title only, such as John George, Viscount Hammersmith, is generally considered to be sufficient.

Baronets are accorded 'Baronet' after the name. Knights Bachelor are accorded 'Knight Bachelor' or 'Knight' after the name.

Membership etc. of Orders of Chivalry is either spelled in full (with or without the honorific prefix of the Order, such as Knight Commander of the Most Excellent Order of the British Empire) or with the recognised abbreviations, such as KBE.

Wives and widows of Baronets and Knights are formally described as 'Dame Frances Elizabeth Smith' or as 'Mary Elizabeth, Lady Smith'. It is incorrect to place 'Lady' before the forename, as this signifies that she is the daughter of a Duke, Marquess or Earl.

Passports

Every passport includes a person's forenames as a means of identification.

Passports for peers have the appropriate abbreviated prefix before the title, which is followed by any letters that signify orders, decorations etc. The first names appear underneath. For example:

> The Rt Hon the Earl of Sonning, MC
> John Henry George

Memorials, Inscriptions and Plaques

These usually contain all the first names of a peer or peeress, with or without the appropriate prefix (The Most Hon, The Rt Hon etc.), which, if included, is usually given in full. A peer's surname and the territorial part of a peerage style may be used if desired. A peer or Baronet is sometimes numbered, particularly when a father and son had identical forenames. It is a matter for the family to decide whether orders, decorations and degrees are to be included, and, if so, which. It is also a matter of choice whether any applicable coats of arms are to be displayed. If there is any doubt about their accuracy, reference should be made to the College of Arms or, for Scottish families, to the Lord Lyon King of Arms.

THE ROYAL FAMILY

THE ROYAL FAMILY

Nearly 300 years ago Queen Anne and her great friend and confidante Sarah, Duchess of Marlborough, formed the habit of addressing each other both verbally and in writing as 'Mrs Freeman' (the Duchess) and 'Mrs Morley' (The Queen). It was the only way they could avoid the strict formality of address, which would otherwise have been inevitable. Today, things are more relaxed, although it is still correct to address the Sovereign and members of the Royal Family who enjoy the style of 'Royal Highness' in a formal style. This should be employed by all except close relatives or close friends who have been instructed to do otherwise. Times are changing swiftly, however, and it may well be that before we reach the middle of the twenty-first century only the Sovereign, the widow or widower of a Sovereign, and the heir apparent will still be accorded the distinctions of such formality.

The Sovereign
Except from personal friends, all communications should be addressed to 'the Private Secretary to Her Majesty The Queen'. These letters should ask him or her to 'submit for Her Majesty's consideration (or approval) . . .'; ask 'if Her Majesty's attention may be directed to'; or suggest that 'it may interest Her Majesty to know that . . .' etc.

Such a letter should be addressed to the holder of the office and not by name, but subsequent correspondence should be sent to the actual writer of the reply, who may be a Lady-in-Waiting. The letter is a straightforward one, commencing 'Dear Sir or Madam', but the first reference to The Queen should be 'Her Majesty', and thereafter 'The Queen'. The phrase 'Her Majesty' should be substituted for 'She' and 'Her Majesty's' for 'Her'.

For those who wish to communicate directly with The Queen, the following style is used.

Beginning of Letter
    Madam, or
    May it please Your Majesty

In the body of the letter 'Your Majesty' should be substituted for 'You' and 'Your Majesty's' for 'Your'.

Ending of Letter
> I have the honour to remain (or to be), Madam,
> Your Majesty's most humble and obedient servant

Envelope
> Her Majesty The Queen or, for formal or state documents only,
> The Queen's Most Excellent Majesty

Verbal Address
'Your Majesty' on first speaking, then 'Ma'am'. This should always rhyme with 'Pam'. Pronunciation to rhyme with 'Palm' has not been correct for some generations. See also Presentation to The Queen, below.

Description in Conversation
Her Majesty or The Queen, as applicable

Presentation to The Queen
On presentation, and on leaving, a bow (from the head only, not from the waist) or curtsy is generally made, but The Queen has let it be known that this is no longer to be considered essential. In conversation with The Queen, the guidelines mentioned under Verbal Address (above) apply. 'Your Majesty' should be substituted for 'You'. References to other members of the Royal Family are made to 'His/Her Royal Highness' or the appropriate title (The Duke of Edinburgh, for instance, or The Prince of Wales). When presenting another person to The Queen, it is necessary only to state the name of the person to be introduced: that is, 'May I present . . ., Your Majesty?'

Official Speeches
At official functions a speech should start 'May it please Your Majesty'. Either 'Your Majesty' or 'Ma'am' may be used during the speech.

Loyal Message
The following is the usual style for a loyal message from an organisation on some special occasion:

On the occasion of the (centenary dinner) of the Society of . . . to be held at . . . on . . . the President with humble duty has the honour to submit loyal greetings to Her Majesty The Queen from all who will be present.

The message should be addressed to the Private Secretary to The Queen, and should be sent in sufficient time before the occasion to allow for a gracious reply.

Queen Elizabeth The Queen Mother
The same instructions as for the Sovereign apply, with 'Queen Elizabeth The Queen Mother' substituted for 'The Queen'.

Other Members of the Royal Family
Unless the writer is known personally to the Prince, Princess, Duke etc. concerned, it is the usual practice to write to the Equerry, Private Secretary, or Lady-in-Waiting of the particular member of the Royal Family.

These letters should be addressed to the holder of the office and not by name, but subsequent correspondence should be sent to the actual writer of the reply.

The letter is a straightforward one, commencing '(Dear) Sir' or '(Dear) Madam', but reference for the first time to the particular member of the Royal Family should be written 'His (Her) Royal Highness' and subsequently 'the Duke of . . .', 'Prince . . .' or 'Princess . . .' as applicable. The phrase 'His (Her) Royal Highness' should be substituted for 'He (She)' as far as possible without peppering the letter with formal descriptions, as was done in the past and making it sound very stilted. Likewise 'His (Her) Royal Highness's' for 'His (Her)'.

If the writer wants to communicate directly with a member of the Royal Family using the prefix His (or Her) Royal Highness, the style given below is used. Orders of Chivalry are now accorded as post-nominal letters to members of the Royal Family, with the exception of The Queen and Queen Elizabeth The Queen Mother.

Beginning of Letter
    Sir, (Madam,)

In the body of the letter 'Your Royal Highness' should be substituted for 'You' and 'Your Royal Highness's' for 'Your'.

Ending of Letter
> I have the honour to remain (or to be), Sir (Madam),
> Your Royal Highness's most humble and obedient servant

Envelope
'His (Her) Royal Highness', followed on the next line by the name:

> The Duke of Edinburgh
> The Prince of Wales
> The Duke of York
> The Prince Edward
> The Princess Royal
> The Princess Margaret, Countess of Snowdon
> Princess Alice, Duchess of Gloucester
> The Duke of Gloucester
> The Duchess of Gloucester
> The Duke of Kent
> The Duchess of Kent
> Prince Michael of Kent
> Princess Michael of Kent
> Princess Alexandra, the Hon Lady Ogilvy

Children of a Sovereign are styled 'The' before 'Prince/Princess'. Members of the Royal Family, apart from the Sovereign's children, who are not peers are addressed according to their particular branch of the Royal Family: for example, 'His Royal Highness Prince Michael of Kent'. The 'of Kent' is included in all written forms, envelopes, invitations etc.

Wives of Princes have a style similar to their husbands: for example, 'Her Royal Highness Princess Michael of Kent'.

Verbally
'Your Royal Highness' for the first time, subsequently 'Sir' (or 'Ma'am'). Pronunciation should be an ordinary 'Sir', or 'Ma'am' to rhyme with 'Pam'. Sire or Ma'am to rhyme with 'Palm' are archaic and not now used.

Presentation to a Member of the Royal Family
On presentation and on leaving, a bow or curtsy may be made, but see above under Presentation to The Queen. The method ranges from the formal to a more informal style. The formal system was the invariable practice in the past and should follow that described under Presentation to The Queen, with, of course, the substitution of 'Your Royal Highness' for 'Your Majesty' and subsequently 'Sir' or 'Ma'am' (to rhyme with 'Pam'). Some members of the Royal Family prefer a more informal method, particularly those of the younger generation.

If there is any doubt concerning which degree of formality is preferred by a particular Prince or Princess etc., reference should be made to the respective Private Secretary, Equerry or Lady-in-Waiting.

Even when the more informal method is adopted, a member of the Royal Family should always be addressed in conversation as 'Your Royal Highness' for the first time, and subsequently as 'Sir' or 'Ma'am', and references to other members of the Royal Family as Her Majesty or His/Her Royal Highness or more informally by their title: the Duke of Kent or Prince Michael, for instance. When presenting another person to a member of the Royal Family, it is necessary only to state the name of the person to be introduced: that is, 'May I present . . ., Your Royal Highness?'

Official Speeches
At official functions a speech should start 'Your Royal Highness(es)'. 'Sir' or 'Ma'am' may be used during the speech.

Her Majesty's Household
The Queen Regnant and The Queen Dowager each appoint a Mistress-of-the-Robes, Ladies-of-the-Bedchamber and Women-of-the-Bed-chamber. By custom, the Mistress-of-the-Robes is usually a Duchess. The present Mistress-of-the-Robes to The Queen is the Duchess of Grafton, but The Queen Mother has not appointed a Mistress-of-the-Robes since the death in 1990 of the last holder, the Dowager Duchess of Abercorn. The others take consecutive turns of duty and are generally known as 'Ladies-in-Waiting'. This duty is usually of a fortnight's duration. The commencement of a tour of duty is notified in the Court Circular in *The Times* and the *Daily Telegraph* that . . . has succeeded . . . as Lady-in-Waiting. The Mistress-of-the-Robes and Ladies-of-the-Bedchamber normally accompany The Queen or

The Queen Mother only on State or other important occasions.

Ladies-in-Waiting are appointed to the members of the Royal Family who are Royal Highnesses. All these Ladies are members of Her Majesty's or other Royal Households. The Ladies should be addressed according to their own rank.

The Queen's Household is headed by three Great Officers – the Lord Chamberlain, the Lord Steward and the Master of the Horse – and is organised into separate departments, which are briefly mentioned below.

The Lord Chamberlain

The Lord Chamberlain is Head of The Queen's Household and supervises all ceremonies, except such State functions as a Coronation, Opening of Parliament or a State Funeral, which are arranged by the Earl Marshal, and a State Banquet, which is arranged by the Lord Steward. The Lord Chamberlain supervises all The Queen's functions except those of a domestic category.

Consequently, on Her Majesty's behalf he organises and sends out invitations to such functions as a Garden Party. He also administers the Ecclesiastical and Medical Households and makes such appointments as the Librarian of Windsor Castle, Keeper of the Jewel House of the Tower of London, the Master of the Queen's Music (formerly spelt 'Musick') and the Poet Laureate.

The Lord Steward

The Lord Steward is in technical control of all The Queen's domestic arrangements and personally is in charge of State Banquets, for which he sends out invitations on Her Majesty's behalf, supervises the function and presents the guests. Day-to-day arrangements are exercised by the Master of the Household. He sends other invitations on Her Majesty's behalf, apart from those issued by the Lord Chamberlain.

The Master of the Horse

The Master of the Horse is responsible for The Queen's safety. At ceremonial occasions, such as The Queen's Birthday Parade, also known as Trooping the Colour, he rides immediately behind the Sovereign. In a procession such the State Opening of Parliament, his carriage immediately follows The Queen's. The Crown Equerry exercises his day-to-day functions.

Departments of the Royal Household
The departments of the Royal Household are as follows:

- The **Private Secretary's Office**, which includes the Press Secretary's Office and the Royal Archives (kept at Windsor Castle).

- The **Privy Purse and Treasurer's Office**, which includes the Royal Almony.

- The **Lord Chamberlain's Office** (at St James's Palace), which includes:
  (a) the Director of the Royal Collection and Surveyor of The Queen's Works of Art and the Surveyor of Pictures and Works of Art,
  (b) the Marshal of the Diplomatic Corps (not to be confused with the Vice-Marshal of the Diplomatic Corps, who is an official of the Foreign and Commonwealth Office) and
  (c) the Central Chancery of the Orders of Knighthood.

- The **Master of the Household's Office**.

- The **Royal Mews**.

Her Majesty has a separate Household in Scotland.

The Keeper of the Privy Purse and Treasurer to The Queen deals with all financial matters.

The Master of the Household supervises The Queen's domestic household not only at Buckingham Palace but wherever Her Majesty is resident at the time.

The Crown Equerry is the senior member of the Royal Household in the Royal Mews Department (after the Master of the Horse) and is responsible for all The Queen's travelling arrangements.

The Vice-Chamberlain of the Household is a political appointment and is appointed on the advice of the Prime Minister. He or she is a Member of Parliament and serves as a government whip. He or she submits to The Queen a daily summary of the proceedings in Parliament.

The Treasurer and the Comptroller of the Household are also political appointments in the Household. In the House of Commons they act as whips and assist Her Majesty at the State Opening of Parliament.

The Captain of the Corps of Gentlemen of Arms and the Captain of the Yeomen of the Guard are also political appointments and are government whips in the House of Lords.

The Lords-in-Waiting are members of the House of Lords. Their female counterparts are known as Baronesses-in-Waiting. By custom, two Lords-in-Waiting are non-political. The remaining five or six, who take their turn for duty for a month at a time, are appointed by the government, being junior government ministers in the House of Lords. Lords-in-Waiting perform duties for the Sovereign, such as representing her at the arrival and departure of visiting heads of state, at memorial services and on special occasions.

Members of Her Majesty's Household should be addressed according to their own rank.

Other Royal Households

Queen Elizabeth The Queen Mother has her own Household at Clarence House, with her Lord Chamberlain, Comptroller, Treasurer, Private Secretary and Equerries.

The Duke of Edinburgh's Household at Buckingham Palace includes his Treasurer and Private Secretary, and Equerries.

The Prince of Wales, The Duke of York, The Prince Edward, The Princess Royal, The Princess Margaret, Countess of Snowdon, Princess Alice, Duchess of Gloucester, the Dukes and Duchesses of Gloucester and Kent, Prince and Princess Michael of Kent, and Princess Alexandra all maintain small Households. Correspondence with these members of the Royal Family is dealt with by the Private Secretary concerned.

Members of these Households should be addressed according to their own rank.

Summary Table

Title	Envelope	Letter (to Private Secretary)	Verbal Address
Her Majesty The Queen	The Private Secretary to Her Majesty The Queen (Letters can be sent direct, but it is simpler to correspond through a Private Secretary)	Dear Sir (or Madam) initially, thereafter by name	Your Majesty, Ma'am

His Royal Highness The Duke of Edinburgh	As above	As above	Your Royal Highness, Sir
Her Majesty Queen Elizabeth The Queen Mother	As above	As above	Your Majesty, Ma'am
His Royal Highness The Prince of Wales	As above	As above	Your Royal Highness, Sir
His Royal Highness The Duke of York	As above	As above	Your Royal Highness, Sir
His Royal Highness The Prince Edward	As above	As above	Your Royal Highness, Sir
Her Royal Highness The Princess Royal	As above	As above	Your Royal Highness, Ma'am
Her Royal Highness The Princess Margaret, Countess of Snowdon	As above	As above	Your Royal Highness, Ma'am
His Royal Highness the Duke of Gloucester	As above	As above	Your Royal Highness, Sir
Her Royal Highness Princess Alice, Duchess of Gloucester	As above	As above	Your Royal Highness, Ma'am
His Royal Highness the Duke of Kent	As above	As above	Your Royal Highness, Sir
His Royal Highness Prince Michael of Kent	As above	As above	Your Royal Highness, Sir
Her Royal Highness Princess Alexandra, the Hon Lady Ogilvy	As above	As above	Your Royal Highness, Ma'am

THE PEERAGE

THE PEERAGE

The most complicated series of titles and styles concern the Peerage, which consists of the following groups:

1. Peer – one of five grades: Duke, Marquess, Earl, Viscount and Baron.

2. Peeress – Duchess, Marchioness, Countess, Viscountess and Baroness, either in her own right or the wife, widow or former wife of a peer (strictly speaking the former wife of a peer is not a peeress, but details are placed here for convenience).

3. Courtesy Lord – son and heir apparent of a Duke, Marquess and Earl and eldest son of the heir apparent.

4. Wife, widow and former wife of a Courtesy Lord.

5. The other sons of a peer with the courtesy style of 'the Lord' or 'the Honourable' before the first name, that is:
i. Younger sons of a Duke and Marquess (the Lord John Brown);
ii. Younger sons of an Earl, and all sons of a Viscount and Baron (the Honourable John Brown, abbreviated to the Hon John Brown).

6. Sons of a Courtesy Lord. They have courtesy styles that follow the same system mentioned above.

7. Wives of sons of a peer or Courtesy Lord – mentioned in group 5 (Lady John Brown or the Hon Mrs John Brown).

8. Daughters of a peer:
i. Daughter of a Duke, Marquess and Earl (Lady Mary Brown);
ii. Daughter of a Viscount and Baron (the Hon Mary Brown, if unmarried, or the Hon Mrs Brown if married).

9. Daughters of a Courtesy Lord. They follow the same system mentioned above.

Peers

There are five grades of the Peerage:

Duke

The highest rank in the Peerage was introduced into England in 1337 when King Edward III created his eldest son Duke of Cornwall. The first non-royal dukedom was created in 1448. In Scotland, the first two dukedoms were created in 1398.

Marquess

The second rank in the Peerage is derived from the German Markgraf, signifying the guardian of a March, or border territory. King Richard II introduced it into England in 1385, and it was introduced into Scotland by King James VI in 1599.

Earl

The third rank in the Peerage, but the oldest. Its origins are traced back to Saxon times, when an Ealdorman administered a shire or province for the king. The present title of Earl, derived from the Scandinavian Jarl, dates from the reign of Canute (1016–35).

Viscount

The fourth rank in the Peerage is derived from the hereditary office of Vice-Comes, that is, the deputy of a Count. King Henry VI introduced it into England in 1440.

Baron

The Normans introduced the fifth and lowest rank of the Peerage into England. A Baron was tenant-in-chief of the king, holding his land directly from him. In Scotland, the equivalent title is Lord of Parliament, as the word 'Baron' relates to Feudal Barons.

The son and heir apparent of a Duke, Marquess or Earl may by courtesy use and be known by the title of one of his father's peerage dignities of lower grade than that by which his father is known. Similarly, the eldest son of a Courtesy Lord of the grade of Marquess or Earl may by courtesy also use and be known by the title of one of his grandfather's peerage dignities, provided that it is of a lower grade than that used by the father. The Peerage, so far as oral and written forms of address are concerned, falls into two sections, each with different rules: Dukes and other peers.

Though known collectively as 'the Peerage', technically it is divided into five separate Peerages: the Peerage of England, of Scotland, of Ireland, of Great Britain and of the United Kingdom. The separate Peerages of England and Scotland continued until 1707, when the two kingdoms combined under the Act of Union. The Peerages were then united and styled the Peerage of Great Britain. From that year, the Peerage of Great Britain and the separate Peerage of Ireland existed until 1801, when Great Britain and Ireland were combined under a second Act of Union. Since 1801 the Peerage has been styled the Peerage of the United Kingdom.

The Peerage of Ireland was not entirely discountinued at the Act of Union of 1801. Creations after that date were made occasionally as a form of reward, but they do not carry the right to sit in the House of Lords (Lord Curzon of Kedleston in 1898, for example).

It is important that the description 'Peerages of Scotland and Ireland' is used only in the technical sense of creation and does not imply that a peer is a Scotsman or Irishman: Lord Fairfax of Cameron in the Peerage of Scotland and Viscount Gage in the Peerage of Ireland both belong to English families, for instance.

The Peerage of Scotland

The term Master is used by the heir apparent, the heir presumptive and, as a courtesy title, by the heir of a Courtesy Lord. See Scottish Title of Master, page 60.

The Peerage of Ireland

If an Irish peer holds a peerage dignity of a lower grade, which enables him or her to sit in the House of Lords, he or she is introduced there by the peerage, which enables him or her to sit. The Earl of Arran, for example, sits in the House as Baron Sudley, and for all other purposes he is known by his higher title, the Earl of Arran.

With a few exceptions, peers are known by the senior peerage they possess. Exceptions include the Earl Brooke and of Warwick, who is known as the Earl of Warwick, Lord Leconfield and Egremont, known as Lord Egremont, Lord Sheffield and Stanley of Alderley, known as Lord Stanley of Alderley, and Lord Trevethin and Oaksey, known as Lord Oaksey. For those who have several peerages of the same grade, the choice of style rests with the peers themselves: the Duke of Richmond, Lennox and Gordon, for instance, is known generally as the Duke of Richmond and Gordon. Some peers use both or all their peerages of the same grade, such as Lord Oranmore and Browne, while others use only one: Lord Henley and Lord Northington, for example, uses only the former, an Irish peerage, except within the House of Lords.

Title of a Peer

Every Viscount and Baron is described in Letters Patent of Creation as being of a place in the United Kingdom, followed by the appropriate county: for example, Baron Redmayne of Rushcliffe in the county of Nottingham. The place may be his residence, domicile, former constituency or some location with which there is a connection. Such description is called the 'territorial designation' and is not used except in very formal documents. A few peers have two territorial designations, of which one at least must be of a place in the United Kingdom (examples are Viscount Allenby, of Megiddo and of Felixstowe in the county of Suffolk; Baron Keyes, of Zeebrugge and of Dover in the county of Kent; Baron Wilson, of Libya and of Stowlangtoft in the county of Suffolk). Some peers have a territorial designation or placename which actually forms part of their title, such as Baron Ritchie of Dundee, Baron Russell of Liverpool and Baron Brassey of Apethorpe. Such titles must always be used in full. They are given as such in the Roll of the House of Lords.

This territorial part of the peerage title may be granted for two main reasons:

i. As a special honour: for example, Earl Mountbatten of Burma.
ii. As a method of differentiation from the title of another peer, such as Baron Erroll of Hale, to distinguish him from the holder of the Earldom of Erroll. This is particularly prevalent now that surnames are so often adopted as peerage titles. Differentiation may also be necessary if the first part of the

title chosen sounds like another existing peerage, even though the spelling may vary: for example, Baron Hylton and Baron Hilton of Upton, Baron Layton and Baron Leighton of St Mellons.

A territorial designation or placename that forms part of a peerage title has not always been that of a place in the United Kingdom (the Earl of Ypres, for instance). War leaders frequently embody the name of their battles or campaigns in their titles.

Some peerages of England and Scotland before the Union of 1707, and of Ireland before the Union of 1801, are duplicated, such as: the Earldom of Arran (Scotland), held by the Duke of Hamilton; the Earldom of Arran (Ireland); the Earldom of Carrick (Scotland), held by The Prince of Wales; the Earldom of Carrick (Ireland); the Earldom of March (England), held by the Duke of Richmond and Gordon; the Earldom of March (Scotland), held by the Earl of Wemyss and March.

Duke
Beginning of Letter

Formal	My Lord Duke
Social	Dear Duke
	Dear Duke of Hamilton may be used if the acquaintanceship is slight.

Envelope

Formal	His Grace the Duke of Hamilton
Social	The Duke of Hamilton
	Note: A few Dukes prefer to be styled 'His Grace' even in social correspondence.

Verbal Address

Formal	Your Grace
Social	Duke

When preceded by other word(s), 'The' or 'the' may be used as preferred, though the Royal Family use the former.

Description in Conversation
A Duke is always so described, unlike the four lower grades of the Peerage – Marquess, Earl, Viscount and Baron – who in speech are all called 'Lord': for example, Lord Bath.

If reference is made only to one Duke, he may be called 'the Duke'. If distinction is necessary, or on introduction, he should be referred to as 'the Duke of Ramsgate', for instance.

List of Directors and Patrons
It is optional whether the formal style (His Grace the Duke of Ramsgate) or the social style (the Duke of Ramsgate) is adopted, so long as the same style is followed for all other patrons etc. in a list. It is recommended that the social style should be used.

Formal Style
The formal style of 'the Most Noble' has given place to the more informal 'His Grace', but the former is still used occasionally in official announcements, documents and on monuments.

Membership of the Privy Council
If a Duke is a Privy Counsellor, the letters PC should be included after his title, since it would not be otherwise apparent that he holds that office. The letters PC follow any orders and decorations he may hold: for example, '(His Grace) the Duke of Dover, KCVO, CBE, PC'.

Ecclesiastical, Ambassadorial or Armed Forces Rank
These precede ducal rank, as in the Very Reverend the Duke of Ramsgate, His Excellency the Duke of Ramsgate and Major the Duke of Ramsgate.

Signature
By title only: Ramsgate, for example.

Wife of a Duke
Beginning of Letter

Formal	(Dear) Madam
Social	Dear Duchess
	Dear Duchess of Somerset may be used if the acquaintanceship is slight.

Envelope
    Formal   Her Grace the Duchess of Norfolk
    Social   The Duchess of Norfolk

Verbal Address
    Formal   Your Grace
    Social   Duchess

Description in Conversation
A Duchess is always so described, unlike the four lower grades of the Peerage, who in speech are called Lady Blank. If reference is made only to one Duchess, she may be called 'the Duchess'. If distinction is necessary, or on introduction, she should be referred to as 'the Duchess of Norfolk', for instance.

List of Directors and Patrons
It is optional whether the formal style (Her Grace the Duchess of Ramsgate) or the social style (the Duchess of Ramsgate) is adopted, so long as the same style is followed for all other patrons etc. in a list. It is recommended that the social style should be used.

Formal Style
The formal style of 'the Most Noble' has given place to the more informal 'Her Grace', but the former is still used occasionally in official announcements, documents and on monuments.

Signature
First name and title: Helen Middlesex, for example.

Widow of a Duke
Officially, the widow of a Duke is known as, say, 'the Dowager Duchess of Southampton', unless there is already a Dowager Duchess in that family still living. In the latter event, the widow of the senior Duke retains this title for life, and the widow of the junior Duke is known by her first name: for example, 'Mary, Duchess of Southampton'. The form 'the Dowager Dowager Duchess' for a senior widow is no longer used.

    Socially, many prefer to use their first name in preference to 'the Dowager Duchess of Southampton'. An announcement is often made in the press; otherwise it will be necessary to discover her wishes. If in doubt, the use of the forename is recommended.

If the present holder of the Dukedom is unmarried, socially the widow of the previous Duke does not use the term of either 'the Dowager Duchess of Southampton' or 'Mary, Duchess of Southampton' but continues to be known as 'the Duchess of Southampton'.

Should the present Duke marry, it is usual for the widowed Duchess to announce the style she wishes to adopt.

Beginning of Letter

Formal	(Dear) Madam
Social	Dear Duchess
	Dear Duchess of Middlesex may be used if the acquaintanceship is slight.

Envelope

Formal	Her Grace the Dowager Duchess of Middlesex or Her Grace Mary, Duchess of Middlesex (as applicable)
Social	The Dowager Duchess of Middlesex or Mary, Duchess of Middlesex

Verbal Address
As for Wife of a Duke, above.

Description in Conversation
As for a Duchess. If distinction from the wife of the present Duke is necessary, or on introduction, she should be described as 'the Dowager Duchess of Middlesex' or 'Mary, Duchess of Middlesex', as applicable.

List of Directors and Patrons

Formal	Her Grace the Dowager Duchess of Southampton or Her Grace Mary, Duchess of Southampton
Social	The Dowager Duchess of Southampton or Mary, Duchess of Southampton

For the choice of formal or social style, see Wife of a Duke, above.

Formal Style
As for Wife of a Duke, above.

Signature
As for Wife of a Duke, above.

Former Wife of a Duke
If a marriage to a Duke has been dissolved, his former wife continues to use her title as a Duke's wife, preceded by her forename. The continuance of her title henceforward is regarded as a name rather than the retention of the attributes and status of the wife of a peer. Accordingly, she is not entitled to the prefix of 'Her Grace'.

In Scotland, due to the difference in laws for divorce, a former wife is legally equivalent to a widow in England. On marriage, as well as adopting her husband's surname, she also retains her maiden name as an alias. Should her marriage to a Duke be dissolved and she marries again, she also retains her first husband's title as an alias. Socially, former wives of Dukes in Scotland are usually treated as former wives of Dukes in general, unless any specific ruling is announced by Lyon King of Arms.

Beginning of Letter
As for Wife of a Duke, above.

Envelope
Formal and Social   Mary, Duchess of Wiltshire

Verbal Address
Formal   (Dear) Madam
Social   Duchess

Description in Conversation
Duchess of Blankshire. If some distinction from the wife of the present Duke is necessary, she should be described as Mary, Duchess of Blankshire.

List of Directors and Patrons
Mary, Duchess of Wiltshire.

Signature
As for Wife of a Duke, above.

Remarriage
She adopts her style from her present husband: Mary, Duchess of Blankshire, for instance, marries Mr Cuthbert Jones and becomes Mrs Cuthbert Jones.

If she has a courtesy style from her father, she will revert to this on remarriage. For example, if Lady Mary Brown marries first the Duke of Blankshire and secondly Mr John Green, on her second marriage she is known as Lady Mary Green. Similarly, if the Hon Mary Brown marries first the Duke of Blankshire and secondly Mr John Green, she becomes the Hon Mrs Green.

Marquess, Earl, Viscount and Baron

Peers of the grades of Marquess, Earl, Viscount and Baron are all referred to in conversation as Lord Blank. The use of their exact rank is socially incorrect, unless for some reason it has to be specifically mentioned. It is, however, used on envelopes, visiting cards and invitations. The only exception to this general rule is at a formal function, when the exact peerage title may be given at the first mention of a peer, but he is usually subsequently referred to, or invited to speak, as 'Lord Blank'.

The fifth grade of the peerage, a Baron, is never referred to by this title except in legal or formal documents, but always as Lord Gretton, for example, both verbally and in correspondence. In the peerage of Scotland, the term 'Lord' (Lord of Parliament) is the legal term of the fifth grade in the peerage, because the term 'Baron' is used in a feudal sense relating to land tenure. The use of 'Baron' is restricted to a foreign title which is never translated as 'Lord Braunvon Cramm'.

Beginning of Letter

Formal	My Lord
Social	Dear Lord Tweeddale

The official spelling of this title is 'Marquess', and this is adopted in the Roll of the House of Lords. Some newspapers spell the word 'Marquis', as for the title in France. In the past, when spelling was not standardised, both forms were adopted in Britain. Some Scottish

Marquesses, in memory of the 'Auld Alliance' with France, prefer to use the French spelling.

Envelope

Formal	The Most Hon the Marquess of Tweeddale
	The Rt Hon the Earl of Gainsborough
	The Rt Hon the Viscount of Falkland
	The Rt Hon the Lord Gretton
Social	The Marquess of Tweeddale
	The Earl of Gainsborough
	The Viscount of Falkland
	The Lord Gretton

Description of a Peer within a Letter, Article etc.
The first formal reference to a peer is usually made to the exact rank. Subsequent references to a peer of all these four grades may be made to Lord Tweeddale, Lord Falkland etc.

References to these peers in social letters usually do not quote the exact rank but give the style of Lord: for example, Lord Tweeddale, not the Marquess of Tweeddale.

Verbal Address

Formal	My Lord
Social	Lord Tweeddale

Description in Conversation
Lord Gainsborough etc. This style applies to all four grades of the Peerage.

List of Directors and Patrons
It is optional whether one adopts the formal style (for example, the Most Hon the Marquess of Findon or the Rt Hon the Earl of Storrington) or the social style (for example, the Marquess of Findon or the Earl of Storrington), as long as the same style is followed for all other patrons etc. in the list. It is recommended that the social style should be used.

Membership of the Privy Council
If a peer is a Privy Counsellor, the letters PC should be included after his name, orders and decorations, since it would not otherwise be apparent that he holds that office. A Marquess still has the prefix or

formal style of Most Hon, and an Earl, Viscount and Baron all have the prefix or formal style of Rt Hon, which is also the attribute of a Privy Counsellor. (See The Privy Council, page 79.)

Ecclesiastical, Ambassadorial or Armed Forces Rank
These precede a peer's rank in correspondence, as in His Excellency the Earl of Storrington, the Rev Canon the Viscount Washington and Major the Lord Ashington.

Signature
By title only: Washington, for example.

Style from Sources other than the Crown
It is not customary in formal usage to combine the style emanating from other sources with titles conferred by the Sovereign. 'Alderman the Lord Jones' and 'Professor the Lord Smith' are solecisms. In social usage this is not uncommon, but deprecated by purists.

Life Peer and Life Peeress
A life peer or peeress and a Law Lord and his wife have exactly the same style and attributes as a hereditary peer.

Children of life peers or peeresses and Law Lords have the same courtesy styles as the children of a hereditary peer. They continue to bear these for life.

Peeress in Her own Right
At present, all peeresses in their own right are either Countesses or Baronesses. In the Peerage of Scotland the term Lady (Lady of Parliament) is the legal term of the fifth grade of the Peerage because the term 'Baroness' is used in a feudal sense relating to land tenure. All peeresses in their own right, whether their peerage is hereditary or for life, are addressed as for the wife of a peer of the applicable grade, but a Baroness has the option of two alternative styles. The use of the Continental style of 'Baroness' for social purposes is of fairly recent origin. It is believed that the first to term themselves 'Baroness' were Baroness Zouche (who styled herself Baroness de la Zouche) and Baroness Burdett-Coutts. As several Life Baronesses have been created since the Peerage Act 1963, its use has now become widespread. It is

40

recommended that the personal wishes of the lady concerned should be ascertained as to which form of address should be used, 'Baroness' or 'Lady'.

A husband derives no title or style from his wife.

Beginning of Letter
As for Wife of a Peer other than a Duke (see page 42), although a Baroness may prefer the style of 'Baroness' to that of 'Lady'. In this case, socially she should be addressed 'Dear Baroness Green'. Most Baronesses in their own right prefer the style 'Dear Lady Green'.

'Baroness' should not be used on its own, as is sometimes done. One would not address a peeress just as 'Lady'. The style is, however, correct for a Continental Baroness.

Envelope
As for Wife of a Peer other than a Duke (see page 42), but if a Baroness prefers the style of 'Baroness' she should be addressed:
Formal	The Rt Hon the Baroness Green
Social	The Baroness Green

Written Description
As for Wife of a Peer other than a Duke (see page 42).

Verbal Address
As for Wife of a Peer other than a Duke (see page 42), with the option for Baronesses of the style 'Baroness Green' instead of 'Lady Green' if preferred. 'Lady Green' is the style usually adopted. *Note:* 'Baroness' should not be used on its own. See Beginning of Letter, above.

Description in Conversation
Formal and Social Lady Teddington or Baroness Teddington

List of Directors and Patrons
It is optional whether one adopts the formal or the social method so long as the same style is followed for all other patrons etc. in the list. It is recommended that the social style should be used.

Signature
By title only: Teddington, for example.

Children

The children of a peeress adopt the same courtesy titles and styles as do the children of a peer: for example, the Countess of Sutherland's son and heir is Lord Strathnaver; Baroness Thatcher's son is the Hon Mark Thatcher.

Wife of a Peer other than a Duke

The wife of a Marquess is a Marchioness

The wife of an Earl is a Countess

The wife of a Viscount is a Viscountess

The wife of a Baron is a Baroness

The last-named title is not used, except in formal documents, the usual style being Lady Blank. The exception is a Baroness in her own right, who has the option of using it in place of Lady Blank. 'Baroness' in Continental titles is never translated as 'Lady Blank'. For nearly all purposes, a peeress of all these four grades of the peerage is referred to in conversation as 'Lady Blank'. The use of the exact rank in speech (for example, Viscountess Blank) is socially incorrect, unless for some reason it needs to be specifically mentioned, but it is always used on envelopes and visiting cards. An exception may be made occasionally at a formal function, such as in the introduction of a speaker who is a peeress, when normally her exact rank is mentioned for the first time only: for example, 'We are very happy to have the Countess of Hallamshire here tonight. Lady Hallamshire, as you know . . .'.

(There is no definite rule concerning the use of the word 'the' before these styles. As some consider the double use of 'the' superfluous, 'Most Hon the Marchioness of Bath' may, if desired, be used. This practice is not, however, recommended.)

Beginning of Letter

Formal	(Dear) Madam
Social	Dear Lady Angmering (irrespective of which of the four grades of peerage is applicable)

Envelope

Formal	The Most Hon the Marchioness of Bath
	The Rt Hon the Countess of Derby
	The Rt Hon the Viscountess Kemsley

	The Rt Hon the Lady Poole
Social	The Marchioness of Bath
	The Countess of Derby
	The Viscountess Kemsley
	The Lady Poole

Written Description

Where a Viscountess or Baroness is referred to in the body of a formal letter, article, caption etc. she may be described as Viscountess Molesey or Lady Surbiton without the prefix 'the'. Any subsequent reference to a peeress can be made to Lady Molesey, without regard to her exact rank in the peerage.

Informal letters again do not usually refer to the exact rank at all, but as Lady Molesey throughout. The second and subsequent reference to a Marchioness or a Countess can be made to Lady Bath, without regard to her exact rank. Informal letters do not usually refer to her exact rank at all, but to Lady Bath throughout.

Verbal Address

Formal	(Dear) Madam (not My Lady)
Social	Lady Poole

Description in Conversation

Formal and Social Lady Poole

List of Directors and Patrons

It is optional whether one adopts the formal or the social method, so long as the same style is followed for all other patrons etc. in the list. It is recommended that the social style should be used.

Signature

By first name and title: Helen Middlesex, for example.

Widow of a Peer other than a Duke

Officially, the widow of a peer of the above-mentioned grades is known as, for instance, 'the Dowager Marchioness Conyngham', 'the Dowager Countess of Pembroke and Montgomery' etc. unless there is already a Dowager peeress of the family still living. In the latter event, the widow of the senior peer of the family retains the title of Dowager for life, and the widow of the junior peer in that family is known by her first name – for example, 'Mary, Marchioness of Hammersmith' – until she becomes the senior widow.

Many Dowager peeresses prefer the use of their first name in preference to the word 'Dowager'. An announcement is often made in the press; otherwise it will be necessary to discover the wishes of the lady concerned. If in doubt, use the style of 'Mary, Lady Blank' (or appropriate rank), as the majority of peers' widows do not like the style of Dowager.

When the present peer is unmarried, by custom the widow of the late peer continues to call herself as she did when her husband was living, that is, without the prefix of Dowager, or her first name. Should the present peer marry, it is usual for the widowed peeress to announce the style by which she wishes to be known in future: for example, 'the Dowager Lady (or appropriate rank) Lancing' or 'Mary, Lady Lancing'.

Beginning of Letter

Formal	(Dear) Madam
Social	Dear Lady Lancing

Envelope

Formal	The Most Hon the Dowager Marchioness of Hammersmith
	The Rt Hon the Dowager Countess of Flintshire
	The Rt Hon the Dowager Viscountess Angmering
	The Rt Hon the Dowager Lady Lancing or
	The Most Hon Mary, Marchioness of Hammersmith (or applicable title) applicable title)
Social	The Dowager Marchioness of Hammersmith
	The Dowager Countess of Flintshire
	The Dowager Viscountess Angmering
	The Dowager Lady Lancing or
	Mary, Marchioness of Hammersmith (or applicable title)

Verbal Address

Formal	(Dear) Madam
Social	Lady Hammersmith

Description in Conversation
Lady Hammersmith. If distinction is necessary, or on introduction, she should be described as 'the Dowager Lady Hammersmith' or 'Mary, Lady Hammersmith'.

List of Directors and Patrons
It is optional whether one adopts the formal or the social method, so long as the same style is followed for all other patrons etc. in the list. It is recommended that the social style should be used.

Signature
By forename and title: Helen Hammersmith, for example.

Remarriage
If the widow of a peer remarries, she adopts her style from her present husband: the Dowager Lady Green having married Mr Edward Brown would be known as Mrs Edward Brown, for instance.

Should a peer's widow who has a courtesy style as a peer's daughter marry again, she reverts to the use of the courtesy style derived from her father. For example, if Lady Mary White (daughter of the Earl of Ditton) marries first the Marquess of Surbiton and secondly Mr Thomas Jones, she will be known as Lady Mary Jones; should the Hon Mary Smith (daughter of Viscount Twickenham) marry first Lord White and secondly Mr Robert Green, she is known as the Hon Mrs Green.

Former Wife of a Peer other than a Duke
If a former wife of a Marquess, Earl, Viscount or Baron does not marry again, she may continue to use the title as she did when she was married to the peer, with the prefix of her first name. She no longer uses the formal style of a peeress:

> The Most Hon for a Marchioness
> The Rt Hon for a Countess, Viscountess and Baroness

On remarriage, she takes her style from her present husband.

In Scotland, due to the difference in divorce laws, a former wife is legally equivalent to a widow in England. On marriage, as well as adopting her husband's surname, she also retains her maiden name as an alias. Should her marriage to a peer be dissolved and she marries again, she also retains her first husband's title as an alias. Socially, former wives of peers in Scotland are usually treated as are former wives of peers in general, unless any specific ruling is announced by Lyon King of Arms.

Beginning of Letter

Formal	(Dear) Madam
Social	Dear Lady Surbiton

Envelope

Formal and Social Mary, Countess of Surbiton

Verbal Address

Formal	(Dear) Madam
Social	Lady Surbiton

Description in Conversation

Lady Surbiton. If distinction from the wife of the present peer is necessary, or on introduction, she should be described as 'Mary, Lady Surbiton'.

List of Directors and Patrons

Mary, Countess of Surbiton

Signature

By forename and title: Mary Surbiton, for example.

Remarriage

On remarriage she adopts her style from her present husband: for example, if the former wife of the Earl of Surbiton marries Mr John Brown, she is known as Mrs John Brown. If she has a courtesy style derived from her father, she will revert to this on remarriage. For example, if Lady Mary Green marries first the Viscount Ferring and secondly Mr John Smith, she becomes Lady Mary Smith; the Hon Mary Smith who marries first the Lord White and secondly Mr John Brown becomes the Hon Mrs Brown.

Widow of one who Would Have Succeeded to a Peerage Had He Survived

The Queen may issue a Royal Warrant conferring on the lady concerned the title, rank, place, pre-eminence and precedence which would have been hers if her late husband had survived and succeeded to the title. This privilege has been granted in certain instances when the lady's husband died on active service.

Children of a Peer

The children of a peer use either:

(a) a peerage title by courtesy, or
(b) a courtesy style.

A courtesy title indicates and reflects a legal right of precedence, unless in particular cases it is confirmed or recognised by the Sovereign.

The Son and Heir Apparent of a Duke, Marquess or Earl

The heir apparent to a dignity is either the eldest son, the eldest surviving son (where a deceased elder brother has left no heir apparent) or the only son of the holder of a dignity. When the heir apparent is deceased, his heir apparent succeeds him in this respect. A woman can be an heir's apparent only when she is the eldest child (without surviving brothers with issue) or the only child of a deceased heir apparent. Legally, the holder of a dignity, so long as he lives, may have a son. Queen Elizabeth I was never heiress apparent to the Crown since she could have been displaced in succession by the birth of a brother. The heir presumptive to a dignity is the next in line, but could be displaced in succession by the birth of an heir apparent. Thus, a relative of a peer is only his heir presumptive until such time as the peer has a son and heir apparent. Alternatively, when a dignity may pass in the female line, the holder's daughter is heiress presumptive until such time as a son is born. If there be more than one daughter, but no son, they are co-heirs to an English Barony created by writ of summons. This falls into abeyance between them or their representatives. Although 'heir' is used loosely for the heir apparent or heir presumptive, legally it means the person in occupation of the title, estate etc. may use one of his father's peerage titles by courtesy provided it is of a lesser grade than that used by his father.

The younger sons of a Duke or Marquess have the courtesy style of 'the Lord' before first name and surname.

The younger sons of an Earl, and all sons of a Viscount or Baron, have the courtesy style of 'the Hon' before first name and surname.

The daughters of a Duke, Marquess or Earl have the courtesy style of 'the Lady' before first name and surname.

The daughters of a Viscount or Baron have the courtesy style of 'the Hon' before first name and surname.

A peer's sons and daughters who are legitimated under the Legitimacy Act 1926, as amended by the Act of 1959, are now, under an Earl Marshal's Warrant, accorded the same courtesy styles as the legitimate younger children of peers, although they have no right of succession to the peerage or precedence from it.

Courtesy styles may continue to be borne by the children of peers who have disclaimed their peerages, if desired.

The children of the younger sons of a peer have no titles or special styles. Children who are or have been adopted by a peer do not acquire any titles, styles and precedence as a result of such adoption.

Bearers of Peerage Titles by Courtesy
Although the bearer of a peerage title by courtesy enjoys none of the privileges of a peer, he is addressed as such with the following exceptions:

- A Marquess by courtesy is not given the formal style of 'the Most Hon': for example, Marquess of Tavistock.

- An Earl, Viscount or Baron by courtesy is not given the formal style of 'the Rt Hon': for example, Earl of Burford, Viscount Sandon and Lord Porchester. (Some Marquessates and Earldoms used as courtesy titles do not contain the word 'of' in their title: Earl Grosvenor, for instance.)

- A peer by courtesy is not addressed as 'the' in correspondence. This is restricted to actual peers.

Normally he is called 'Lord Blank', but if there is a special reason for a Marquess or an Earl by courtesy to be referred to by his exact courtesy title, he is called verbally 'the Marquess of Blandford' or 'the Earl of

Burford', this being the usual colloquial form of reference. The definite article is never given to courtesy Viscounts and Barons.

The eldest (or only) son and heir apparent of a Duke, Marquess or Earl may by courtesy use a title in the peerage of a rank junior to his father. This is usually, but not invariably, the second senior peerage borne by the peer (the son and heir apparent of the Duke of Rutland is known as the Marquess of Granby, for instance).

Second Heir to a Peerage

When a Marquess or an Earl by courtesy has an eldest (or only) son (who consequently is the second heir apparent), he too may use a courtesy title in the peerage, provided that it is junior in rank to that by which his father is known: Lord Howland, for instance, is the son of the Marquess of Tavistock, who is son and heir of the Duke of Bedford.

(For the eldest son of an Earl by courtesy in the peerage of Scotland, see Scottish Title of Master, page 60.)

Grandson Who Is Heir Apparent of a Peer

When the heir apparent of a Duke, Marquess or Earl is deceased but has left a son (who then becomes the heir apparent to the peer), the son is allowed to use the courtesy title borne by his father. In 1955 Viscount Swinton was created Earl of Swinton; his son and heir, the Hon John Cunliffe-Lister, had died of wounds in 1943, leaving male issue. On the creation of the Earldom, the elder of these sons, the present Earl of Swinton, became heir apparent to his grandfather and known by courtesy as Lord Masham.

If the eldest son of a Viscount or Baron predeceases his father, his children do not use the courtesy style of 'the Honourable'. Thus, the present Lord Kingsale, who succeeded his grandfather, did not have the style of 'the Honourable' when his grandfather was the peer.

Peerage Titles Borne by Courtesy

There is no hard-and-fast rule about which title borne by a peer is selected for use by his eldest son as a peer by courtesy, although in most families custom is followed. If the Marquess of Lansdowne has a son, his heir is usually known as Earl of Kerry or Earl of Shelburne in alternate generations. When the sixth Marquess of Ailesbury died, he

49

was succeeded in that dignity by his eldest son, known by courtesy as Earl of Cardigan. The latter's son, however, preferred to retain the use of his courtesy title of Viscount Savernake and was not known as Earl of Cardigan. He has since succeeded as the eighth Marquess of Ailesbury.

The following examples of (1) the peer, (2) his son and heir apparent and (3) the heir's eldest son are included to show how the system varies according to the particular peerage. Each example given consists of a different sequence of rank in the courtesy titles. Where a rank has been omitted, this is usually because the peer does not possess a peerage dignity of that grade (for example, the Marquess of Bath is not also an Earl but is also Viscount Weymouth; by courtesy his eldest son is styled Viscount Weymouth). In two instances the peerage ranks shown in parentheses do not exist at present, but they are normally used as courtesy titles.

The third heir in line of succession has not been included in the examples, but if a courtesy Earl is the second heir and he has sons, the eldest would also use a courtesy title, a Viscountcy or Barony, as applicable.

1. The Duke of Leinster
2. Marquess of Kildare
3. (Earl of Offaly)

1. The Duke of Abercorn
2. Marquess of Hamilton
3. (Viscount Strabane)

1. The Duke of Bedford
2. Marquess of Tavistock
3. Lord Howland

1. The Earl of Lindsay
2. Viscount Garnock

1. The Earl of Westmorland
2. Lord Burghersh

Peers by courtesy are eligible to sit in the House of Commons: the Earl of Ancram (son and heir of the Marquess of Lothian), for instance, sits as Mr Michael Ancram.

Wife of a Peer by Courtesy

The wife of a peer by courtesy is addressed as the wife of a peer of the same rank but with the following exceptions (also mentioned under Bearers of Peerage Titles by Courtesy, above):

- The wife of a Marquess by courtesy is not given the formal style of 'the Most Hon': for example, Marchioness of Kildare.

- The wife of an Earl, Viscount or Baron by courtesy is not given the formal style of 'the Rt Hon': for example, Countess of Ronaldshay.

- The wife of a peer by courtesy is not given the prefix 'the' in correspondence.

Widow of a Peer by Courtesy

The widow of a peer by courtesy is addressed as the widow of a peer of the identical rank, with the following exceptions:

- Without the prefix of 'the Most Hon' (Marchionesses) or 'the Rt Hon' (peeresses of lower grades).

- Without the prefix 'the' before the title.

If the courtesy title has passed to her late husband's brother or other relation, she would prefix her title by her first name. If it has passed to her son or stepson, she would prefix the title by her first name when he marries.

Former Wife of a Peer by Courtesy

She is styled as the former wife of a peer other than a Duke.

Younger Sons of a Duke or Marquess

The younger sons of a Duke or a Marquess are known by the courtesy style of Lord, followed by their first name and surname, such as Lord Edward FitzGerald.

Beginning of Letter
    Formal   My Lord

ˌSocial	Dear Lord Edward
	The surname may be added if the acquaintance-
	ship is slight.

Envelope
Formal and Social   The Lord Edward FitzGerald

Verbal Address

Formal	My Lord
Social	Lord Edward

Description in Conversation
Lord Edward. If distinction is necessary, or on introduction, he is described as Lord Edward FitzGerald. He should never be described as Lord FitzGerald.

List of Directors and Patrons
The Lord Edward FitzGerald

Membership of the Privy Council
Precede his style with 'the Rt Hon': for example, the Rt Hon the Lord Edward FitzGerald (see The Privy Council, page 79).

Ecclesiastical, Ambassadorial or Armed Forces Rank
These should precede his rank: for example, His Excellency the Lord Edward FitzGerald; Rear-Admiral the Lord Edward FitzGerald.

Signature
Edward FitzGerald

Wife of a Younger Son of a Duke or Marquess
The wife of a younger son of a Duke or Marquess is known as Lady, followed by her husband's first name and surname: the wife of Lord Edward FitzGerald is known as Lady Edward FitzGerald, for instance. This style is identical for the wife of a younger son of a courtesy Marquess. If she derives senior precedence as the daughter of a Duke or Marquess from that which she acquired on marriage, she may continue to use her prefix instead of his: Lady Mary Jones, married to Lord Edward Brown, may, if she wishes, be known as Lady Mary Brown

instead of Lady Edward Brown, but this is seldom done today. This form should be used only if it is known that it is preferred. It is, however, generally used by such ladies whose marriage has been dissolved.

Beginning of Letter

Formal	(Dear) Madam
Social	Dear Lady Edward
	The surname may be added if the acquaintance-ship is slight: Dear Lady Edward FitzGerald.

Envelope

Formal and Social   The Lady Edward FitzGerald

Verbal Address

Formal	(Dear) Madam
Social	Lady Edward

Description in Conversation

Lady Edward. If distinction is necessary, or on introduction, she should be described as Lady Edward FitzGerald. She should not be described as Lady FitzGerald, and would be described as Lady Mary FitzGerald only if she were senior in precedence to her husband and prefers to use her own style.

List of Directors and Patrons

The Lady Edward FitzGerald

Widow of a Younger Son of a Duke or Marquess

Her style in widowhood doesn't change, except on remarriage, when she adopts her style from her husband.

Former Wife of a Younger Son of a Duke or Marquess

She continues to be known by the same title she held on marriage: the former wife of Lord George Jones is still known as Lady George Jones, for instance. If she has a courtesy style derived from her father, it is probable that she will revert to its use on dissolution of her marriage: Lady Mary Green, formerly married to Lord George

Black, will probably be known as Lady Mary Black.

Younger Son of an Earl

The style of 'the Honourable' is only used on the envelope in correspondence, in written descriptions or in formal documents. It is never used in conversation or on invitations or visiting cards, when the correct style is 'Mr' or his ecclesiastical, Armed Forces rank etc. The more usual abbreviation is 'the Hon'.

Sons of Earls by courtesy have the same style as sons of Earls.

Beginning of Letter

Formal	(Dear) Sir
Social	Dear Mr Brown

Envelope

Formal and Social The Hon John Brown

Verbal Address

Mr Brown (or appropriate rank, such as Major Brown)

Description in Conversation

Mr Brown

Ecclesiastical, Ambassadorial or Armed Forces Rank

These precede his rank in correspondence, as in the Rev and Hon John Brown, His Excellency the Hon John Brown and Major the Hon John Brown.

Wife of a Younger Son of an Earl

The wife of a gentleman with the courtesy style of 'the Honourable' is known by her husband's first name and surname, with the addition of 'Mrs' as a prefix. Thus, the wife of 'the Hon John Brown' is 'the Hon Mrs John Brown'.

If she is the daughter of a Duke, Marquess or Earl, with the style of 'Lady' followed by her forename, she continues to use this style with her husband's surname: Lady Mary Brown, for example. If she is the daughter of a Viscount or Baron, with the style of 'the Hon', she does not use her husband's forename: if the Hon Jane White, for instance, marries Mr John Brown, she is known as the Hon Mrs Brown. There is no difference in her style if her husband also has the style of 'the Hon'.

'The Hon' is never used in conversation, on invitations or visiting cards.

Beginning of Letter
Formal   (Dear) Madam
Social   Dear Mrs Brown

Envelope
Formal and Social The Hon Mrs John Brown

Verbal Address
Mrs Brown

Description in Conversation
Mrs Brown

Widow of a Younger Son of an Earl
There is no difference in the form of address in widowhood. Should she remarry, she adopts her style from her new husband.

Former Wife of a Younger Son of an Earl
There is no difference in the form of address on the dissolution of her marriage, but, should she remarry, she adopts her style from her new husband.

Many former wives of Hons now prefer to drop the courtesy title and simply become Mrs Mary Smith. This is to be recommended in cases where the former husband has remarried and avoids the incidence of two or more Hon Mrs John Smiths.

Son of a Viscount or Baron
All the sons of a Viscount or Baron, and of those who by courtesy enjoy the style and title of Viscount or Baron, have the courtesy style of 'the Honourable'.

In all respects, the forms of address are identical to those accorded to a younger son of an Earl (see page 54).

For the elder son of a Viscount or Baron in the peerage of Scotland, see Scottish Title of Master, page 60.)

Wife of a Son of a Viscount or Baron
There is no difference in the form of address from that of the wife of a younger son of an Earl. See Wife of a Younger Son of an Earl, above.

Widow of a Son of a Viscount or Baron
There is no difference in her form of address as a widow from when her husband was alive, provided that she does not remarry. In this case she adopts her style from her new husband. See Wife of a Younger Son of an Earl, above.

Former Wife of a Son of a Viscount or Baron
There is no difference in the form of address on the dissolution of her marriage, provided that she does not remarry. If she does so, she adopts her style from her new husband. See Wife of a Younger Son of an Earl, above.

Daughter of a Duke, Marquess or Earl
A daughter of a Duke, Marquess or Earl has the style of 'the Lady' before her first name and surname: the eldest daughter of the Duke of Norfolk is the Lady Tessa Balfour, for instance. A daughter of those who by courtesy enjoy the title of a Marquess or Earl has the identical style of 'Lady'. On marriage she continues to use the same style, with her husband's surname: if the Lady Mary Brown marries Mr John Black, she becomes Lady Mary Black. In no case does she drop from 'the Lady Mary Brown' to 'the Hon Mrs Brown', even though her husband has this prefix. Should she marry a peer, she adopts his title: if the Lady Mary Brown marries the Earl of Flintshire, she becomes the Countess of Flintshire, even though his precedence is lower than hers. If she marries a courtesy lord, and the precedence she derives from this is lower than that she derives from her father, she has the option of adopting the usual style of the wife of a courtesy lord – Viscountess Molesey; for example – or continuing her own style

followed by the courtesy title: the Lady Mary Molesey. In practice very
few ladies now adopt the second course unless the marriage has been
dissolved, as it is difficult to determine the relative degree of
precedence. It was generally used a generation ago.

If she marries the younger son of a Duke or Marquess, who has the
courtesy style of Lord John Jones, again she has the option of adopting
the usual style of the wife of a younger son of a Duke or Marquess –
the Lady John Jones, for example – or continuing her own style followed
by her surname: the Lady Mary Jones.

Beginning of Letter
Formal   (Dear) Madam
Social   Dear Lady Mary
                The surname may be added if the acquaintance-
                ship is slight: Dear Lady Mary Jones

Envelope
Formal and Social   The Lady Mary Smith

Verbal Address
Social   Lady Mary

Description in Conversation
Lady Mary. If distinction is necessary, or on introduction, she is
described as Lady Mary Smith.

List of Directors and Patrons
The Lady Mary Smith

Daughter of a Viscount or Baron

A daughter of a Viscount or Baron, or of those who by courtesy use the
style and title of a Viscount or Baron, bears the courtesy style of 'the
Honourable'. When she is unmarried, this style is followed by her
forename (the Hon Mary Brown, for example). After marriage, she
drops the use of her forename and uses her surname only, following
Mrs (for example, the Hon Mrs Smith). The style of 'the Honourable'
is not used before 'Miss'.

The style of 'the Hon' is used only on an envelope, in written
descriptions (usually only on the first mention) and in formal docu-

ments. It is never used in conversation, or on invitations or visiting cards, where the correct style is 'Miss' or 'Mrs'. A husband does not derive any style or title from his wife.

Beginning of Letter

Formal	(Dear) Madam
Social	Dear Miss Brown or Dear Mrs Brown (as applicable)

Envelope

Formal and Social The Hon Mary Brown (unmarried ladies only) or the Hon Mrs Brown

Verbal Address
Miss Brown or Mrs Brown (as applicable)

Description in Conversation
Miss Brown or Mrs Brown (as applicable)

List of Directors and Patrons
The Hon Mary Brown (unmarried ladies only) or the Hon Mrs Brown

Brothers and Sisters of a Peer, Whose Father Did Not Live to Succeed to a Peerage
The Queen may issue a Royal Warrant, which confers on the brothers and/or sisters of a peer the style and precedence (of the sons or daughters of the dead peer) that would have been theirs had their father lived and succeeded to his title.

Disclaimed Peer
Under the Peerage Act 1963, it is possible to disclaim a hereditary peerage of England, Scotland, Great Britain or the United Kingdom for life. The disclaimer is irrevocable and operates from the date by which an instrument of disclaimer is delivered to the Lord Chancellor. When a peerage has been disclaimed, no other hereditary peerage shall be conferred. Two examples of this have occurred. The second Viscount Hailsham disclaimed his hereditary peerages for life in 1963 in order to sit in the House of Commons. As the Rt Hon Quintin Hogg, he was

elected as Member for St Marylebone. In 1970 he was appointed Lord Chancellor and received the customary life peerage, becoming Lord Hailsham of St Marylebone. Sir Alec Douglas-Home, previously the fourteenth Earl of Home, was created Lord Home of the Hirsel (life peerage) in 1974. A life peerage cannot be disclaimed.

As soon as a peer has disclaimed his peerage, he reverts to the status held before he inherited the peerage and is not accorded any courtesy title or style that he previously possessed deriving from that peerage. Even if he disclaims the peerage within a few days after succession, he must first have succeeded as a peer immediately on his predecessor's death, and for that interval he will figure in the numbering in works of reference: for example, twelfth Earl of Flintshire.

Should he also be a Baronet or Knight, these dignities and appropriate styles are retained, being unaffected by his disclaiming the peerage.

Examples
John E P Grigg, Esq (previously the Lord Altrincham); the Rt Hon Anthony Wedgwood Benn (previously the Viscount Stansgate).

Wife of a Disclaimed Peer
Immediately her husband disclaims his peerage, she reverts to the same style as her husband: if he becomes Mr John Jones, she becomes Mrs John Jones, for instance.

If her husband is also a Baronet or has been knighted, she will use the title of 'Lady Jones'. If she inherited any courtesy style from her father, she may revert to its use. For example, if Lady Mary White marries Lord Blank who disclaims his peerage and thereby becomes Mr Blank, she may then revert to the style of Lady Mary Blank; the Hon Mary White who marries Lord Blank similarly reverts to the Hon Mrs Blank.

Children of a Disclaimed Peer
The children of a disclaimed peer retain their precedence as the children of a peer, and any courtesy titles and styles borne while their father was a peer. It is open to any child of a disclaiming peer to say that he or she no longer wishes to be known by these styles. The children of the late Sir Max Aitken (previously Lord Beaverbrook) and the late Mr Victor Montagu (previously the Earl of Sandwich) have retained such styles,

whereas those of Dr William Collier (previously Lord Monkswell) and the Rt Hon Anthony Wedgwood Benn (previously Viscount Stansgate) decided not to use them.

Scottish Title of Master

There are three kinds of Master, all of which are connected with the Peerage of Scotland. They are:

- the **heir apparent** (usually the eldest son) of a peer, or a peeress in her own right,

- the **heir presumptive** of a peer, or a peeress in her own right, and

- the **son and heir of an heir apparent** (as above), who bears a peerage by courtesy.

Heir Apparent

He bears the title of Master, which is a legal dignity in its own right. As such he was ineligible to sit in the old Scottish Parliament, or for a Scottish seat in the House of Commons at Westminster, but only for an English seat, until the law was amended in the late eighteenth century.

Generally, the Master's designation is the same as the peerage title, having evolved to show whose heir he was: the son of Lady Sempill, for example, is the Master of Sempill. If the peer is known by more than one peerage or designation – Lord Belhaven and Stenton, for instance – his son and heir is known by the first designation: the Master of Belhaven in this case.

As the eldest sons of the first three grades of peers (Dukes, Marquesses and Earls) use courtesy titles, heirs apparent fall into two categories.

Heir Apparent of a Duke, Marquess, Earl or Countess in Her own Right

Although socially he is generally known by his courtesy title in the peerage, he is referred to by his substantive title of Master in all legal documents, commissions or proceedings in court: for example, the son and heir of the Marquess of Lothian is referred to as Michael, Master of Lothian, commonly called the Earl of Ancram.

Heir Apparent of a Viscount, Lord or Lady of Parliament
The title of Master is borne both legally and socially.

Heir Presumptive

The heir presumptive of a peer of Scotland may bear the title of Master, which he gives up when he ceases to be heir to the peerage. One historic case was the heir presumptive to Lord Glamis. For two periods, Sir Thomas Lyon was designated Master of Glamis, but he first gave up the title on the birth of his nephew. Later, he became heir presumptive for eighteen years and was again Master of Glamis until his great-nephew was born. If the heir presumptive is not a close relation of the peer, it is necessary for the Lord Lyon to approve his use of the title.

See also Titles Borne by Scottish Peers and Masters, Page 62.

Son and Heir of an Heir Apparent Who Has a Peerage by Courtesy

The grandson of a peer of Scotland bears by courtesy the title of Master. In practice this usage is limited to an Earl's grandson, since a grandson of a Duke or Marquess is generally known by a courtesy title. The Master's designation is usually the same as his father's courtesy title, since the title evolved to show whose heir he was. Thus, when the Earl of Strathmore has a son and a grandson, the son and heir is Lord Glamis, and the latter's son and heir is the Master of Glamis. If the designation does not follow the usual practice, it is by family arrangement and by the decision of the Lord Lyon.

The following are exceptions to the general custom: the Earl of Crawford (Chief of the Lindsays) is father of Lord Balniel. Prior to the succession in 1975 of Lord Balniel as twenty-ninth Earl of Crawford, his son and heir was the Master of Lindsay. In the lifetime of the Countess of Seafield, her son and heir was Viscount Reidhaven, and the latter's son and heir was the Master of Deskford.

See also Titles Borne by Scottish Peers and Masters, page 62.

Beginning of Letter
> Formal   Sir
> Social   Dear Master of Glamis

Envelope
The Master of Glamis; Major the Master of Glamis

Verbal Address
Formal	Sir
Social	Master

Description in Conversation
The Master. If distinction is necessary, or on introduction, he is described as the Master of Glamis.

Signature
Thomas, Master of Glamis

Wife of Master
The wife of a Master is called by the appropriate peerage style, if applicable. The wife of the Master of Polwarth is known as the Hon Mrs Andrew Hepburne-Scott. If a Master, as heir presumptive to a peer, has no alternative peerage style, then as Mrs John Blank.

Mistress
When the Mastership is held by a woman, the official designation is 'Mistress of Blank': for example, Mistress of Mar. For obvious reasons the style is not much favoured nowadays and is seldom used.

Titles Borne by Scottish Peers and Masters
The Scottish Parliament ruled that a peer who belonged to a cadet (younger) branch must not use his surname only for his peerage, as this is restricted to the chief of the whole name; consequently, he must be Lord Blank 'of' somewhere to distinguish him. There are several examples in the peerage: Lord Hay of Yester, a title of the Marquess of Tweeddale, and Lord Forrester of Corstorphine, a title of the Earl of Verulam. Today, this rule still applies for United Kingdom peerages. Even though the chief is not a peer, someone else of his name cannot use the undifferenced name for his title. Thus, when Lord Mackintosh of Halifax was created a peer in 1948, he could not be styled Lord Mackintosh alone, as he was not Chief of Clan Mackintosh. Masters

who belong to cadet (younger) branches may not use only that part of their father's titles which is identical to the surname.

During the seventeenth century the Earl of Roxburghe (forebear of the Duke) and then Chief of the Kers obtained a pronouncement in Parliament that his heir apparent alone was to be known as Lord Ker. The Earl of Lothian's heir, a Ker cadet, was to be known in distinction as Lord Ker of Newbottle. (Subsequently, the Marquess of Lothian succeeded as Chief of the Kerrs and Kers, the Dukes of Roxburghe having become Chiefs of the Innes family.)

These lengthy titles became abbreviated for ordinary purposes, and the peer came to use only the latter part of his title. Thus, Lord Ker of Newbottle became known as Lord Newbottle. Today, the heir apparent of the Earl of Wemyss (who is also Lord Douglas of Neidpath) is known as Lord Neidpath.

Summary Table

Name	Envelope	Letter	Verbal Address
Peers, Baronets and Knights			
Duke	The Duke of Westminster	Dear Duke or Dear Duke of Westminster	Duke
Duchess	The Duchess of Westminster	Dear Duchess or Dear Duchess of Westminster	Duchess
Eldest son of a Duke (usually takes his father's second title as a courtesy title)	Marquess of Annandale	Dear Lord Annandale	Lord Annandale
Younger son of a Duke	The Lord Edward Family Name	Dear Lord Edward	Lord Edward
Wife of younger son of a Duke	The Lady Edward Family Name	Dear Lady Edward	Lady Edward
Daughter of a Duke	The Lady Catherine Family Name	Dear Lady Catherine	Lady Catherine
Marquess	The Marquess of Northumberland	Dear Lord Northumberland	Lord Northumberland
Marchioness	The Marchioness of Northumberland	Dear Lady Northumberland	Lady Northumberland

63

Eldest son of a Marquess (usually takes his father's second title as a courtesy title)	Viscount Malverne	Dear Lord Malverne	Lord Malverne
Younger son or daughter of a Marquess	Same form as younger son or daughter of Duke		
Earl	The Earl of Bessborough	Dear Lord Bessborough	Lord Bessborough
Countess	The Countess of Bessborough	Dear Lady Bessborough	Lady Bessborough
Eldest son of an Earl (usually takes his father's second title as a courtesy title)	Viscount Allanbrooke	Dear Lord Allanbrooke	Lord Allanbrooke
Younger son of an Earl	The Hon James Family Name	Dear Mr Family Name	Mr Family Name
Wife of younger son of an Earl	The Hon Mrs James Family Name	Dear Mrs Family Name	Mrs James Family Name
Daughter of an Earl	The Lady Elizabeth Family Name	Dear Lady Elizabeth	Lady Elizabeth
Viscount	The Viscount Petersham	Dear Lord Petersham	Lord Petersham
Viscountess	The Viscountess Petersham	Dear Lady Petersham	Lady Petersham
Son of a Viscount	The Hon Charles Family Name	Dear Mr Family Name	Mr Family Name
Baron	The Lord Butterworth	Dear Lord Butterworth	Lord Butterworth
Baron's wife	The Lady Butterworth	Dear Lady Butterworth	Lady Butterworth
Children of a Baron	Same form as children of Viscounts		
Life peer	The Lord Brenton of Parry	Dear Lord Brenton	Lord Brenton
Wife of a life peer	The Lady Brenton of Parry	Dear Lady Brenton	Lady Brenton
Children of a life peer	The Hon Peter/Jessica Family Name	Dear Mr/Miss Family Name	Mr/Miss Family Name

Wife of a Viscount's son	The Hon Mrs Charles Family Name	Dear Mrs Family Name	Mrs Family Name
Daughter of a Viscount	The Hon Mary Family Name	Dear Miss Family Name	Miss Mary Family Name

Women's Titles

Hereditary peeress in her own right	The Countess of Dysart	Dear Lady Dysart	Lady Dysart
Life peeress	The Baroness Johnston of Calderwood	Dear Lady Johnston	Lady Johnston
Widow of a hereditary peer	The Dowager Marchioness of Reading. Some widowed peeresses now prefer to be styled with their own forenames, such as Victoria, Duchess of Grafton	Dear Lady Reading	Lady Reading
Former wife of a hereditary peer	Catherine, Countess of Ranfurly	Dear Lady Ranfurly	Lady Ranfurly

OTHER TITLES AND STYLES

OTHER TITLES AND STYLES

Baronet

The hereditary title of Baronet, ranking below that of Baron and above that of Knight, was instituted by King James I in 1611. The king's original object was to raise money for the settlement of Ireland by requiring those on whom the honour was conferred to pay a sum equivalent to three years' pay for thirty soldiers.

The holder of this dignity is accorded the prefix of 'Sir' and the suffix of 'Baronet' to his name. The suffix is invariably abbreviated in correspondence to 'Bt'.

Scottish Baronets sometimes use their territorial titles in conjunction with their surnames. In this case, 'Bt' should appear at the end: for example, Sir John Macmillan of Lochmillan, Bt.

Beginning of Letter
    Formal   (Dear) Sir
    Social   Dear Sir John
                   If the person is known only slightly, the surname may be used as well: Dear Sir John Brown.

Envelope
    Formal and Social Sir John Brown, Bt

Verbal Address
    Formal and Social Sir John

Description in Conversation
Sir John. If distinction is necessary, or on introduction, he can be described as Sir John Brown.

Membership of the Privy Council
The Rt Hon Sir John Brown, Bt. It is unnecessary to add the letters PC, since 'the Rt Hon' is sufficient indication.

Ecclesiastical, Ambassadorial or Armed Forces Rank
These should precede 'Sir', as in His Excellency Sir John Brown, Bt, the Hon Sir John Brown, Bt, the Rev Sir John Brown, Bt and Major Sir John Brown, Bt.

All the letters after the name follow 'Bt': Lt-Gen Sir John Brown, Bt, KCB, CBE, DSO and the Rev Sir John Brown, Bt, DCL.

Signature
John Brown

Wife of a Baronet

The wife of a Baronet has the style of 'Lady' before her surname. The old-fashioned style of 'Dame' followed by her forenames and surname (such as Dame Edith Brown) is no longer in general use. It is, however, retained for legal documents, where it is useful for these purposes in that it allows for the identification of a particular Lady Brown by the use of her forenames; an alternative legal style is for the forenames to be placed before 'Lady'. For correspondence, where confusion with others of the same surname could arise, 'Lady' may be followed by the forename in brackets, as mentioned below. This form is often used in publications.

If a Baronet's wife has a courtesy style of Lady Mary, this is used in full: Lady Mary Brown, for instance. If she has the courtesy style of 'the Honourable', this precedes 'Lady Brown', as in the Hon Lady Brown.

The wife of a Scottish Baronet who uses his territorial designation should be so addressed, as in Lady Macmillan of Lochmillan.

Beginning of Letter
    Formal   (Dear) Madam
    Social   Dear Lady Brown

Envelope
    Formal and Social Lady Brown

If it is necessary to distinguish the wife of a particular Baronet from another with the same title and surname, such as at a hotel or conference, the forename may be added in brackets: for example, Lady (Edith) Brown. This form should be used only in special circumstances.

Verbal Address
  Formal and Social   Lady Brown

Description in Conversation
  Formal and Social   Lady Brown

Widow of a Baronet

Officially, the widow of a Baronet immediately becomes the Dowager Lady Brown on the death of her husband, unless the widow of a senior Baronet of the same creation is still alive, when she becomes Mary, Lady Brown.

Many Dowager ladies prefer to use their forename rather than the word 'Dowager', so the wishes of the lady concerned should be ascertained. If in doubt, use the style of 'Mary, Lady Brown', which the majority prefer. Should she remarry, she takes her style from her new husband.

By custom, when a Baronet is unmarried, the widow of his predecessor continues to call herself Lady Blank, the same style as when her husband was living. Should the Baronet marry, it is usual for the widow of his predecessor to announce the style by which she wishes to be known: either 'Dowager Lady Brown' or 'Mary, Lady Brown'.

The widow of a Scottish Baronet who uses his territorial title should be so described: for example, Dowager Lady Macmillan of Lochmillan or Mary, Lady Macmillan of Lochmillan.

Beginning of Letter
  Formal   (Dear) Madam
  Social   Dear Lady Brown

Envelope
  Formal and Social   Dowager Lady Brown or Mary, Lady
                      Brown

The word 'the' should not be included as a prefix as this would imply that the lady was a peeress.

Verbal Address
  Formal and Social   Lady Brown

71

Description in Conversation

Formal and Social Lady Brown. If distinction is necessary, or on introduction, she should be described as Mary, Lady Brown.

Former Wife of a Baronet

As the widow of a Baronet, she is addressed with the style of Mary, Lady Brown, provided that she does not remarry.

Widows of Those Who Would Have Succeeded to a Baronetcy Had Their Husbands Survived

The Queen may issue a Royal Warrant, by which the lady concerned may enjoy the same title, rank, place, pre-eminence and precedence as if her late husband had survived and succeeded to the title. This privilege is usually granted only when her late husband died in active service.

Children of a Baronet

They do not have any special style, but follow the rules for addressing untitled ladies or gentlemen. Children who are or have been adopted are not in line of succession to a baronetcy by reason of such adoption.

Knight

The dignity of knighthood, which dates from medieval times, is the one most frequently conferred. It carries the prefix of 'Sir', but unlike a baronetcy is held only for life. The recipient is allowed to use this prefix and also the appropriate letters for those of Orders of Chivalry from the date of the announcement in the *London Gazette*; he does not wait for the accolade to be conferred on him.

There are two kinds of knighthood conferred by the Sovereign: Knights of the various Orders of Chivalry, identified by the appropriate letters after the name, and Knights Bachelor, which in ordinary correspondence carry no letters after the name.

Beginning of Letter

Formal   (Dear) Sir
Social   Dear Sir John

If the person is known only slightly, the surname may be used as well: Dear Sir John Smith.

Envelope
>   Formal and Social   Sir John Smith (with the appropriate letters after his name)

Verbal Address
>   Formal and Social   Sir John

Description in Conversation
Sir John. If distinction is necessary, or on introduction, he is described as Sir John Smith.

Membership of the Privy Council
The Rt Hon John Smith It is unnecessary to add the letters PC, since 'The Rt Hon' is sufficient indication.

Ecclesiastical, Ambassadorial or Armed Forces Rank
These precede 'Sir', as in the Hon Sir John Brown, KCB, His Excellency Sir John Brown, KCMG and Major Sir John Brown.

A clergyman of the Church of England, if appointed a Knight of one of the Orders of Chivalry, does not receive the accolade and is thus not accorded the prefix 'Sir' before his name, but he places the appropriate letters of the Order of Chivalry concerned after his name, as in the Rt Rev the Lord Bishop of Sevenoaks, KCVO.

Clergy of other Churches may receive the accolade and thus use 'Sir'.

A Knight of an Order of Chivalry who is subsequently ordained a clergyman of the Church of England has no need to relinquish the prefix of 'Sir': for example, the Rev Sir (George) Herbert Andrew, KCMG, CB.

Signature
John Smith. A peer who receives a knighthood of an Order of Chivalry adds the appropriate letters of the Order after his name: for example, the Viscount Angmering, KCVO.

Style from Sources other than the Crown

It is not customary in formal usage to combine the style emanating from other sources with titles conferred by the Sovereign. Alderman Sir William Brown and Professor Sir Edward Hailstorm are solecisms. In social usage this is not uncommon, though deprecated by purists.

Honorary Knighthood

When a foreign national receives an honorary knighthood of an Order of Chivalry, he is not entitled to use the prefix 'Sir', but he may place the appropriate letters after his name: for example, Bob Geldof, KBE. Should he subsequently become a naturalised British subject, he will be entitled to receive the accolade. Having become a full Knight of the appropriate Order, he will then use 'Sir' before his name.

Knights of the Orders of Chivalry

The two senior Orders of Chivalry are exclusive. Unlike the other Orders (see below), they consist of one class only. They carry the following letters after the name: Knight of the Garter: KG; Knight of the Thistle: KT. Ladies of these Orders carry the letters LG and LT after the name.

At the time of going to press the only non-royal Lady of the Order of the Thistle is accorded the style of Lady Marion Fraser, although she is not the daughter of a Duke, Marquess or Earl.

The remaining Orders of Chivalry consist of several classes, of which the first two carry knighthoods: Knight Grand Cross or Knight Grand Commander, and Knight Commander.

The appropriate letters for the various Orders of Chivalry are as follows in order of precedence:

	Knight Grand Cross or Knight Grand Commander	Knight Commander
Order of the Bath	GCB	KCB
Order of the Star of India	GCSI	KCSI
Order of St Michael and St George	GCMG	KCMG
Order of the Indian Empire	GCIE	KCIE
Royal Victorian Order	GCVO	KCVO
Order of the British Empire	GBE	KBE

For lower classes of the Orders of Chivalry which do not carry knighthoods, see Members of the Orders of Chivalry below the Rank of Knight, page 82.

There is no difference in the form of address of a Knight Grand Cross (or Knight Grand Commander) and a Knight Commander. In both cases the appropriate letters are placed after the names.

Should a Knight be promoted within the same Order, he ceases to use the appropriate titles of his lower rank. For example, if John Brown, KCB, is raised to a GCB, he becomes John Brown, GCB. The same applies to a Knight of an Order of Chivalry who previously belonged to the same Order but of a class that did not carry a knighthood. Thus, Colonel John Brown, CB, on promotion to a KCB becomes Colonel Sir John Brown, KCB, and drops the CB.

When a Knight receives more than one Order of the same class, the letters appear in order of precedence of the Orders concerned, and not according to the date on which he received them. Thus, a Knight Grand Cross of the Bath, the Royal Victorian Order and the British Empire is addressed as follows: Field Marshal Sir John Brown, GCB, GCVO, GBE.

When a Knight receives more than one Order of a different class, the higher grade of a junior Order is placed before the lower grade of a senior Order: for example, Lt-Gen Sir John Brown, GBE, KCMG, CB, CVO. Where a Knight has received several Orders of Chivalry, all the appropriate letters must be included after his name in correspondence. The style 'etc, etc,' after the first letters mentioned is a slight both to the individual and to the Orders concerned. It is, however, permissible in social correspondence with a KG or KT to omit other letters after the name.

An honorary Knight of an Order of Chivalry uses the appropriate letters after his name, but without the prefix 'Sir' because he is not eligible to receive the accolade.

Knight Bachelor

In legal and official documents 'Knight' may be added after the name of a Knight Bachelor. Otherwise neither 'Knight', nor 'Kt', nor 'KB' should be added.

Knighthood does not affect the use of letters already borne. If a Mr John Brown, CB, CVO, OBE, is created a Knight Bachelor, he becomes Sir John Brown, CB, CVO, OBE.

Precedence of Letters

Victoria Cross (VC)
George Cross (GC)

This is not always identical to the precedence to which the person is entitled. For example, no precedence has been accorded to holders of the Victoria Cross.

Knight of the Garter (KG)
Knight of the Thistle (KT)
Knight Grand Cross of the Order of the Bath (GCB)
Order of Merit (OM)
Knight Grand Commander of the Star of India (GCSI)
Knight Grand Cross of the Order of St Michael and
    St George (GCMG)
Knight Grand Commander of the Indian Empire (GCIE)
Knight Grand Cross of the Royal Victorian Order (GCVO)
Knight Grand Cross of the British Empire (GBE)
Companion of Honour (CH)
Knight Commander of the Bath (KCB)
Knight Commander of the Star of India (KCSI)
Knight Commander of St Michael and St George (KCMG)
Knight Commander of the Indian Empire (KCIE)
Knight Commander of the Royal Victorian Order (KCVO)
Knight Commander of the British Empire (KBE)

Wife of a Knight

The wife of a Knight is known as 'Lady' followed by her surname, and she is addressed as is the wife of a Baronet.

The old-fashioned style of 'Dame' followed by forename and surname – Dame Edith Brown, for instance – is no longer in general use but is retained for legal documents. It is useful for this purpose because it allows for the identification of the particular Lady Brown by the use of her forenames. An alternative legal style is for her forenames to be placed before 'Lady'. For correspondence, where confusion with others of the same surname could arise, 'Lady' may be followed by the forename in brackets. This form is often used in publications. She should never be styled Lady Edith Brown, unless she is the daughter of a Duke, Marquess or Earl.

If a Knight's wife has the courtesy style of 'Lady', this is used in full: Lady Mary Smith, for instance.

If a Knight or the wife of a Knight has the courtesy style of 'the Honourable', this style precedes 'Lady Smith', as in the Hon Lady Smith.

The wife of a Church of England clergyman who receives a knighthood but is not eligible to receive the accolade continues to be addressed as Mrs John Smith, but she has the precedence of a Knight's wife.

The wife of an honorary Knight continues to be addressed as Mrs John Brown.

Beginning of Letter
    Formal   (Dear) Madam
    Social   Dear Lady Brown

Envelope
    Formal and Social Lady Brown

Where there may be more than one lady of the same title and surname, such as at a hotel or conference, the forename may be added in brackets: for example, Lady (Edith) Brown. This form should be used only in special circumstances.

Verbal Address
    Formal and Social Lady Brown

Description in Conversation
Lady Brown

Widow of a Knight
She is addressed as the wife of a Knight, provided she does not remarry, when she will take her style from her new husband.

Former Wife of a Knight
She is addressed as the wife of a Knight, provided that she does not remarry, when she will take her style from her new husband.

Children of a Knight
They do not have any special style, but follow the rules for addressing untitled ladies and gentlemen.

Dame
A Dame is the female equivalent of a Knight of an Order of Chivalry. Similarly, the title is always used in conjunction with the forename.

The recipient is allowed to use the prefix and appropriate letters from the date of the announcement in the *London Gazette*.

Dames are appointed to the following Orders of Chivalry, and, as for Knights, there are two classes:

	Dame Grand Cross	*Dame Commander*
Order of the Bath	GCB	DCB
Order of St Michael and St George	GCMG	DCMG
Royal Victorian Order	GCVO	DCVO
Order of the British Empire	GBE	DBE

The rule for promotion in the same Order of Chivalry and the precedence of the Orders applies as for a Knight (see pages 75–6).

A peeress (including holders of a peerage title by courtesy) who is appointed a Dame adds the appropriate letters after her name, as in the Countess of Dorking, DCVO. The daughter of a Duke, Marquess or Earl, with the style Lady Mary Brown, adds the appropriate letters after her name, as in Lady Mary Brown, DBE.

As a Dame, the wife or widow of a Baronet or Knight is usually known as, say, Dame Irene Smith, DBE, but a few ladies prefer to continue their former style of Lady Smith, DBE (as did Baroness Spencer-Churchill when Lady Churchill). She should be addressed as Dame Irene Smith, DBE, unless her preference for the latter style is known.

Letters that signify membership of the Most Venerable Order of the Hospital of St John of Jerusalem are not included after the name. Dames Grand Cross and Dames of Justice and of Grace do not bear the title of 'Dame' before the name.

A lady styled 'the Hon' is addressed 'the Hon Dame Mary Jones, DBE'. As a Dame is the female equivalent of a Knight, the style of 'Mrs' is incorrect.

A husband does not derive any style or title from his wife.

When a Dame of an Order of Chivalry is gazetted by her professional, rather than her legal, name, she usually prefers to be so addressed: for example, Dame Margot Fonteyn, DBE.

When a Dame is the wife or widow of a Knight, she generally prefers to separate the honour acquired in her own right from that derived from her husband. For example, when Miss Daphne du Maurier (widow of Sir Frederick Browning) was raised to the rank of a Dame of the British Empire, she chose to be addressed either as Lady Browning, DBE, or Dame Daphne du Maurier, DBE.

Beginning of Letter

Formal	(Dear) Madam
Social	Dear Dame Mary
	When the person is known only slightly, the surname may be used: Dear Dame Mary Smith.

Envelope

Formal and Social   Dame Mary Smith, DBE (or applicable Order)

Verbal Address

Social   Dame Mary

Description in Conversation
Dame Mary. If distinction is necessary, or on introduction, she should be described as Dame Mary Smith.

Children of a Dame
They do not have any special style but follow the rule for addressing untitled ladies and gentlemen.

The Privy Council
The Privy Council, the ancient executive governing body of the United Kingdom, is presided over by the Sovereign and exercises many functions, some entrusted to it by Acts of Parliament, which may be legislative, administrative or judicial. Its decisions are usually embodied in Orders in Council or in Proclamations.

Membership is for life, with the style of 'Right Honourable'. Privy

Counsellors are appointed by the Crown from persons distinguished in various walks of public life, at home and in the Commonwealth, including members of the Royal Family, the Archbishops of Canterbury and York, the Bishop of London, the Lord Chancellor, members of the judiciary such as Lords of Appeal, all Cabinet Ministers, and some overseas Prime Ministers. The Lord President of the Council is usually a senior member of the Cabinet.

A full Council is now assembled only for the accession of a new Sovereign, and a member does not attend any Council unless specially summoned. Those summoned are generally, though not invariably, members of the government. A routine Council meeting is usually held at Buckingham Palace by the Sovereign (or, in her absence abroad, by Counsellors of State) and must be attended by at least three Privy Counsellors and the Clerk of the Council.

The Cabinet owes its origin to the Privy Council, of which it was an 'inner Council' or committee.

Much of the work of the Privy Council is done in committee, of which the most important is the Judicial Committee, the final Court of Appeal outside the United Kingdom (where the House of Lords is the Supreme Court of Appeal), although certain Commonwealth countries, such as Canada, have abolished appeals to the Privy Council and established instead their own Supreme Courts of Appeal. The Queen does not preside at meetings of committees of the Privy Council.

Privy Counsellor

The spelling Privy 'Councillor' is also used, but as the Privy Council Office prefers the spelling 'Counsellor' this has been adopted throughout the book.

The letters PC follow all honours and decorations awarded by the Crown. This is because membership of the Privy Council is an appointment or office held rather than an honour conferred. By precedence, a Privy Counsellor immediately follows a Knight of the Garter or the Thistle (in Scotland), and the letters PC are often incorrectly given next position after KG or KT. The position of letters after the name is not always identical with precedence: for example, VC is given first place by Royal Warrant, although such precedence has not been accorded.

Beginning of Letter
    Formal and Social No special form is used when writing to a
                           member of the Privy Council.

Envelope
Peer or Peeress
He or she is addressed according to the peerage rank, with the letters
PC after the title and any Orders conferred.
    Formal   The Rt Hon the Earl of Dorking, KCVO, PC
    Social   The Baroness Jones, PC

Others
'The Rt Hon' is always placed before the name both in formal and
social usage. There is no need to add the letters PC after the name,
since 'the Rt Hon' is sufficient indication of membership of the Privy
Council.
    Other ranks, such as ecclesiastical, ambassadorial, Armed Forces
etc. precede 'the Rt Hon' (see below).
    Ladies who are Privy Counsellors drop the use of Miss/Mrs/Ms.
    Example: the Rt Hon Harriet Harman, MP; the Most Rev and Rt
Hon Archbishop of Canterbury.

Verbal Address
Membership of the Privy Council does not affect verbal address in any
way. A peer, peeress, Baronet, Knight or an untitled lady or gentleman
is addressed as any other person of the same rank who is not a Privy
Counsellor: Lord Blank, Lady Blank, Admiral Blank, Mr Blank, Mrs
Blank or Miss Blank, for instance.

Description in Conversation
Membership of the Privy Council does not affect description in any
way. The Rt Hon Sir John Cummings is known as 'Sir John Cummings',
Lt-Col the Rt Hon John Jones as 'Colonel Jones' and the Rt Hon
Margaret Beckett, MP, as 'Mrs Beckett'.

Wife (or Husband) of a Privy Counsellor
They acquire no style or title.

Members of the Orders of Chivalry below the Rank of Knight, and Recipients of Decorations and Medals Conferred by the Crown

They are addressed according to their rank, with the appropriate letters after their names in order of precedence. The use of all these letters is obligatory: for example, John Brown, Esq, CBE, MVO, TD.

The recipient is allowed to use the appropriate letters for the Order from the date of announcement in the *London Gazette*.

Those promoted within the same Order of Chivalry do not continue to show the letters of the lower class of that Order. If Brigadier John Smith, OBE, is promoted to CBE, he is addressed as Brigadier John Smith, CBE, and the OBE is dropped.

Precedence of Letters

The full list of honours and awards in order of precedence of letters is given below. A Baronet has the letters Bt immediately after the name and before any letters that signify honours.

Decorations and Medals

Victoria Cross (VC)	The abbreviation takes precedence over all other decorations and honours
George Cross (GC)	Follows VC but takes precedence over all other decorations and honours
Order of Merit (OM)	Follows Knight Grand Cross of the Order of the Bath (GCB)
Companion of Honour (CH)	Follows the first degree of the Order of the British Empire (GBE)

Order of Precedence

The following is the list of Orders etc., conferred by the Crown below the rank of Knight, in order of precedence of letters. The abbreviation is in parentheses.

Victoria Cross (VC); George Cross (GC); Order of Merit (OM); Order of Victoria and Albert (VA); Order of the Crown of India (CI); Companion of Honour (CH); Companion of the Order of Bath (CB); Companion of the Order of the Star of India (CSI); Companion of the

Order of St Michael and St George (CMG); Companion of the Order of the Indian Empire (CIE); Commander of the Victorian Order (CVO); Commander of the Order of the British Empire (CBE); Distinguished Service Order (DSO); Member of the Royal Victorian Order (if Class IV) (MVO); Officer of the Order of the British Empire (OBE); Imperial Service Order (ISO); Member of the Royal Victorian Order (if Class V) (MVO); Member of the Order of the British Empire (MBE); Indian Order of Merit (Military) (IOM); Royal Red Cross (RRC); Distinguished Service Cross (DSC); Military Cross (MC); Distinguished Flying Cross (DFC); Air Force Cross (AFC); Associate, Royal Red Cross (ARRC); Order of British India (OBI); Distinguished Conduct Medal (DCM); Conspicuous Gallantry Medal (CGM); George Medal (GM); Indian Distinguished Service Medal (IDSM); Distinguished Service Medal (DSM); Military Medal (MM); Distinguished Flying Medal (DFM); Air Force Medal (AFM); Medal for Saving Life at Sea (SGM); Indian Order of Merit (Civil) (IOM); Colonial Police Medal for Gallantry (CPM); Queen's Gallantry Medal (QGM); British Empire Medal (BEM); King's Police Medal (KPM); King's Police and Fire Service Medal (KPFSM); Queen's Fire Service Medal (QFSM); Colonial Police Medal for Meritorious Service (CPM); Army Emergency Reserve Decoration (ERD); Volunteer Officer's Decoration (VD); Territorial Decoration (TD); Efficiency Decoration (ED); Air Efficiency Award (AE); Canadian Forces Decoration (CD).

Some Commonwealth countries have their own Orders, which are awarded to their citizens and indicated in the same way as the British system.

Order of Canada
Companion of the Order of Canada (CC); Officer of the Order of Canada (OC); Member of the Order of Canada (CM).

Order of New Zealand
Order of New Zealand (ONZ).

This post-nominal immediately follows VC or GC in their appointed order.

Companions of the Queen's Service Order (QSO); the Queen's Service Medal (QSM). The letters QSO precede OBE; QSM follow QGM.

Order of Australia
Knight (or Dame) of the Order of Australia (AK, AD); Companion of the Order of Australia (AC); Officer of the Order of Australia (AO); Member of the Order of Australia (AM). These follow OM, GBE, KBE and DSO.

Orders of Canada, New Zealand and Australia may be conferred on British subjects who have done some service of some sort in any Commonwealth country. These letters or distinguishing titles are usually used only while in the country that conferred them.

Untitled Gentleman
It is for the writer to decide whether to address his correspondents as John Brown, Esq, or Mr John Brown. The writer's usage should always be consistent. The former style is now customary in most walks of life in Great Britain and Ireland, but in the United States, Canada, Australia and New Zealand the style of Mr is generally used. John Brown used to be considered impolite, except for schoolboys, but is now common, and has always been the form of address adopted by Quakers.

Beginning of Letter
Formal	(Dear) Sir
Social	Dear Mr Brown

Ending of Letter
Formal	Yours faithfully
Social	Yours sincerely

Envelope
John Brown, Esq
Mr John Brown

Verbal Address and Description in Conversation
Mr Brown. On formal occasions the following distinction is often made, unless a prefix, such as 'Captain', makes this unnecessary:

Head of the family	Mr Brown
Others	Mr John Brown

Schoolboys
The usual style of addressing the envelope is 'John Brown', but at Eton and some other public schools they are often given 'Esq' after the name. The style of 'Master John Brown', at one time given to boys up to the age of twelve or thirteen, has largely gone out of fashion. If adopted at all, this form is now restricted to small boys up to the age of about eight, but they generally dislike it. It is more sensible to use just 'John Brown' until old enough to add the title 'Esq'.

Untitled Married Lady

Beginning of Letter

Formal	(Dear) Madam
Social	Dear Mrs Brown

Ending of Letter

Formal	Yours faithfully
Social	Yours sincerely

Envelope
Wife or widow of the head of the family (provided no senior widow is living): Mrs Brown.

Wives or widows of other members of the family: Mrs John Brown or Mrs J W Brown (her husband's initials).

Divorced ladies: Mrs Mary Brown or Mrs M J Brown.

It is incorrect for a widow to be addressed by her own forename or initials, as this implies that her marriage was dissolved.

If the forename of the lady's husband (living or dead) is unknown, it is better to address her as Mrs Brown rather than Mrs Mary Brown.

If the senior lady of the family has a title (Lady Mary Brown, say), this is sufficient identification for the next senior lady to be known as Mrs Brown.

Verbal Address and Description in Conversation
Mrs Brown. On formal occasions the following distinction can be made: wife or widow of the head of the family, and divorced ladies: Mrs Brown; wives of younger sons: Mrs John Brown, Mrs Edward Brown.

Use of Ms

In business 'Ms' (pronounced 'Muz') is often used as a convenient female equivalent of 'Mr' and is acceptable to most women. It is, however, always better to find out if someone prefers to be styled as Miss, Mrs or Ms, as they all have their advocates. Some women are happy to be referred to as 'Ms' in social situations as well.

When a woman marries, she may, for the sake of convenience, continue to work under her maiden name. If she does so, she should still be called Miss unless she makes it clear that she prefers otherwise. It is also common for women to take their husband's surname but continue to use their own forename at work.

Position of Letters after the Name

The abbreviations 'Bt' or 'Bart' (for a Baronet) and 'Esq', if applicable, precede all other letters. Other letters are grouped either by regulations or by custom, as follows:

1. Orders and decorations conferred by the Crown.

2. Appointments in the following order: Privy Counsellor, Aide de Camp to The Queen, Honorary Physician to The Queen, Honorary Surgeon to The Queen, Honorary Dental Surgeon to The Queen, Honorary Nursing Sister to The Queen and Honorary Chaplain to The Queen: PC, ADC, QHP, QHS, QHDS, QHNS and QHC.

3. Queen's Counsel, Justice of the Peace and Deputy Lieutenant: QC, JP and DL.

4. University degrees.

5. (a) Religious orders.
   (b) Medical qualifications.

6. (a) Fellowships of learned societies.
   (b) Royal Academicians and Associates.
   (c) Fellowships, memberships etc. of professional institutions, associations etc.
   (d) Writers to the Signet.

7. Member of Parliament: MP.

8. Membership of one of the Armed Forces, such as RN or RAF.

It is important to keep the group order, even if the individual series of letters in Groups 3, 4 and 5 present difficulties. For further details see the appropriate section.

The nature of the correspondence determines which series of letters should normally be included under Groups 3, 4 and 5. For instance, when writing a professional letter to a Doctor of Medicine one would normally add more medical qualifications than in a social letter.

On a formal list, all the appropriate letters are usually included after each name.

Those who have letters signifying Crown honours and awards are usually given only the principal letters in Groups 3, 4 and 5 (MD, FRCS, FRS, for example)

A peer who is a junior officer in the Armed Forces is not usually addressed by his service rank in social correspondence unless he so wishes, or a letter is forwarded to him at a service address or club.

Orders and Decorations
All the appropriate letters are obligatory in correspondence and lists. The order is laid down for Knights, Dames and others.

Privy Counsellors and Appointments to The Queen
For peers the letters PC are obligatory. For other Privy Counsellors, 'the Rt Hon' before the name is sufficient identification. As the other appointments to the Crown (QHP, QHS etc.) are held for a limited period only, recipients do not always use them.

Appointments
The letters QC are always shown for a Queen's Counsel, including a County Court judge but not a High Court judge.

The letters JP for a Justice of the Peace and DL for a Deputy Lieutenant may be included in that order. In practice they are often omitted for a peer, or for one with several honours and awards.

Note: There is no official abbreviation for a Lord-Lieutenant, HM Lieutenant or a Vice-Lieutenant (see Local Government, page 174).

University Degrees

Doctorates in the Faculties of Divinity and Medicine (DD, MD) and Masters degrees in the latter (for example, MS) are given in all correspondence. Other divinity degrees (for example, BD) are sometimes included.

Other degrees in medicine, such as MB or BS, are sometimes included, especially in professional correspondence, but if one progresses in the same degree only the higher is given.

Doctorates in other faculties are sometimes given, especially if the correspondence concerns the particular profession or subject (for example, LLD, DSc). Alternatively, except for surgeons, the envelope may be addressed as 'Doctor' before the name, without giving his or her degrees.

Other degrees are seldom, and MA and BA never, used in social correspondence, but they are generally included in a formal list.

For further information see Academics, page 107, and Medicine, page 192.

Religious Orders

Letters for members of religious communities, when used, should be included: SJ, for example. Some Members of the Order of St Benedict do not normally use the letters OSB, as the prefix of 'Dom' or 'Dame' is held to be a sufficient identification.

Medical Qualifications

Fellowships are given in all correspondence: FRCP, FRCS, for example.

Other qualifications are sometimes given, especially those that are the highest held. They are usually included when writing professionally.

When all letters signifying qualifications are included, as for example in a nominal list, they should appear in the following order (*Note:* Fellows and Members of each category precede the next category): medicine; surgery (except MRCS); obstetrics, gynaecology and other specialities; qualifying diplomas, such as MRCS and LRCP, and other diplomas, such as DPH, DObst and RCOG.

In practice, a maximum of three series of letters, including MD (see University Degrees, above), is usually sufficient in ordinary correspondence: for example, MD, MS, FRCS. See also Medicine, page 192.

Fellowships of Learned Societies

Fellowships fall into two categories: honorific – that is, nomination by election – and nomination by subscription.

Normally, only honorific fellowships are used in social correspondence, as in FRS or FBA.

Fellowships by subscription are generally restricted to correspondence concerning the same field of interest: a writer to a Fellow of the Zoological Society on the subject of zoology will include FZS after the name, for example.

There is no recognised order for placing these letters. Strictly speaking, they should be arranged according to the date of foundation or incorporation of the societies concerned, but some hold that those with a Royal Charter should precede others. In practice the following is usually adhered to.

Where one society is indisputably of greater importance than another, the letters may be placed in that order. Alternatively, the fellowship of the junior society may be omitted. If such precedence cannot be determined, the letters may be placed in order of conferment. Where this is not known, they may be placed in alphabetical order.

Where a fellow is pre-eminent in a particular subject, his fellowship of a society connected with this interest may either be placed first or his other fellowships omitted. The following are some of the principal learned societies, with their dates of incorporation:

Fellow of the Royal Society	FRS	1662
Fellow of the Society of Antiquaries	FSA	1707
Fellow of the Royal Society of Edinburgh	FRSE	1783
Fellow of the Royal Society of Literature	FRSL	1823
Fellow of the British Academy	FBA	1901

Presidents of some societies have special letters to signify their appointment. The President of the Royal Society has PRS after his name, for instance, but these letters are used only within the particular society.

The Royal Society of Literature bestows an award limited to ten recipients, the Companion of Literature. The letters CLit are placed before the fellowship.

Royal Academy of Arts, the Royal Scottish Academy etc.
It is not suggested that Royal Academicians yield in precedence to fellows of learned societies. In practice the two lists do not coincide. The President and Past Presidents are indicated as follows:

President of the Royal Academy	PRA
Past President of the Royal Academy	PPRA
President of the Royal Scottish Academy	PRSA
Past President of the Royal Scottish Academy	PPRSA

Royal Academicians and Associates are included as follows:

Royal Academician	RA
Royal Scottish Academician	RSA
Associate of the Royal Academy	ARA
Associate of the Royal Scottish Academy	ARSA

Similarly with other academies, such as President of the Royal Hibernian Academy (PRHA) and Academicians (RHA).

Honorary Academicians and Associates do not normally use the relevant letters.

Fellowships and Memberships of Professional Institutions, Associations etc.
These letters are usually restricted to correspondence concerning the particular profession. It is not suggested that professional societies as such yield precedence to learned societies, but in point of fact the two groups do not coincide to any great extent. Most of the senior learned societies that elect fellows are senior in age and importance to the professional. Those whose fellowships are by subscription are generally used only in the particular field of interest. For example, if Mr John Smith is a Chartered Engineer and a Fellow of the Royal Historical Society, he would normally be described professionally as John Smith, Esq, CEng, FIMechE. When corresponding on historical subjects, he is normally described as John Smith, Esq, FRHistS. If both series of letters are placed after his name, it is usual to place first those that concern the particular function or subject.

As there is no recognised order for placing qualifications awarded by different bodies, a recipient usually places these letters on headed paper, business cards etc. in order of importance to his particular profession.

Council of Engineering Institutions

The Council of Engineering Institutions (CEI), which was granted a Royal Charter in 1965, is a federation of fifteen chartered engineering institutions (see below). In 1971 the Privy Council approved changes to the council's charter so that CEI could set up the Engineers' Registration Board (ERB), which enables chartered engineers, technical engineers and technicians to be registered and to use the designatory letters CEng, TEng (CEI) and Tech (CEI) respectively. These titles are based on nationally recognised academic examinations, training and experience. The designatory letters CEng, denoting chartered engineer, follow immediately after an individual's name and are followed in turn by the letters F (Fellow) or M (Member), identifying him with the particular institutions to which he belongs. Thus, J Smith, CEng, FICE, MIMechE, is a chartered engineer who is a Fellow of the Institution of Civil Engineers and a Member of the Institution of Mechanical Engineers. *Note:* Some chartered engineers are also Masters of Engineering (a university degree). They are shown as MEng, CEng etc.

The constituent members of CEI are the Royal Aeronautical Society, Institution of Chemical Engineers, Institution of Civil Engineers, Institution of Electrical Engineers, Institution of Electronic and Radio Engineers, Institute of Fuel, Institution of Gas Engineers, Institute of Marine Engineers, Institution of Mechanical Engineers, Institution of Mining Engineers, Institution of Mining and Metallurgy, Institution of Municipal Engineers, Royal Institution of Naval Architects, Institution of Production Engineers and Institution of Structural Engineers.

Chartered Societies of the Land

Three chartered societies of the land – the Royal Institution of Chartered Surveyors, the Chartered Land Agents' Society and the Chartered Auctioneers' and Estate Agents' Institute – united in June 1970 to become the Royal Institution of Chartered Surveyors. Fellows and Professional Associates respectively have the letters FRICS and ARICS.

Incorporated Society of Valuers and Auctioneers

The Incorporated Society of Auctioneers and Landed Property Agents united in April 1968 with the Valuers Institution to form the Incorporated Society of Valuers and Auctioneers, with the letters FSVA and ASVA.

Writers to the Signet
It is customary for the letters WS to follow the name after university degrees and those that signify fellowship or membership of a society or institution, despite the fact that the WS Society (an ancient society of solicitors in Scotland) is frequently considerably older than many institutions. This is a way of indicating the profession. It is not customary for the letters WS to be used socially.

Members of Parliament
The letters MP are always shown for a Member of Parliament.

Membership of one of the Armed Forces
Royal Navy. The letters 'RN' (or 'Royal Navy', which this service prefers) are placed after the names of serving officers of and below the rank of Captain. They are also placed after the names of retired Captains, Commanders and Lieutenant-Commanders where they are prefixed by naval rank. The letters RNR are likewise used by officers of the Royal Naval Reserve.

Army. The appropriate letters which signify a regiment or corps may be placed after the name for officers on the active list of and below the rank of Lieutenant-Colonel, but are often omitted in social correspondence. These letters are not used for retired officers. Corps have letter abbreviations: for example, RE, RAMC, RAOC, RAPC. Most regiments are written in full.

Royal Air Force. The letters RAF are placed after serving and retired officers, except for Marshals of the Royal Air Force. Officers above the rank of Group Captain do not often use these letters. Similarly with RAFVR.

Royal Marines. The letters 'RM' (or 'Royal Marines', which some officers prefer) are placed after the names of serving and retired officers of and below the rank of Lieutenant-Colonel. Similarly RMR (Royal Marines Reserve).

For further information, see Armed Forces, page 120.

Scottish Titles and Territorial Designations
According to Scottish law there are some special titles which are recognised by the Crown. These fall into two divisions: those of the peerage of Scotland with the title of Master and recognised chiefly styles and territorial designations of chieftains and lairds, which are

strictly speaking part of their surnames. These are under the jurisdiction of the Lord Lyon King of Arms and by statute form part of the name, so should always be used.

These titles are as follows:

- Chiefs of clans (Highlands)
- Chiefs of names (Lowlands)
- A few independent heads of considerable houses who are recognised as chiefs (for example, Fraser of Lovat, Macdonald of Clanranald, Macdonald of Sleat)
- Chieftains (branch chiefs)
- Lairds

Some of the above are also feudal barons with precedence before esquires. They may be known by their baronial status (usually on the Continent, where Baronets and the other designations mentioned above are not understood). For this reason the fifth grade in the Peerage of Scotland is a Lord of Parliament and not a Baron as in other Peerages. There is no English equivalent for the formal style of William Stirling, Baron of Keir.

The traditional prefix to which chiefs, chieftains and lairds are entitled is 'the Much Honoured', but is seldom used today.

Chiefships and chieftaincies descend to the nearest heir of the blood and name, unless there is a family settlement on a different line of succession. The ruling chief may nominate his successor, but in such a case Crown confirmation, through the Lord Lyon permitting such a successor to matriculate the chiefly arms, must be obtained.

Where a chiefship has long been dormant and no heir can prove his right to the succession, Lyon may grant and confirm the chiefly arms to a suitable person of the name who is officially recognised as chief (usually after a petition from the leading men of the clan), subject to challenge by an heir coming forward and proving his claim within twenty years.

If the name of a laird is recognised, it does not necessarily imply that the estate is now in possession of the laird concerned, as with MacDonell of Glengarry. Subsequent owners with the same surname must use some other designation. In the case of Glengarry, for example, he must make this stipulation against all future purchasers, even of other surnames, in the deed of sale. Someone could become 'Black of Kintail', but no Mackenzie, except the chief, can become by purchase 'Mackenzie of Kintail'.

Scottish Chief, Chieftain or Laird

Surnames were adopted by the Anglo-Normans in the twelfth and thirteenth centuries from either placenames or nicknames. In the Lowlands, Braes and part of the Highlands, territorial surnames are adopted to match (for example, Sir Matthew of Moncreiffe). The chief, as head of the family and owning the name-place, described himself as 'Sir John of Moncreiffe of that Ilk' (which became standardised in charter Latin as 'dominus Johannes de Moncreiffe de eodem'). By the sixteenth century the 'of' became omitted before Moncreiffe (William Moncreiffe of that Ilk). By the second half of the sixteenth century, Highland chiefs were styled by the Crown as 'of that Ilk', to make their chiefly status clear, and they so styled themselves (for example, MacGregor of that Ilk). Some varied between this form and a territorial designation (such as Maclean of Duart). After the Union of 1707, Highland chiefs moved to a straightforward reduplication of the name (as in Macdonald of Macdonald) because of the difficulty in explaining 'of that Ilk' in England. Most other families have since followed suit.

In recent years the Lord Lyon has recognised landless chiefs as 'of that Ilk', although their ancestors never bore that designation.

For centuries some chiefs have abbreviated their style and adopted the initial 'the': for example, Chisholm of Chisholm is known as 'the Chisholm', and Macnab of Macnab as 'the Macnab'. Others use 'the' as well as the clan or territorial designation: for example, the Maclaren of Maclaren, the MacKinnon of MacKinnon, and the Macneil of Barra. The use of 'the' by certain chiefs, in place of the forename, is recognised officially by the Lord Lyon. Macdonald of Clanranald is formally styled the Captain of Clanranald, 'captain' being a medieval word for 'chief', literally 'headman'. Similarly, the Mackintosh chief of Clan Chattan is formally styled the Captain of Clan Chattan (pronounced 'Hattan').

The use of 'the' arose in two ways. Occasionally, 'le' was a corruption of 'de': for example, Robert of Bruce was incorrectly called Robert the Bruce. Usually it implied the chief of the clan or name, much in the same way as today we speak of 'the Mr Ford'. Though this form was used both in the Highlands and Lowlands, its survival is now restricted to chiefs of Highland clans.

In Scotland the following chiefly designations are used:

- Direct reduplication of the name, as in Henry Borthwick of Borthwick, the MacKinnon of MacKinnon

- Single designation, as in the Menzies (pronounced 'Ming-iz')

- 'Of that Ilk': for example, Sir Iain Moncreiffe of that Ilk, Bt

- Territorial designation: for example, Colonel Donald Cameron of Lochiel, the Macneil of Barra

Forms of Address
In Scotland it is normal to write to chiefs, chieftains and lairds by their designation or estate and not by their surname. The English 'Esquire' is not added to the name on the envelope.

Beginning of Letter

Formal	(Dear) Sir
Social	Dear Chisholm, Dear Lochiel, Dear Drum
	A member of a clan or name writes to his chief, Dear Chief.

Envelope
The Chisholm
Colonel Donald Cameron of Lochiel TD (Territorial Officers' Decoration)
The MacNeil of Barra Henry Forbes Irvine of Drum
Peter Barclay of that Ilk

Verbal Address
By clan or territorial designation, and not by the surname: Lochiel, Mackintosh.

On introduction, 'the' can be used if applicable (for example, the Macnab), or simply 'This is Lochiel'.

Description in Conversation
As for Verbal Address, except for those styled 'the' (for example, the Chisholm) are so described.

Chief, Chieftain or Laird (Woman)

There is no separate feminine equivalent for a lady who is a chief, chieftain or laird, and a woman has exactly the same status as a man, except that one does not write to her by her estate only.

Beginning of Letter

Formal	(Dear) Madam
Social	Dear Madam Maclachlan of Maclachlan or
	Dear Mrs Maclachlan of Maclachlan(whichever
	form is adopted)
	Dear Miss Rose of Kilravock

If she possesses a title, she is addressed as such. A letter to the former Chief of Clan MacLeod will be addressed 'Dear Dame Flora (MacLeod of MacLeod)'.

Envelope

Madam Maclachlan of Maclachlan or Mrs Stewart of Ardvorlich. If she possesses a title, then as such: for example, Dame Flora MacLeod of MacLeod, DBE, or Miss Rose of Kilravock.

Wife of a Chief etc.

Until the end of the eighteenth century, a wife of a chief or laird was invariably described as 'Lady', followed by her husband's territorial designation: for example, the wife of Cameron of Lochiel was called Lady Lochiel.

As the difference between 'Lady' plus the estate, and 'Lady' plus the surname (for example, a Knight's wife) was not understood by English officials, this title for a chief's wife died out early last century, becoming restricted to the peerage, baronetage and knightage. For the same reason, a chief's or laird's wife came to adopt her husband's full surname and not just the territorial designation part.

Today, some wives of chiefs or chieftains use the designation of 'Mrs'; others have adopted the Irish style of 'Madam' – for instance, Madam Chisholm – which has met with the Lord Lyon's approval. To be certain of the designation preferred, one needs to check with an individual family.

Widow of a Chief etc.

The style of the Dowager Madam (or Mrs) Maclean of Ardgour is now seldom used, but when the widow of a previous chief etc. is under the same roof as the wife of the current chief, this identification is useful.

Eldest Son and Heir Apparent of a Chief

He is known by his father's territorial designation, with the addition of 'younger', abbreviated to 'yr' (so that it will not be mistaken for a surname). This may follow the surname, but it is more usually placed after the territorial designation: Ranald Macdonald of Castleton, yr, or Ranald Macdonald, yr of Castleton.

If the forename of the heir apparent is different from his father, 'yr' may be omitted.

Wife of the Eldest Son

She is known by her husband's style – that is, with 'yr' but without his forename, as in Mrs MacGregor of MacGregor, yr – unless she is sufficiently distinguished from her mother-in-law, as in Lady Mary MacGregor of MacGregor.

Other Sons

They are not known by their father's territorial designation but as an Esquire – for example, John Macdonald, Esq – unless they are recognised as lairds in their own right: for example, Sir Thomas Innes of Learney's younger son became Sir Malcolm Innes of Edingight, being laird of that old family estate.

Eldest Daughter

As an unmarried daughter, she uses the territorial designation of her house without her forename, as in Miss MacLeod of Glendale, unless a senior lady is still living, such as an unmarried daughter of a previous chief etc., when she will use her forename as well as the territorial designation, as for younger daughters.

Other Daughters
All other unmarried daughters bear the designation of their house: for example, Miss Janet MacLeod of Glendale.

Irish Chieftainries
Chieftains of Irish Tribes and Septs are known by their titles.

About the beginning of the nineteenth century, some of the representatives of the last holders of these chieftainries resumed the appropriate designations that had lapsed with the destruction of the Gaelic order.

The use of 'the' as a prefix, though convenient and generally used, lacks official recognition by the Chief Herald of Ireland.

Gaelic Chiefs of the Name Recognised by the Chief Herald of Ireland

O'Long of Garranelongy
O'Ruairc of Breifne
O'Conor Don (descended from the kings of Connacht)
O'Donovan
O'Donoghue of the Glens
O'Grady of Kilballyowen
MacDermot, Prince of Collavin
McGillycuddy of the Reeks
O'Callaghan
The Fox; in Irish, An Sionnach
O'Neill of Clannaboy (descended from the kings of Ulster)
O'Donnell of Tirconnell
O'Kelly of Gallagh and Tycooly
O'Morchoe
O'Brien (descended from the kings of Munster)
Macquire of Fermanagh
MacCarthy Mor
O'Dogherty of Inis Eoghain
O'Carroll of Eile
MacDonnell of the Glens
MacMorrough Kavanagh (descended from the kings of Leinster)

Beginning of Letter
    Formal   (Dear) Sir
    Social   Dear O'Conor

Envelope
Armed Forces rank precedes the style: for example, Lt.-Col. the O'Grady, MC.

Verbal Address
O'Conor
    On introduction the full title is used: the O'Conor Don.

Description in Conversation
By the title: for example, the O'Conor Don; O'Morchoe.

Signature
As a peer: O'Grady, for example.

Wife of an Irish Chieftain
She is referred to and addressed as Madam, as in Madam O'Donoghue.
    The form of 'Madam' probably originated because several Roman Catholic chieftains of Jacobite sympathies left Ireland in the eighteenth century to live abroad. They usually spoke French through entering service abroad, being prevented as Catholics from holding commissions in the British Army. In France 'Madame' is the equivalent of both 'Lady' and 'Mrs'.
    A non-Irishman who writes to a chieftain with a Service rank, especially when he is younger or junior in rank, would write 'Dear Colonel the O' Grady'.

Children of an Irish Chieftain
They do not have any special form of address.

Irish Hereditary Knights
There are three Irish hereditary Knights, feudal dignities, which were conferred on the FitzGerald family: the Knight of Kerry (the Green Knight), the Knight of Glin (the Black Knight) and the White Knight.

The last of these, whose surname became fixed as FitzGibbon, is dormant, though there is a claimant. The Knight of Kerry, who is a Baronet, prefers to be addressed 'the Knight of Kerry', his older title.

Beginning of Letter
Formal	Dear Sir
Social	Dear Knight

Envelope
The Knight of Glin
Major the Knight of Kerry, Bt, MC

Verbal Address
Knight

Description in Conversation
The Knight of Glin
The Knight of Kerry

Wife of an Irish Hereditary Knight
She is addressed as the wife of an Irish chieftain, with 'Madam' before her surname.

Joint Form of Address
The Knight of Glin and Madam FitzGerald; the Knight of Kerry and Lady FitzGerald

The Aga Khan
The Aga Khan received the personal title of His Highness from The Queen in 1957 on succeeding his grandfather, His Highness the late Rt Hon the Aga Khan, GCSI, GCIE, GCVO, and is therefore styled 'His Highness the Aga Khan'. The wife of the Aga Khan is styled 'Her Highness Begum Aga Khan'.

The widow of the late Aga Khan is styled 'Her Highness Begum Sultan Mohamed Shah Aga Khan'.

Indian Princes

The principal Indian princes and chiefs, and their wives, may by courtesy be styled His or Her Highness, though the Princely Order in India was abolished by a presidential decree on 31 December 1971.

The Maltese Nobility

The nobility of Malta consists of titles of the following degrees: Marquis, Count and Baron. They take precedence among themselves according to the date of creation as a noble, irrespective of title. They are all addressed 'the Most Noble' followed by the title. If the title of Marquis is of Italian origin, the Italian form comprising 'Marchese' is sometimes used in place of 'Marquis'. The eldest sons and heirs apparent of nobles have the courtesy title of 'Marchesino', 'Contino' or 'Baroncino' before the title, depending on its degree. If the heir is a daughter, she has the courtesy title of 'Marchesina', 'Contessina' or 'Baroncina'. They are addressed by these titles, which are untranslatable, followed by the family title (for example, Marchesino St George).

The younger sons and all daughters of nobles are styled by courtesy 'the Noble' before the forename and title.

Other members of a noble's family are styled 'dei Marchesi', 'dei Conti' or 'dei Baroni', followed by their forename and surname or title. When a woman who has succeeded to a title marries an untitled commoner named Smith, she is addressed 'the Most Noble Countess Smith Montalto' (Montalto being her maiden name). When a daughter with the style of 'the Noble' marries Mr Smith, she is styled 'the Noble Mrs Smith'.

These titles are no longer recognised by the Republic of Malta.

The Canadian Nobility

There is one French title that is recognised by the British Crown, the Baron de Longueuil (of Longueuil in the Province of Quebec). This was created in 1700 by King Louis xiv for the services rendered in Canada by Charles le Moyne, whose descendants still hold it.

Commonwealth Sovereigns

In Southern Africa there are the Kingdoms of Lesotho and Swaziland, and in the Pacific the Kingdom of Tonga. The Supreme Head of

Malaysia has the style of 'His Majesty'. He is elected for a term of five years by the rulers of the Malay states from among their number. Other rulers include the Sultan of Brunei and the Head of State of Western Samoa.

Kings are addressed as 'His Majesty', and both the Sultan of Brunei and the Head of State of Western Samoa as 'His Highness'.

Summary Table

Name	Envelope	Letter	Verbal Address
Baronet	Sir Nigel Gordon, Bt	Dear Sir Nigel	Sir Nigel
Wife of a Baronet	Lady Gordon	Dear Lady Gordon	Lady Gordon
Children of a Baronet	These have no titles		
Knight	Sir Arthur Webster *Note:* Knights other than Knights Bachelor, i.e. Knights of the various Orders of Chivalry, also take post-nominal letters after the name on the envelope, e.g. GCB and KCVO	Dear Sir Arthur	Sir Arthur
Knight's wife	Lady Webster	Dear Lady Webster	Lady Webster

Women's Titles

Widow of a hereditary peer	The Dowager Marchioness of Reading Some widowed peeresses now prefer to be styled with their own forenames, e.g. Victoria, Duchess of Grafton	Dear Lady Reading	Lady Reading
Former wife of a hereditary peer	Catherine, Countess of Ranfurly	Dear Lady Ranfurly	Lady Ranfurly
Dame	Dame Lucinda Fosterington-Parkes	Dear Dame Lucinda	Dame Lucinda
Widow of a Baronet	Dowager Lady Garsington	Dear Lady Garsington	Lady Garsington

Special Scottish and Irish Titles

Eldest son of a Scottish peer (or peeress in her own right)	The Master of Clackmannan or Lord Clackmannan	Dear Master of Clackmannan or Dear Lord Clackmannan	Master or Lord Clackmannan
Irish hereditary Knight	The Knight of Glin	Dear Knight	Knight of Glin
Wife of an Irish hereditary Knight	Madam Glin	Dear Madam Glin	Madam Glin
Scottish chief or chieftain	The McCartney of McCartney	Dear McCartney of McCartney	McCartney of McCartney
Woman chief	Madam/Mrs McCartney of McCartney	Dear Madam/Mrs McCartney of McCartney	Madam/Mrs McCartney of McCartney
Wife of a Scottish chief	Madam/Mrs McCartney of McCartney	Dear Madam/Mrs McCartney of McCartney	Madam/Mrs McCartney of McCartney
Eldest son of a chief	Angus McCartney of McCartney, yr	Dear McCartney of McCartney, yr	McCartney of McCartney, yr
Wife of eldest McCartney son of a chief	Mrs Angus McCartney McCartney, yr	Dear Mrs McCartney of McCartney, yr	Mrs McCartney of McCartney, yr
Other children of a chief	Sons are addressed without any title, e.g. Hamish McCartney, Esq. However, daughters would be Miss McCartney of McCartney (the eldest daughter) or Miss Ruth McCartney of McCartney (any others)		
Irish chieftains	The O'Brien of Fermanagh	Dear O'Brien	O'Brien
Wife of an Irish chieftain	Madam O'Brien of Fermanagh	Dear Madam O'Brien	Madam O'Brien
Children of Irish chieftains	Have no special titles		

Untitled people

Men	Peter Flemming, Esq	Dear Mr Flemming	Mr Flemming
Married women	Mrs Peter Flemming	Dear Mrs Flemming	Mrs Flemming
Unmarried women	Miss Michelle Howden	Dear Miss Howden	Miss Howden
Widows	Mrs Peter Flemming	Dear Mrs Flemming	Mrs Flemming
Divorcees	Mrs Lucy Flemming	Dear Mrs Flemming	Mrs Flemming

STYLES BY OFFICE

ACADEMICS

The majority of universities were created by Royal Charter or an Act of Parliament. They are self-governing institutions which have academic freedom and are responsible for their own academic appointments, student entries, curricula and their own degrees.

In the UK there are currently eighty-eight universities. Prior to the Further and Higher Education Acts 1992, however, only forty-seven were in existence. Although the pre-1992 universities each have their own system of internal government, broad similarities exist between the old and new institutions.

The Open University provides nationwide courses that lead to degrees. It is uniquely non-residential, and courses are taught through a mixture of television and radio programmes, correspondence, tutorials, short residential courses and local audio-visual centres.

Chancellor of a University
The Chancellor has specific duties by statute in relation to conferring titles of degrees, presiding over the university Council (at Oxford 'Hebdomadal Council'), hearing appeals alleging infringement of statutes, and dealing with disciplinary matters.

The Chancellor of a university is addressed according to rank and name. If a letter concerns his or her university, the style 'Dear Chancellor' may be used both formally and socially.

The following is the form of address used on matters pertaining to the university.

Beginning of Letter

Formal	My Lord or Lady or Dear Sir or Madam (as applicable) or Dear Chancellor
Social	Dear Lord Blank, Dear Sir Henry (Smith) or Dear Dr (Mrs) Jones (as applicable) or Dear Chancellor (this is a more distant style than by name)

Envelope

Formal	The Chancellor of the University of Huntingdon
Social	Sir John Jones, CH, KBE, LLD, Chancellor of the University of Huntingdon

Verbal Address

Formal	Chancellor (on a platform; otherwise according to rank or name: 'My Lord', 'Dame Elizabeth' etc.)
Social	By name, or Chancellor

Description in Conversation
The Chancellor, or by name

High Steward of the Universities of Oxford and Cambridge

There are no specific duties attached to the offices of High Steward, Deputy High Steward or Commissary, but the High Steward may in certain circumstances deputise for the Chancellor. These last three offices are, in effect, principally honorific.

If the subject of the letter concerns his or her university, the style of 'Dear High Steward' may be used both in formal and social correspondence.

Envelope

Formal	The High Steward of the University of Oxford or The Rt Hon the Viscount Blank, High Steward of the University of Oxford
Social	The High Steward of the University of Oxford or the Viscount Blank, High Steward of the University of Oxford

Deputy High Steward of the University of Cambridge

The Deputy High Steward is addressed according to his or her rank and name. If the subject of the letter concerns the university, the form of address is as for the High Steward, with the addition of the word 'Deputy'.

Executive Head of a University, including Vice-Chancellor

The Executive Head of a university is the generic term that covers the Vice-Chancellor, President, Principal or Rector, irrespective of what the individual title may be.

The Vice-Chancellor, President etc. of a university is addressed according to rank and name. If the subject of the letter concerns the university, the formal and social style of 'Dear Vice-Chancellor', 'Dear President' etc. may be used.

In newer universities it is more usual to write to him or her by name.

In Cambridge the correct formal title for the Vice-Chancellor is 'the Right Worshipful the Vice-Chancellor'. These terms apply to women as well as men.

For the University of Oxford the designation of the Vice-Chancellor is: The Reverend the Vice-Chancellor of the University of Oxford (irrespective of whether he/she is in Holy Orders and normally now only on formal occasions).

The Executive Head of a Scottish university is sometimes jointly appointed Vice-Chancellor and Principal. He or she is then addressed as Principal.

Beginning of Letter

Formal	Dear Sir or Madam (or according to rank) or
	Dear Vice-Chancellor, Principal, Rector etc.
	(on a matter concerning his or her university)
	Dear Mr Vice-Chancellor (for Oxford)
Social	Dear Sir Henry (Jones)
	Dear Dr Jones etc. or
	Dear Vice-Chancellor, Principal, Rector etc.
	(on a matter concerning his or her university; this is a more distant style than by name)

Envelope

Formal	The Vice-Chancellor (including Oxford)
	The University of Milton Keynes
Social	Sir Philip Jones, CBE, LLD, Vice-Chancellor,
	The University of Milton Keynes

Verbal Address

Formal	Vice-Chancellor (on a platform etc.)
	or by name, Principal . . . etc. (if applicable)

       or by name: Sir Henry etc.
Social   Vice-Chancellor or by name, Principal . . . etc.
       (if applicable) or by name

Description in Conversation
The Vice-Chancellor, Principal etc. or by name
Deputy Chancellor, Pro-Chancellor, Deputy Vice-Chancellor or Pro-Vice-Chancellor
Or Vice-Chancellor of the University of . . .

Head of a University College

The title of the Head varies from college to college.

 The correct form of epistolary address is 'Dear Master of Caius', 'Dear Principal of Newnham' etc.

 The issue of gender does not therefore arise, and variations of marital status do not occur.

 In a Scottish university, a Rector has a unique meaning as the students' representative.

 The following shows the principal titles adopted, together with some examples of colleges etc. under each appropriate appointment.

Principal	*Master*	*President*
Brasenose College, Oxford	Balliol College, Oxford	Corpus Christi College, Oxford
Hertford College, Oxford	Pembroke College, Oxford	
Jesus College, Oxford	University College, Oxford	Magdalen College, Oxford
St Edmund Hall, Oxford	St Catherine's College, Oxford	
Linacre College, Oxford		St John's College, Oxford
Mansfield College, Oxford	St Cross College, Oxford	Trinity College, Oxford
Regent's Park College, Oxford	St Peter's College, Oxford	Wolfson College, Oxford
St Hilda's College, Oxford	St Benet's Hall, Oxford	Clare Hall, Cambridge
	Campion Hall, Oxford	Lucy Cavendish Collegiate Society, Cambridge
Newnham College, Cambridge	All other Colleges at Cambridge except King's, Queens' and those that were originally colleges for women	New Hall, Cambridge
		Queens' College, Cambridge
The Chief Administrative Officer, University of London		University College, Cambridge
Heythrop College, London	Birkbeck College, London	
King's College, London		University Colleges of Dublin, Cork and Galway
Royal Holloway College, London		Magee University College, Londonderry
Royal Veterinary College		

(*Principal and Dean*)
Queen Mary and Westfield
   College, London
Wye College, London

All Colleges of Durham University
   except University, Collingwood,
   Grey, Hatfield

Rector
Exeter College, Oxford
Lincoln College, Oxford

Imperial College of Science,
   Technology and Medicine,
   London

Director
London School of

Mistress
Girton College, Cambridge
   Economics and
   Political Science,
   London
School of Oriental and
   African Studies,
   London

Dean	*Warden*	*Provost*
Christ Church, Oxford	All Souls College, Oxford	Oriel College, Oxford
	Greyfriars Hall, Oxford	Queen's College, Oxford
King's College, Theological	Keble College, Oxford	Worcester College,
Department, London	Merton College, Oxford	Oxford
School of Pharmacy, London	New College, Oxford	
London School of Hygiene and	Nuffield College, Oxford	King's College,
Tropical Medicine	St Anthony's College, Oxford	Cambridge
The Heads of the Medical	Wadham College, Oxford	
Schools and Colleges, London		Trinity College, Dublin
	Goldsmith's College, London	
The Heads of the Institutes of		University College,
the British Postgraduate		London
Medical Federation		

Beginning of Letter

Formal   Dear Sir or Madam

Social   By name (Dear Dr Smith etc.) or by appointment: Dear Dean, Director, Master, Mistress, President, Principal, Provost, Warden etc.

Envelope

Formal   The Master,
                   Pepys College,
                   Cambridge

Social   Sir James Smith, PhD, Master of Pepys
                   College, Cambridge

Clergymen

When the head of a college is a clergyman, the ecclesiastical rank is shown before the name or appointment: for example,
The Very Reverend the Dean, Christ Church, or
The Very Reverend John Smith, DD, Dean of Blank Hall.

Verbal Address
Sir or Madam, Dean, President, Master, Provost, Warden etc. or by name.

Description in Conversation
By appointment – that is, The Master (of Blank College) – or by name.

Professor

A professor is addressed by name: Professor Meredith Jones, for instance. Though he or she may also hold a doctorate, the address continues to be the same as a professor while he or she has a chair.

Should a professor be in Holy Orders, he or she is addressed as the Reverend Professor John Smith and known verbally as Professor Smith.

Should a professor be a canon (or have higher ecclesiastical rank), he or she is sometimes known as Professor Smith, but strictly speaking the ecclesiastical rank supersedes the academic. Thus, a canon should be known as Canon Smith rather than as Professor Smith, but in practice this is a matter of personal choice. The academic style is used more often within a university, and the ecclesiastical style outside.

When a professor retires from his or her chair at a university and emeritus rank is conferred, the Professor Emeritus or Emeritus Professor continues to be addressed as previously in correspondence.

Beginning of Letter

Formal	Dear Sir or Madam
Social	Dear Professor Jones. Should he or she be a peer, Dear Lord or Lady Kirkcudbright should be used; if a Knight, Dear Sir Henry; if a Dame, Dear Dame Elizabeth (Jones)

Envelope
Professor John Smith. 'Professor' precedes any title held: for example, Professor Lord Blank or Professor Sir Henry Smith, Professor Dame

Mary Smith or Professor the Hon John Robinson.

Should he or she be in Holy Orders, the ecclesiastical rank precedes the academic, as in the Reverend Professor John Jones.

If a canon, 'the Reverend Canon Edward Jones' or 'the Reverend Professor Edward Jones', as desired (usually on a university matter the latter is used; otherwise the former). The form 'the Reverend Canon Professor Edward Jones' is never used, as it is too cumbersome.

Verbal Address
Professor Jones. Should he or she possess a title, he or she is known as Lord or Lady Blank, or Sir John Jones etc. If a canon, Canon Jones or Professor Jones, as desired.

Description in Conversation
As for Verbal Address.

Doctor
The recipient of a doctorate conferred by a university or other body, such as the Council for National Academic Awards, is entitled to be addressed as 'Doctor'. The exception to this is a surgeon, who is known as 'Mr/Mrs/Miss'.

The recipient of an honorary doctorate is entitled to the style of 'Doctor'. In practice, when a well-known figure outside the academic world receives an honorary doctorate (or doctorates) the recipient does not always use this style if he or she has other prefixes: for example, a peer, a high-ranking Service officer, a judge etc. This, however, is a matter of the recipient's choice.

Beginning of Letter

Formal	Dear Sir or Madam
Social	Dear Doctor Jones
If a peer	Dear Lord or Lady Blank
If a Baronet, Knight or Dame	Dear Sir Henry or Dame Elizabeth (Jones)

Envelope
It is a matter of choice whether the appropriate degree(s) should be placed after his or her name or to address the doctor as Dr John or Dr Mary Smith, though by custom a Doctor of Divinity always has the

letters DD appended after his or her name. This arises because many recipients, such as an archbishop or bishop, are not normally addressed as Dear Doctor Blank.

In the University of Oxford the appropriate letters are usually omitted, and the envelope is addressed 'Dr John Smith', irrespective of the particular doctorate. In the University of Cambridge both forms are used, and in the University of London the letters to signify the particular doctorate are usually given. It is, however, recommended that the letters, where known, are used to distinguish him or her from a medical practitioner who is known as 'Doctor', whether or not he is a Doctor of Medicine.

Examples: the Very Rev John Jones, DD; Lord Blank, DLit; Sir Henry Robinson, MusD; John Smith, Esq, LLD; Mrs Joan Smith, PhD.

Verbal Address
Dr Smith, unless he or she is a peer, Baronet, Knight or Dame, then by the appropriate rank.

Description in Conversation
As for Verbal Address.

Other Academic Appointments
The following are the usual appointments.
Boys' Schools Headmaster, although there are certain variations:

* High Master   of St Paul's, Manchester Grammar School etc.
* Head Master   of Westminster
* Master   of Dulwich, Marlborough, Wellington etc.
* Rector   of Edinburgh and Glasgow Academies etc.
* Warden   of Radley, St Edward's School, Oxford, etc.

Girls' Schools. Usually Headmistress or Principal.
Training and Technical Colleges and Schools. Usually Principal or Warden.
Teaching Hospitals, Medical Colleges, Schools and Institutes. Usually Dean.

Adult Education Centres and University Settlements. Usually Warden.

Beginning of Letter
The Head of a college, school, educational centre etc. may be addressed by his or her appointment if the letter concerns the college etc., but more usually by name. If the former style is adopted, then:

> Dear Headmaster,
> Dear Principal,
> Dear Warden, etc.
> Others holding staff appointments are addressed by name.

Envelope
By appointment: that is,
The Headmaster
The Principal
The Bursar
The Secretary to the Principal etc.
or by name.

Verbal Address
Headmaster, Principal, Warden, Dean etc. or by name.

Description in Conversation
The Headmaster, Principal, Warden, Dean etc. or by name.

University Degrees
Letters that denote a particular degree often vary according to the conferring university. First degrees also vary, but are often BA in arts and BSc in science. At the old Scottish universities of St Andrews, Glasgow, Aberdeen, Dundee and Edinburgh, the first arts degree is MA.

In social correspondence it is generally necessary only to place letters after the name to denote a doctor's degree, and even then the term 'Dr John Smith' is sometimes used on the envelope. Lesser degrees are usually omitted. An exception is generally made for the inclusion of the degree of Bachelor of Divinity (BD), and in the Faculty of Medicine.

Some graduates add their universities in parentheses after their degrees, such as in a school prospectus: for example Mr John Smith, MA (Cantab). The university is usually omitted in lists of names etc.

Lists of University Graduates

In a formal list, such as of patrons, officers and directors of societies and firms, all degrees may be placed after the name (with the exceptions mentioned below), but if a person has several Crown or other honours and awards it is a matter of personal choice or discretion which, if any, should be included. This is particularly applicable to well-known public figures who have acquired many honorary degrees.

The following rules are normally applied.

The degree of a Bachelor or Master is not accorded to those who have proceeded to the corresponding second or final degree. Therefore, one does not include BA and MA, BSc and MSc, MSc and DSc or LLB and LLD.

The degree of MA is not accorded to a doctor of the Universities of Oxford and Cambridge, where a doctor's degree is considered to include the MA degree.

Order of Placing Degrees

The order of placing the appropriate letters after the name depends on:

- The precedence of faculties within the conferring university, and

- whether a particular university places the degrees conferred in 'descending order' (in order of seniority) or in 'ascending order' (in the order by which they are taken).

The 'descending order' follows the same system applied to other honours and qualifications. Most universities, however, adopt the 'ascending order' system, which has the advantage of following the sequence of events.

Not only does the position of the appropriate letters vary according to the awarding university, but also either the name of the degree or the letters to indicate it:

Doctor of Civil Law   Oxford   DCL

Doctor of Law	Cambridge	LLD
Doctor of Laws	Other universities	LLD
Doctor of Letters	Cambridge	LittD
	Leeds	LittD
	Liverpool	LittD
	Manchester	LittD
	Sheffield	LittD
Doctor of Letters	Oxford and other universities	DLitt
Doctor of Literature	London and Belfast	DLit
Doctor of Music	Cambridge and Manchester	MusD
Doctor of Music	Oxford and other universities	DMus
Doctor of Philosophy	Oxford, Sussex, Ulster and York	DPhil
	Other universities	PhD

Cambridge has adopted the 'descending order'. Oxford, London and Birmingham, and most other universities, adopt the 'ascending order', and are included as being representative of those who use this system.

The following is a list in ascending order of the most common degree qualifications taken from the Universities of Oxford, Cambridge, London and Birmingham.

First Degrees

BED/EdB	Bachelor of Education
BA	Bachelor of Arts
BPhil	Bachelor of Philosophy
BMus/MusB	Bachelor of Music
BLitt	Bachelor of Literature
BS	Bachelor of Surgery
BM/MB	Bachelor of Medicine
BCL	Bachelor of Civil Law
BD	Bachelor of Divinity
BDS	Bachelor of Dental Surgery
BChir	Bachelor of Surgery
BCom	Bachelor of Commerce
BSocSc	Bachelor of Social Science
LLB	Bachelor of Laws
VetMB	Bachelor of Veterinary Medicine
BSc	Bachelor of Science

Master's Degrees

MA	Master of Arts
MSc	Master of Science
MS	Master of Surgery
MPhil	Master of Philosophy
MLitt	Master of Letters
MusM	Master of Music
LLM	Master of Laws
MEd	Master of Education
MPharm	Master of Pharmacy
MCom	Master of Commerce
MSocSc	Master of Social Science

Doctorate/Higher Doctorate

PhD	Doctor of Philosophy
MusD/DMus	Doctor of Music
ScD/DSc	Doctor of Science
LittD/DLitt	Doctor of Literature
DSocSc	Doctor of Social Science
DLit	Doctor of Letters
MD	Doctor of Medicine
LLD	Doctor of Laws
DD	Doctor of Divinity

New degrees may be conferred from time to time, according to changes in faculty.

Honorary Degrees

Recipients of honorary degrees are entitled to the same letters as university graduates. In certain universities, such as Essex, York and Stirling, an honorary doctorate is conferred 'of the university', according to the system in France, instead of in a particular faculty. The appropriate letters after the name are 'DUniv', except Essex where 'DU' is used.

Non-University Degrees

The most usual of these degrees are those conferred by the Council for National Academic Awards. These are the first degrees of BA, BEd and BSc, those for postgraduate study – MA, MEd and MSc – and for research – MPhil and PhD. In addition to honorary degrees conferred, the higher doctorates of DSc, DLitt and DTech are awarded for work of high distinction.

The Royal College of Art confers the following degrees:

Doctor	DrRCA
Doctor of Philosophy	PhD(RCA)
Master of Design	MDes(RCA)
Master of Arts	MA(RCA)

These letters are placed after the name as in Caroline Smith, DRCA.

THE ARMED FORCES

Titled Officers

Officers with a title, or a courtesy title or style, are addressed in the beginning of the letter and in speech in the same way as others with the same style.

Correspondence

	Formal	Social
Peer or peer by courtesy	My Lord or Lady	Dear Lord or Lady Blank
Courtesy style of 'Lord' or 'Lady' before their full name	My Lord or Lady	Dear Lord or Lady Smith (the surname may be added if the acquaintance is slight)
Baronet, Knight or Dame	Dear Sir or Madam	Dear Sir Guy or Dame Elizabeth (the surname may be added)

Some officers who have inherited or received a title or style prefer to be addressed by their Service rank. If Admiral Sir Guy Jones expresses his preference to be addressed 'Dear Admiral Jones' instead of 'Dear Sir Guy', this should be followed.

Envelope

According to the title or style. The Service rank appears before the title, except 'His or Her Excellency'. The appropriate letters that signify orders, decorations etc. immediately follow the name, except that if the person is a Baronet or Dame, the abbreviation immediately follows the name, followed by letters which signify orders etc.

Examples: His Excellency Admiral the Lord Chiswick, KCB; Colonel Lord Edward Brown, DSO, MC; Wing Commander the Hon Edward Smith, DFC, RAF; Lieutenant Commander Sir John Brown, Bt, DSO, Royal Navy (or RN).

Verbal Address
According to the title or style, unless the officer prefers to be addressed by his or her Service rank.

'The Honourable' is never used in speech: for example, Major the Honourable Mary Young is known as Major Young.

Use of an Officer's Rank without the Surname
In informal correspondence, certain officers are sometimes addressed at the beginning of a letter by only their rank – 'Dear Admiral' in place of 'Dear Admiral Smith', for instance – but some officers dislike this practice, especially from those outside the Services. In any case this practice is limited to the following:
Royal Navy. Commodore and above (Rear Admiral, Vice Admiral and Admiral of the Fleet being shortened to 'Admiral').
Army. Lieutenant Colonel and above (Lieutenant Colonel being shortened to 'Colonel' and Major General and Lieutenant General to 'General').
Royal Air Force. Flight Lieutenant and above (Air Vice Marshal and Air Chief Marshal being shortened to 'Air Marshal' and Marshal of the Royal Air Force to 'Marshal').

Relative Ranks in the Armed Forces

Royal Navy	Army	Royal Air Force
Admiral of the Fleet	Field Marshal	Marshal of the RAF
Admiral	General	Air Chief Marshal
Vice Admiral	Lieutenant General	Air Marshal
Rear Admiral	Major General	Air Vice Marshal
Commodore* and Captain of six years or more	Brigadier	Air Commodore
Captain of less than six years' seniority	Colonel	Group Captain
Commander	Lieutenant Colonel	Wing Commander
Lieutenant Commander	Major	Squadron Leader
Lieutenant	Captain	Flight Lieutenant
Sub Lieutenant	Lieutenant	Flying Officer

Midshipman	Second Lieutenant	Pilot Officer

*This rank is held by Captains during their tenure of certain specific appointments. On completion they revert to the rank of Captain.

Officers of the same rank show seniority between themselves depending on length of service.

The WRAC (1991), WRNS (1993) and WRAF (1994) have been integrated into the regular services, and women are eligible to achieve promotion on equal terms with men.

The Royal Navy

All officers of the Royal Navy below the rank of Rear Admiral are entitled to the words 'Royal Navy' or the letters 'RN' after their name, preceded by decorations etc., whether on the active or retired lists. The Royal Navy prefers this to be written in full, but the abbreviation 'RN' is widely used. It should also be noted that as the Senior Service, naval officers should be considered senior to their equals in the other services.

Admiral of the Fleet

This is a rank held for life.

Beginning of Letter
According to their title
  Formal:
  If a peer   My Lord or Lady
  Otherwise   Dear Sir or Madam
  Social:
  If a peer   Dear Lord or Lady Blank
  Baronet, Knight
    or Dame   Dear Sir John or Dame Elizabeth (the surname may be added if the acquaintance is slight)
  Otherwise   Dear Admiral Smith

Envelope
According to rank, with the appropriate letters after the name: for example, Admiral of the Fleet the Duke of Flintshire, GCB, CBE; Admiral of the Fleet Sir John Brown, GBE, KCB.

Verbal Address
According to their title: Lord Brown, Dame Elizabeth.

They may prefer to be known by their naval rank, which is socially abbreviated to 'Admiral'. A younger person or a more junior officer in any of the Armed Forces addresses him or her as 'Sir' or 'Ma'am'.

Description in Conversation
Lady Flintshire
Sir John Brown

If reference is made to rank, Admiral of the Fleet is used in full and should not be abbreviated.

Admiral, Vice Admiral, Rear Admiral (R Adm, V Adm, Adm)

All three ranks are known socially as Admiral (unlike the Army). The exact rank is given within the Royal Navy, on the envelope or in a formal description.

Beginning of Letter

Formal	Dear Sir or Madam
Social:	
If a Knight or Dame	Dear Sir William or Dame Elizabeth (the surname may be added if the acquaintance is slight)
Otherwise	Dear Admiral Robinson

Envelope
This is addressed to the exact rank, with the appropriate letters following the name: for example, Admiral Sir William Smith, GCB; Vice-Admiral Dame Mary Brown, DBE, MVO; Rear-Admiral John Robinson, VC, CB, OBE.

If they prefer their naval rank to be used, letters begin 'Dear Admiral Blank', and the verbal address is 'Admiral Blank' or 'Admiral'.

Verbal Address

If a Knight or Dame	Sir William or Dame Margaret
Otherwise	Admiral Blank

A younger person or a more junior officer in any of the Armed Forces addresses him or her as 'Sir' or 'Ma'am'.

Description in Conversation
    If a Knight or
        Dame   Sir William Smith or Dame Margaret Smith
        Otherwise   Admiral Robinson

Should social reference be made to only one Admiral, Vice Admiral or Rear Admiral, he or she may be called informally 'the Admiral'.

Commodore or Captain (Cdre, Capt)

Beginning of Letter
Formal   Dear Sir or Madam
Social   Dear Commodore Smith
                  Dear Captain Smith

Envelope
Commodore John Smith, CBE, Royal Navy
Chief Commandant Jennifer Smith, CB, Royal Navy

Verbal Address
Commodore Smith
Captain Smith

A younger person or a more junior officer in any of the Armed Forces addresses him or her as 'Sir' or 'Ma'am', never by rank.

Description in Conversation
Commodore Smith
Chief Commandant Smith

Commander or Lieutenant Commander (Cdr, Lt Cdr)
In the Royal Navy he or she is styled Commander or Lieutenant-Commander, as applicable. The exact rank is given on the envelope or in a list.

Beginning of Letter

Formal	Dear Sir or Madam
Social	Dear Commander Smith (this rank should not be abbreviated)

Envelope
Commander John Smith, OBE, Royal Navy
Lieutenant Commander Mary Jones, Royal Navy

Verbal Address
Commander Smith
Lieutenant Commander Jones

A younger person or a more junior officer in any of the Armed Forces addresses him or her as 'Sir' or 'Ma'am'

Description in Conversation
Commander Smith

Lieutenant (Lt)
As for a Commander, with the substitution of Lieutenant in all places.

Sub-Lieutenant (S-Lt)
A Sub-Lieutenant is equivalent in the Army to a full Lieutenant so should be accorded the same dignity.

Beginning of Letter

Formal	Dear Sir or Madam
Social	Dear Mr or Miss/Mrs/Ms Smith

Envelope
Sub-Lieutenant John Smith, Royal Navy

This rank should not be abbreviated.

Verbal Address
Sub-Lieutenant Smith

Description in Conversation
Sub-Lieutenant Smith

Midshipman (Mid)
A Midshipman is addressed as with a Sub-Lieutenant, except called Mr/Mrs/Miss/Ms in conversation and on envelopes, where they should be addressed according to rank, as in Midshipman John Smith, Royal Navy (or RN).

Women retain the title Midship**man**.

Officer cadets exist only at BRNC Dartmouth and gain rank on passing out.

Medical, Dental and Instructor Officers
The ranks of naval Medical Officers are preceded by 'Surgeon': for example, Surgeon Rear-Admiral Sir John Green, KBE.

The ranks of naval Dental Officers are preceded by 'Surgeon' and suffixed '(D)': for example, Surgeon Lieutenant (D) Judith Green, RNR.

The ranks of Naval Instructor Officers are preceded by 'Instructor': for example, Instructor Commander James Smith, Royal Navy.

Retired and Former Officers
Admirals of the Fleet remain on the active list for life and so continue to hold this rank. Other officers of the rank of Lieutenant Commander and above customarily use, and are addressed by, their rank after being placed on the retired list. More junior officers who are no longer actively employed do not do this.

The word 'retired' (abbreviated to 'Ret' or 'Rtd') should not be added after an officer's name in ordinary correspondence or in lists, but only when it is specifically necessary to indicate that an officer is on the retired list: for example, one employed in a civilian capacity in a Ministry of Defence establishment, when it facilitates postal arrangements.

Royal Naval Reserve

Forms of address are as for the Royal Navy except for 'Royal Naval Reserve' (or 'RNR') after the name. But most officers use their ranks only when under training or when called up for service with the Royal Navy. The Royal Naval Volunteer Reserve (RNVR) was merged with the RNR shortly after the Second World War.

Non-Commissioned Rates

The principal rates, excluding technical and specialist rates, are as follows:

Warrant Officer (WO)
Chief Petty Officer (CPO)
Petty Officer (PO)
Leading Seaman (Ldg Smn)
Able-Bodied Seaman (A/B)

Beginning of Letter
Dear Mr or Miss/Mrs/Ms Smith (for a Warrant Officer); otherwise according to rate: for example, Dear Chief Petty Officer Smith.

Envelope
According to rate.
   Rates should not be abbreviated to prevent confusion with initials of first names.

Verbal Address
According to rate.

Royal Marines

Forms of address are as for the Army.
   Those of the rank of Lieutenant Colonel and below place RM (some prefer 'Royal Marines' in full) after their name.
   Retired Royal Marine officers may place Royal Marines or RM after their names.

Non-Commissioned Ranks
The principal ranks are as follows:

> Warrant Officer Class 1 (WO 1)
> Warrant Officer Class 2 (WO 2)
> Colour Sergeant (CSgt)
> Sergeant (Sgt)
> Corporal (Cpl)
> Lance Corporal (LCpl)
> Marine (Mne)

Beginning of Letter
> Warrant Officer   Dear Mr or Miss/Mrs/Ms Smith
> Colour Sergeant   Dear Colour Sergeant Smith
> Otherwise, as for the Army.

Envelope
According to rank.

Verbal Address
As for Beginning of Letter (omitting 'Dear').

The Army
The Army categorises letters as formal, semi-official and routine. Formal letters are not common and are usually handwritten. They should be styled in the following way:

Beginning of Formal Letter
Sir/Madam
(subject of letter as appropriate)
I have the honour to . . .

Ending of Formal Letter
I have the honour to be
Sir/Madam
Your obedient servant
(signature) (rank in block capitals)

Field Marshal
This rank is held for life.

Beginning of Letter
According to his or her title (he or she would almost certainly be a peer, Baronet, Knight or Dame).

Formal:
If a peer	My Lord or Lady
Otherwise	Dear Sir or Madam

Social:
If a peer	Dear Lord or Lady Blank
Otherwise	Dear Sir John or Dame Margaret (the surname may be added if the acquaintance is slight)

Envelope
According to rank with the appropriate letters after the name, as in Field Marshal (the Rt Hon) the Lord Blank, GCB; Field Marshal Sir John Brown, KCB.

Verbal Address
According to title:
Lord or Lady Blank
Sir John or Dame Margaret
  A younger person or a more junior officer in any of the Armed Forces addresses him or her as 'Sir' or 'Ma'am'.
  When he or she prefers military rank to be used, the verbal address is 'Field Marshal Blank' or 'Field Marshal'.

Description in Conversation
Lord or Lady Horsham
Sir John Brown or Dame Margaret Smith or the Field Marshal
  If reference is made to rank, Field Marshal is used in full and should not be abbreviated.

General, Lieutenant General, Major General
All three ranks are referred to as General, except on the envelope, or formally, such as in a list, when the exact rank is given.

Beginning of Letter
    Formal   Dear Sir or Madam
    Social:
    If a Knight or
       Dame   Dear Sir John or Dame Margaret (the surname
                       may be added if the acquaintance is slight)
      Otherwise   Dear General Smith

Envelope
According to the exact rank, with the appropriate letters after the name, as in General Sir Edward Jones, GCB; Lieutenant General Sir John Smith, KCB; Major General John Jones, CB, CBE; Brigadier General Sarah Robinson, CIE, CMG.
    The ranks should not be abbreviated.

Verbal Address
    If a Knight or
       Dame   Sir John or Dame Margaret
      Otherwise   General Jones or General

A younger person or a more junior officer in any of the Armed Forces addresses him or her as 'Sir' or 'Ma'am'.

Description in Conversation
    If a Knight or
       Dame   Sir John Smith or Dame Margaret Jones
      Otherwise   General Jones

Should social reference be made to only one General Officer, he or she may be called 'the General'.

Brigadier
Beginning of Letter
    Formal   Dear Sir or Madam
    Social   Dear Brigadier Smith

This rank should not be abbreviated.
    If he or she prefers military rank to be used, letters begin 'Dear General Blank', and the verbal address is 'General Blank' or 'General'.

Envelope
Brigadier John Brown, DSO, MC

Verbal Address
Brigadier Brown or Brigadier
    A younger person or a more junior officer in any of the Armed Forces addresses him or her as 'Sir' or 'Ma'am'.

Description in Conversation
Brigadier Brown
    Should social reference be made to only one Brigadier, he or she may be called 'the Brigadier'.

Colonel or Lieutenant-Colonel

Both ranks are referred to as Colonel, except on the envelope, or in a formal description, such as a list, when the exact rank is given.
    These ranks should not be abbreviated.

Beginning of Letter

Formal	Dear Sir or Madam
Social	Dear Colonel Robinson

Envelope
The Regiment or Corps (or abbreviations) may be added to an officer on the active list: Lieutenant-Colonel Edward Black, MC, Grenadier Guards.

Verbal Address
Colonel Brown or Colonel
    A younger person or a more junior officer in any of the Armed Forces addresses him or her as 'Sir' or 'Ma'am'.

Description in Conversation
Colonel Brown

Major or Captain

The form of address is as for a Colonel, with the substitution of Major or Captain.

Lieutenant or Second Lieutenant
Beginning of Letter

Formal	Dear Sir or Madam
Social	Dear Mr or Miss/Mrs/Ms Jones

Envelope
The Regiment or Corps may be added on the next line, as for a Lieutenant Colonel:
Lieutenant Margaret Smith
Grenadier Guards

Verbal Address
Mr or Miss/Mrs/Ms Brown
The verbal use of the terms 'Cornet' for a Second Lieutenant of the Blues and Royals, and 'Ensign' for a Second Lieutenant of Foot Guards is restricted to within the Household Division.

Description in Conversation
Mr Brown

Retired and Former Officers
Field Marshals remain on the active list for life and so continue to use this rank. Other regular officers of the rank of Major and above may use, and be addressed by, their rank after being placed on the retired list. More junior officers who do so are lacking in *savoir-vivre*, which applies also to temporary officers of all ranks (such as those with war service only).

The word 'retired' (abbreviated to 'Ret' or 'Rtd') should not be added after an officer's name in ordinary correspondence or in lists, but only when it is specifically necessary to indicate that an officer is on the retired list: for example, one employed in a civilian capacity in a Ministry of Defence establishment, when it facilitates postal arrangements.

Territorial, Auxiliary and Volunteer Reserve
Officers should only use, and be addressed by, their ranks in correspondence etc. relevant to their TA and VR role. Forms of address are then as for the Army.

Non-Commissioned Ranks
Full stops between letters of abbreviation are no longer used within the Service, as in CSM.

Some ranks vary according to the Regiment or Corps. The Household Division, which comprises the Household Cavalry and the Guards' Division, differs considerably from the rest of the Army (see below).

The principal ranks in the British Army (apart from the Household Division) are:

> Warrant Officer Class 1 (WO 1)
> Warrant Officer Class 2 (WO 2)
> Staff Sergeant (SSgt) or Colour Sergeant (CSgt) in the infantry
> Corporal (Cpl)
> Lance Corporal (LCpl) or Lance Bombardier (LBdr)
> Private (Pte)

Beginning of Letter
Ranks are not abbreviated.

> Warrant Officer Class 1   Dear Mr or Miss/Mrs/Ms Smith
> Warrant Officer Class 2   Dear Sergeant Major Smith
> Staff Sergeant   Dear Staff Sergeant Smith
> Sergeant   Dear Sergeant Smith
> Corporal and Lance-Corporal   Dear Corporal Smith
> Private and equivalent ranks   Dear Private (Gunner etc.) Smith

Envelope
According to rank, which may be abbreviated. Initials rather than the first name are used, as in RSM J Jones, MC, MM; CSM W Jones; Sgt J Brown.

Verbal Address
According to Corps and Regimental custom.

A Warrant Officer Class 1 is called 'Mr or Miss/Mrs/Ms Smith'. If he or she has the appointment of Regimental Sergeant Major, they may be called either 'Regimental Sergeant Major' or 'RSM Jones'.

A Warrant Officer Class 2 who has the appointment of Company Sergeant Major may be called either 'Sergeant Major' or 'CSM Brown'. Other Warrant Officers Class 2 by their appointment: for example, 'RQMS Brown'.

NCOs are called according to their rank. A Lance Corporal is called 'Corporal'. These ranks may be used with or without the surname.

For Privates or equivalent rank, the surname must always be added.

The Army, Household Division
This comprises **the Household Cavalry** and **the Guards' Division**.

(A) The Household Cavalry (the Life Guards and the Blues and Royals)
The principal ranks are as follows:

> Warrant Officer Class 1 – Regimental Corporal Major (RCM)
> Warrant Officer Class 2 – Squadron Corporal Major (SCM)
> Staff Corporal and Squadron Quartermaster Corporal (SQMC)
> Corporal of Horse (CoH)
> Lance Corporal of Horse (LCoH)
> Lance Corporal (LCpl)
> Trooper (Tpr)

Beginning of Letter
> Regimental Corporal Major   Dear Mr Smith
> Squadron Corporal Major   Dear Corporal Major Smith
> Corporal of Horse   Dear Corporal Smith
> Otherwise as for the Army in general.

Envelope
According to rank, which may be abbreviated, as in CMS.

Verbal Address
As for Beginning of Letter (omitting 'Dear'). NCOs may be addressed with or without their surname. Troopers are always addressed with their surname.

(B) The Guards' Division
The principal ranks are as follows:

> Warrant Officer Class 1 (RSM)

Warrant Officer Class 2 (CSM etc.)
Colour Sergeant (CSgt) and Company Quartermaster
Sergeant (CQMS)
Sergeant (Sgt)
Lance Sergeant (LSgt)
Lance Corporal (LCpl)
Guardsman (Gdsm)

Drum Major (D Maj)
Pipe Major (P Maj)
Drummer (Drmr)
Musicians (Mus)
Master Tailor (M Tlr)

Beginning of Letter
Ranks or appointments are not abbreviated.

Regimental Sergeant Major   Dear Sergeant Major Brown
Other Warrant Officers   By their appointment and name
Colour Sergeant and
    Company Quartermaster Sergeant   By their rank and name
Sergeant and Lance Sergeant   Dear Sergeant Smith
Lance Corporal   Dear Corporal Smith

Envelope
According to rank, which may be abbreviated, as in Sgt.

Verbal Address
As for Beginning of Letter (omitting 'Dear'). Alternatively, some ranks
may be abbreviated (such as CQMS Brown).

NCOs may be addressed with or without their surname. Guardsmen
are always addressed with their surname.

The Royal Air Force
Entrants to the RAF College, Cranwell, are commissioned on arrival.

Marshal of the Royal Air Force
This rank is held for life.

Beginning of Letter
According to his or her title (he or she would almost certainly be a peer, Baronet, Knight or Dame).

Formal:	
If a peer	My Lord or Lady
Otherwise	Dear Sir or Madam
Social:	
If a peer	Dear Lord or Lady Blank
Otherwise	Dear Sir John or Dame Margaret (the surname may be added if the acquaintance is slight)

When he or she prefers Air Force rank to be used, letters begin 'Dear Air Marshal Blank' and the verbal address is 'Air Marshal Blank' or 'Air Marshal'. The style of 'Marshal' is also used, but is unofficial.

Envelope
Marshal of the Royal Air Force (the Rt Hon) Viscount Dorking, GCB
Marshal of the Royal Air Force Sir John Jones, GCB

Verbal Address
According to his or her title: Lady Sachs, Sir John.
    A younger person or a more junior officer in any of the Armed Forces addresses him or her as 'Sir' or 'Ma'am'.

Description in Conversation
Lady Sachs
Sir John Jones

Air Chief Marshal, Air Marshal or Air Vice-Marshal
All these ranks are referred to as Air Marshal, except on the envelope or in a formal description, such as in a list, when the exact rank is given.
    The letters RAF may follow the name, and any letters signifying orders etc.

Beginning of Letter
Formal	Dear Sir or Madam

Social:

If a Knight or Dame	Dear Sir John or Dame Margaret (the surname may he added if the acquaintance is slight)
Otherwise	Dear Air Marshal Smith

When he or she prefers Air Force rank to that appropriate for his or her title, letters begin 'Dear Air Marshal Brown'.

Envelope
According to the exact rank, with the appropriate letters after the name: for example, Air Chief Marshal Sir John Brown, GBE, RAF; Air Vice Marshal Edward Grey, CB, CBE, RAF.
  These ranks should not be abbreviated.

Verbal Address

If a Knight or Dame	Sir John or Dame Margaret
Otherwise	Air Marshal Grey

A younger person or a more junior officer in any of the Armed Forces addresses him or her as 'Sir' or 'Ma'am'.

Description in Conversation

If a Knight or Dame	Sir John Brown or Dame Margaret
Otherwise	Air Marshal Grey

Should social reference be made to only one Air Chief Marshal, Air Marshal or Air Vice-Marshal, he or she may be called 'the Air Marshal'.

Air Commodore, Group Captain, Wing Commander, Squadron Leader or Flight Lieutenant
These ranks are always used in full. The letters RAF follow the name, and any letters that signify orders etc.

Beginning of Letter

Formal	Dear Sir or Madam
Social:	Dear Air Commodore Davis

Dear Group Captain Smith
Dear Wing Commander Jones
Dear Squadron Leader Robinson
Dear Flight Lieutenant Brown

Envelope
Air Commodore David Davis, CB, RAF
Group Captain John Smith, CBE, RAF
Wing Commander Mary Jones, DFC, RAF
Squadron Leader Richard Robinson, MBE, RAF
Flight Lieutenant Jennifer Brown, RAF

Verbal Address
Air Commodore Davis
Group Captain Smith
Wing Commander Jones
Squadron Leader Robinson
Flight Lieutenant Brown
     A younger person or a more junior officer in any of the Armed
Forces addresses him or her as 'Sir' or 'Ma'am'.

Description in Conversation
As for Verbal Address.

Flying Officer or Pilot Officer
The letters RAF follow the name, and any letters that signify orders
etc.

Beginning of Letter
| Formal | Dear Sir or Madam |
| Social | Dear Mr or Miss/Mrs/Ms Smith |

Envelope
John Smith, Esq, AFC, RAF or Flying Officer John Smith, AFC, RAF

Verbal Address
Mr Smith

Description in Conversation
Mr Smith

Retired and Former Officers

Marshals of the Royal Air Force remain on the active list for life and so continue to use this rank. Other officers of the rank of Flight Lieutenant and above may use, and be addressed by, their rank after being placed on the retired list.

The word 'retired' (or the abbreviation 'Ret' or 'Rtd') need not be added after an officer's name, but officially it has been the practice for the Ministry of Defence to use the abbreviation 'Retd' for officers on the retired list.

Royal Air Force Volunteer Reserve

Officers should only use, and be addressed by, their ranks when under training or when called up for service. Forms of address are then as for the Royal Air Force except that the letters RAFVR follow the name (in lieu of RAF).

Non-Commissioned Ranks

The principal ranks are as follows:

Warrant Officer	WO
Flight Sergeant	FS
Chief Technician	Chf Tech
Sergeant	Sgt
Corporal	Cpl
Junior Technician	Jnr Tech

Senior Aircraftman	SAC
Leading Aircraftman	LAC
Aircraftman	AC

Beginning of Letter
    Warrant Officer
       (formally)   Dear Warrant Officer Smith
       Otherwise   Dear Mr or Miss/Mrs/Ms Smith

Other ranks   According to rank

Envelope
According to rank, with 'RAF' (or 'RAFVR') after the name

Verbal Address
As for Beginning of Letter (omitting 'Dear').

Queen Alexandra's Royal Naval Nursing Service
An officer of Queen Alexandra's Royal Naval Nursing Service adds any letters signifying orders etc. after his or her name and then QARNNS.
   The ranks are as follows:

Captain
Director of Naval Nursing Services
Matron-in-Chief QARNNS

Commander
Lieutenant Commander
Lieutenant
Sub-Lieutenant

Beginning of Letter
Formal   Dear Sir or Madam
Social   Dear Mr or Miss/Mrs/Ms Smith

Envelope
Professional   Miss Rosemary Smith, Matron-in-Chief, QARNNS
Private   Mr Roger Smith, QARNNS

Verbal Address
Miss/Mrs/Ms or Mr Smith

Description in Conversation
Miss Smith

Nursing Rates
The rates of nurses are as follows:

> Warrant Officer Naval Nurse
> Chief Petty Officer Naval Nurse
> Petty Officer Naval Nurse
> Leading Naval Nurse
> Naval Nurse
> Probationary Student Nurse

Ratings are referred to at the beginning of a letter, as in Dear Leading Naval Nurse Smith.

Queen Alexandra's Royal Army Nursing Corps

Ranks for officers and other ranks of Queen Alexandra's Royal Army Nursing Corps have Army ranks, with the letters QARANC after the name.

The Director of the QARANC holds the rank of Colonel but takes the rank of Brigadier when he or she holds the post of Director of Defence Nursing Services.

The ranks are as follows:

> Brigadier
> Colonel
> Lieutenant Colonel
> Major
> Captain
> Lieutenant

A Matron or Sister may also be so addressed and described.

Titled officers are addressed as such – Dear Dame Mary, for example – or if the acquaintance is slight as Dear Dame Mary Green, unless the recipient is unknown to the writer, in which case the Service Rank should be used: Dear Brigadier Green. Otherwise, all officers are addressed by their rank (except when mentioned below), which should not be abbreviated. The letters QARANC follow the name.

Beginning of Letter
Formal   Dear Sir or Madam or Dear Colonel Smith

Social   Dear Colonel Smith or Dear Colonel (for Majors and above)

Envelope
Initials rather than first names are customarily used, as in Major M Brown QARANC

Verbal Address
According to rank, except for Lieutenants, who are referred to as Mr or Miss/Mrs/Ms Jones. Matrons and Sisters may be so addressed and described instead of military rank.

Retired and Former Officers
Officers placed on the retired list, or who leave the Service, do not normally continue to use their ranks.

Non-Commissioned Officers
They have Army ranks.

Beginning of Letter
  Warrant Officers Dear Mr or Miss/Mrs/Ms Smith
Others according to rank Dear Corporal Jones

Envelope
Address according to rank, with QARANC after the name

Verbal Address
  Warrant Officers Mr or Miss/Mrs/Ms Smith
Others according to rank

Princess Mary's Royal Air Force Nursing Service
The Princess Mary's Royal Air Force Nursing Service (PMRAFNS) offers commissions to Registered General Nurses (RGNs) with a minimum of two years' experience after obtaining RGN and normally with a second qualification. RGNs with no additional experience or qualification are recruited as non-commissioned officers in the grade of Staff Nurse.

An officer of Princess Mary's Royal Air Force Nursing Service adds the letters PMRAFNS after his or her name, preceded by any letters signifying orders etc.

The appointments and ranks are as follows:

Director of RAF Nursing Services
   and Matron-in-Chief   Group Captain
Deputy Director of
   RAF Nursing Services Wing Commander
Matron   Wing Commander
Ward Manager   Squadron Leader
Nursing Sister   Flight Lieutenant/Flying Officer

Beginning of Letter
Formal   Dear Madam or Sir
Professional   Dear Wing Commander Smith
             (or appropriate rank)
Private   Dear Mr or Miss/Mrs/Ms Smith

Envelope
Professional   Squadron Leader Mary Smith, ARRC,
             PMRAFNS
Private   Miss Mary Smith, ARRC

Verbal Address
Professional   Squadron Leader Smith
Private   Miss Smith

Description in Conversation
As for Verbal Address.

Non-Commissioned Ranks
All non-commissioned ranks of the PMRAFNS are as for the regular Royal Air Force service.

Summary Table

Name	Envelope	Letter	Verbal Address
The Royal Navy			
Admiral of the Fleet	Admiral of the Fleet, the Earl of Bessborough, GCB, KBE	Dear Lord Bessborough	Lord Bessborough
Admiral	Admiral Sir Victor White, GCB	Dear Sir Victor or Admiral White (if not a Knight)	Sir Victor or Admiral White (if not a Knight)
Commodore	Commodore Graham Morgan, CBE, Royal Navy (or RN)	Dear Commodore Morgan	Commodore
Captain, Commander, Lieutenant-Commander, Lieutenant Sub-Lieutenant	As for Commodore, but with appropriate title		
Midshipman, Officer Cadet	Midshipman (Mid)/ Officer Cadet (O/C) Roger Vickers, Royal Navy (or RN)	Dear Mr Vickers	Mr Vickers
Royal Marine	The rank of Lieutenant Colonel and below takes 'Royal Marines' or 'RM' after any decorations		
The Army			
Officers from Field Marshal to Captain	Same form as naval ranks, e.g. Major General Nicholas Henstridge	Dear General (or Dear Sir Nicholas)/Dear General Henstridge (if not a Knight)	Sir Nicholas Henstridge/General Henstridge (if not a Knight)
Lieutenants and lower ranks	Colin Henderson, Esq, Royal Defence Regiment	Dear Mr Henderson	Mr Henderson

The Royal Air Force

Air Marshal	Air Marshal Sir Oliver Huntley, KCB, CBE, RAF	Dear Sir Oliver/Dear Air Marshal Huntley (if not a Knight)	Sir Oliver/Air Marshal Huntley (if not a not a Knight)

Flying Officers and Pilot Officers are addressed as Esq on the envelope and Mr in correspondence.

Other form is as for the other two forces.

Envelopes for official use carry the rank, title and decorations.

DIPLOMATIC SERVICE

A Foreign Ambassador Accredited to the United Kingdom and a Commonwealth High Commissioner

An Ambassador accredited to the Court of St James's is accorded the style of 'His or Her Excellency' within the United Kingdom and Colonies. A Commonwealth High Commissioner in the United Kingdom is accorded the same style and precedence as an Ambassador.

The partner of an Ambassador or High Commissioner is not entitled to the style of 'His or Her Excellency' and is referred to and addressed by name in official documents, unless titled in their own right.

Precedence within the Diplomatic Corps is accorded to an Ambassador and High Commissioner in a common roll from the time they take up their duties in London. The London Diplomatic List, published at two-monthly intervals by HMSO, contains, after the alphabetical list, a list of the heads of diplomatic missions in London in order of precedence.

Chargés d'Affaires rank after all Ambassadors and High Commissioners. If two or more are present, they rank among themselves in accordance with the precedence to their respective Ambassadors.

Other members of the Diplomatic Corps of equal rank are usually placed in alphabetical order, but the relative importance of their countries may be taken into account.

It is always correct to describe an Ambassador or High Commissioner by adding the country after the name: for example, 'His Excellency the Ambassador of Jordan' or 'His Excellency the High Commissioner for Canada'. (Note the word 'for' in respect of Commonwealth countries.)

In a letter to an Ambassador or High Commissioner, it is usual to mention 'Your Excellency' in the opening paragraph. In a long letter, subsequent references may be made to 'you' or 'your', as in 'I am most grateful to you for your assistance', but 'Your Excellency' is again stated in the closing section.

Traditionally, letters to Ambassadors have tended to be very formal. However, this is now thought of as old-fashioned and, although still technically correct, is rarely used. Therefore, it is acceptable to use the social form in almost all correspondence.

Beginning of Letter
    Formal   Your Excellency
    Social   Dear Ambassador
                    Dear High Commissioner

Ending of Letter: Ambassador
    Formal   I have the honour to be, with the highest consideration,
                    Your Excellency's obedient servant
    Social   Yours sincerely

Ending of Letter: High Commissioner
    Formal   I have the honour to be
                    Your Excellency's obedient servant
    Social   Yours sincerely

Envelope
His or Her Excellency always precedes all other styles; titles or ranks – Señor etc. – precedes Don or Doctor. An Armed Forces rank immediately follows His or Her Excellency, as in:

    His Excellency General . . .
    Her Excellency Doctor . . .
    His Excellency Monsieur, Mr, Herr, Signor, Señor, Senhor . . . etc.

If an Ambassador is His or Her Royal Highness, His or Her Highness or His or Her Serene Highness, 'His or Her Excellency' is unnecessary. 'Esq' cannot be used after 'His Excellency'.
    Formal and Social His or Her Excellency, the Ambassador of Finland or His or Her Excellency, the Finnish Ambassador

Alternatively, the envelope may be addressed to 'His or Her Excellency Herr/Frau Schmidt', followed by any letters, if known (especially if British Orders of Chivalry have been received). In such a case, where a recipient also has foreign honours, 'etc. etc.' may be added for the latter. This alternative form is to be preferred when the address that follows is not that of the embassy or when the letter is purely private.

Verbal Address
Formal   'Your Excellency' should be mentioned at least
       once in conversation, and thereafter 'Sir' or
       'Ma'am' or by name
Social   Ambassador or High Commissioner or by name

Description in Conversation
Formal   His or Her Excellency
Social   The French Ambassador or the Ambassador of
       the Ivory Coast or the Ambassador or by name
       The Canadian High Commissioner or the High
       Commissioner for Canada or the High Com-
       missioner or by name

Joint Form of Address
His or Her Excellency the French Ambassador and Madame or
Monsieur le Blanc (or appropriate title). Similarly for a High Com-
missioner and his or her partner.

British Ambassador Accredited to a Foreign Country
A British Ambassador accredited to a foreign country is known as 'His
or Her Excellency' within the country to which he or she is accredited
and often by courtesy when travelling outside it on duty, but not in the
United Kingdom. Similarly, an Ambassador who is Head of a United
Kingdom Mission abroad (for example, to the United Nations) is styled
'His or Her Excellency'.

 A lady Ambassador is called Ambassador, and not Ambassadress.
Her husband is not given any style as such.

Beginning of Letter
Formal   Sir or Madam
Social   Dear Ambassador

Ending of Letter
Formal   I have the honour to be, Sir or Madam,
       Your Excellency's obedient servant
Social   Yours sincerely

149

Envelope

Peer	His Excellency Viscount Flintshire, KCMG
	Her Excellency Viscountess Flintshire, DBE
Privy Counsellor	His Excellency the Rt Hon John Jones, CMG
	Her Excellency the Rt Hon Margaret Smith, CMG
Knight or Dame	His Excellency Sir William Smith
	Her Excellency Dame Elizabeth Jones
Esquire	His Excellency Mr John Smith, CMG
	His Excellency Major-General John Brown, CMG. 'Esq' is not used with His Excellency

Verbal Address

Formal	'Your Excellency' should be mentioned at least once in conversation, and thereafter 'Sir' or 'Ma'am' or by name
Social	Ambassador or by name

Description in Conversation

Formal	His or Her Excellency
Social	The British Ambassador or the Ambassador or by name (as applicable)

British High Commissioner in a Commonwealth Country

A High Commissioner is accorded the same style and precedence as an Ambassador and is styled 'His or Her Excellency'.

Deputy High Commissioner

Within the Commonwealth it is usual to appoint a Deputy High Commissioner to assist the High Commissioner and to act for him or her when absent. He or she has no prefix and may be addressed and referred to by name or, perhaps more commonly, as Deputy High Commissioner. A letter may be addressed by name or Dear Deputy High Commissioner.

Chargé d'Affaires and Acting High Commissioner
A Chargé d'Affaires is the style for the Deputy Ambassador. In the temporary absence of the permanent head of a diplomatic mission, or between appointments as such, a Chargé d'Affaires *ad interim* (ai) is generally appointed to conduct business.

Within the Commonwealth, he or she is generally appointed as and styled Acting High Commissioner.

When there are no plans to accredit an Ambassador, the Chargé d'Affaires *en titre* is occasionally named as the permanent head of a mission.

Chargés d'Affaires and Acting High Commissioners represent their governments rather than their Heads of State and are not accorded the style of Excellency.

An Acting High Commissioner is usually addressed by name, but it is not incorrect to address him or her by appointment thus. 'My dear Acting High Commissioner'.

Beginning of Letter
Formal	Sir or Madam
Social	Dear Chargé d'Affaires or by name

Ending of Letter
Formal:	
Foreign	I have the honour to be, Sir or Madam, with high consideration, Your obedient servant
British	I have the honour to be, Sir or Madam, your obedient servant
Social	Yours sincerely

Envelope
John Brown, Esq,
Chargé d'Affaires,
British Embassy . . .

Monsieur Georges Van Cleef,
Chargé d'Affaires
. . . Embassy

John Brown, Esq,
Acting High Commissioner,
British High Commission . . .

Shri K Singh,
Acting High Commissioner,
. . . High Commission

Verbal Address
Chargé d'Affaires
or by name

Description in Conversation
The Guatemalan Chargé d'Affaires or the Chargé d'Affaires of Guatemala
The British Chargé d'Affaires or by name (as applicable)
The Acting High Commissioner for Sri Lanka or by name

Other Members of Diplomatic Staffs, including Service Attachés
Ministers Plenipotentiary, Ministers, Minister-Counsellors, Counsellors, Advisers, First, Second and Third Secretaries, Attachés etc. and
Diplomats who are not head of their mission are usually addressed by
name, but Consuls and Consul-Generals are usually addressed as such.

Consul General, Consul or Vice Consul
A Consul General, Consul or Vice-Consul who holds Her Majesty's
Commission is entitled to the letters 'HM' before the appointment.

Other Consuls, Vice-Consuls and Consular Agents, appointed other
than by the Crown, are known as the British Consul, Vice Consul etc.
and do not have the prefix 'HM'.

The officer in charge of a Consular appointment, during the absence
of the incumbent, temporarily takes on the incumbent's rank but is
addressed as 'the Acting British Consul General, Consul' etc.

Consuls of the other Commonwealth countries are addressed as 'the
Australian Consul' etc.

Envelope
John H Brown, Esq, CMG,
HM Consul General,
British Consulate General

Mrs Margaret Smith,
HM Consul,
British Consulate

William Jones, Esq,
British Consul,
British Consulate
Otherwise as an Esquire or appropriate style.

Agent General
Each province in Canada and the Australian states of Victoria, Queensland, South Australia and Western Australia are represented in London by an Agent General. New South Wales has a Government Office but does not have diplomatic status

The state badges appear in the order New South Wales, Victoria, Queensland, South Australia, Western Australia and Tasmania.

An Agent General is not accorded any special form of address, but his or her appointment should be placed after the name, as in John Jones, Esq, Agent General for . . .

When more than one Agent General for the provinces in Canada are listed, they should be placed according to the alphabetical order of the provinces.

Governor General, Governor or Lieutenant-Governor
A Governor General or Governor is styled 'His or Her Excellency', which precedes all other titles and ranks, while administering a government and within the territory administered.

The Lieutenant Governors of Jersey, Guernsey and the Isle of Man are accorded the same style. A Lieutenant Governor of a Canadian province is accorded the style of 'the Honourable' for life. The Governor General of Canada has the rank of 'Right Honourable' for life.

Beginning of Letter

Formal	Sir or Madam
	My Lord or Lady (if a peer)
Social	Dear Lord or Lady Smith (if a peer)
	Dear Sir John (Smith) (if a Knight)
	Dear Dame Margaret (Jones) (if a Dame)

Dear Mr or Miss/Mrs/Ms Smith
or My dear Lieutenant-Governor (Canada)

Ending of Letter
    Formal   I have the honour to be, Sir or Madam (My
                          Lord or Lady, if a peer), Your Excellency's
                          obedient servant
    Social   Yours sincerely

Envelope
    Peer   His Excellency the Lord Blank, KCB, or Her
                          Excellency the Lady Blank, CBE, Governor
                          General of Australia
    Knight or Dame   His Excellency Sir John Brown, KCB, or
                          Her Excellency Dame Elizabeth Green,
                          DBE, Governor of New South Wales
    Esquire   His Excellency Mr William Robinson, CMG,
                          Governor of St Helena
                          The Hon John Smith, Lieutenant-Governor
                          of . . .
    or   His Honour the Lieutenant-Governor of . . .

Verbal Address
    Formal   Your Excellency
    Social   By name

For Canadian provinces
    Formal   Your Honour or Sir or Ma'am
    Social   By name

Description in Conversation
    Formal   His or Her Excellency or the Governor (General)
    Social   The Governor (General) or by name
                        The Lieutenant-Governor or by name

Embassies

For more specific guidelines governing etiquette within the Diplomatic Service, it is advisable to contact the Protocol Office/Department of each individual embassy.

A

Embassy of the Islamic State of Afghanistan	0171 589 8891
Embassy of the Republic of Albania	0171 730 5709
Embassy of Algeria	0171 221 7800
Embassy of the Republic of Angola	0171 495 1752
Embassy of the Republic of Argentina	0171 318 1300
Embassy of the Republic of Armenia	0171 938 5435
Australian High Commission	0171 379 4334
Austrian Embassy	0171 235 3731

B

High Commission for the Commonwealth of the Bahamas	0171 408 4488
Embassy of the State of Bahrain	0171 370 5132/3
High Commission for the People's Republic of Bangladesh	0171 584 0081
Barbados High Commission	0171 631 4975
Belgian Embassy	0171 470 3700
Belize High Commission	0171 499 9728
Bolivian Embassy	0171 235 4248/2257
Embassy of the Republic of Bosnia Herzegovina	0171 255 3758
Botswana High Commission	0171 499 0031
Brazilian Embassy	0171 499 0877
Brunei Darussalam High Commission	0171 581 0521
Embassy of the Republic of Bulgaria	0171 584 9400/9433
Embassy of The Republic of Burundi (based in Brussels)	230-45-35, 230-45-48, 230-46-76

C

High Commission for the Republic of Cameroon	0171 727 0771
Canadian High Commission	0171 258 6600
Embassy of the Central African Republic (based in Paris)	42-24-42-56
The Embassy of the Republic of Chad (based in Brussels)	215-19-75
Embassy of Chile	0171 580 6392

Embassy of the People's Republic of China	0171 636 9375/5726
Colombian Embassy	0171 589 9177/5037
Embassy of the Republic of Congo (based in Paris)	45-00-60-57
Embassy of the Democratic Republic of Congo	0171 235 6137
Embassy of the Republic of Croatia	0171 387 2022
Embassy of the Republic of Cuba	0171 240 2488
Cyprus High Commission	0171 499 8272
Embassy of the Czech Republic	0171 243 1115

D

Royal Danish Embassy	0171 333 0200
Office of the High Commissioner for the Commonwealth of Dominica	0171 370 5194/5
Embassy of the Dominican Republic	0171 727 6285

E

Embassy of Ecuador	0171 584 2648/1367/ 8084
Embassy of the Arab Republic of Egypt	0171 499 2401/3304
Embassy of El Salvador	0171 436 8282
Embassy of the Republic of Estonia	0171 589 3428
Embassy of the Federal Democratic Republic of Ethiopia	0171 584 7054

F

High Commission for the Republic of Fiji	0171 584 3661
Embassy of Finland	0171 838 6200
French Embassy	0171 201 1000

G

The Gambia High Commission	0171 937 6316/7/8
Embassy of Georgia	0171 937 8233
Embassy of the Federal Republic of Germany	0171 824 1300
Office of the High Commissioner for Ghana	0171 235 4142
Embassy of Greece	0171 229 3850
High Commission for Grenada	0171 373 7809
Embassy of Guatemala	0171 351 3042
Embassy of the Republic of Guinea (based in Paris)	47-04-81-48/ 45-53-85-45

High Commission for Guyana   0171 229 7684

H

Embassy of the Republic of Haiti closed on
    30 March 1987
Embassy of Honduras   0171 486 4880
Embassy of the Republic of Hungary   0171 235 5218

I

Embassy of Iceland   0171 730 5131/2
Office of the High Commissioner for India   0171 836 8484
Indonesian Embassy   0171 499 7661
Embassy of the Islamic Republic of Iran   0171 225 3000
Iraq. Following the break in diplomatic relations
    with the Republic of Iraq in February 1991,
    the Embassy of the Hashemite Kingdom of
    Jordan has undertaken the task of protecting
    Iraqi interests in the UK. Iraqi Interests
    Section   0171 584 7141/6
Irish Embassy   0171 235 2171
Embassy of Israel   0171 957 9500
Italian Embassy   0171 312 2200

J

Jamaican High Commission   0171 823 9911
Embassy of Japan   0171 465 6500
Embassy of the Hashemite Kingdom of Jordan 0171 937 3685

K

Embassy of the Republic of Kazakhstan   0171 581 4646
Kenya High Commission   0171 6636 2371/5
Embassy of the Republic of Korea   0171 227 5500
Embassy of the State of Kuwait   0171 590 3400

L

Embassy of the Republic of Latvia   0171 312 0040
Lebanese Embassy   0171 229 7265/6
Embassy of the Republic of Liberia   0171 221 1036
Libya. Following the break in diplomatic
    relations with the Socialist People's Arab

Jamahiriya in April 1984, the Royal Embassy
of Saudi Arabia has undertaken the task of
protecting Libyan interests in the UK. Libyan
Interests Section   0171 486 8387
Embassy of the Republic of Lithuania   0171 486 6401/2
Embassy of Luxembourg   0171 235 6961

M

Embassy of the Former Yugoslav Republic of
  Macedonia   0171 499 5152/1854
Embassy of the Republic of Madagascar (based
  in Paris)   45-04-62-11
High Commission for the Republic of Malawi   0171 491 4172/7
Malaysian High Commission   0171 235 8033
High Commission of the Republic of Maldives   0171 224 2135
Malta High Commission   0171 292 4800
Mauritius High Commission   0171 581 0294/5
Embassy of Mexico   0171 499 8586
Embassy of Mongolia   0171 937 0150
Embassy of the Kingdom of Morocco   0171 581 5001/4
High Commission of the Republic of
  Mozambique   0171 383 3800

N

High Commission for the Republic of Namibia   0171 636 6244
Royal Nepalese Embassy   0171 229 1594/6231
Royal Netherlands Embassy   0171 590 3200
New Zealand High Commission   0171 839 4580
Embassy of the Republic of Niger (based in
  Paris)   45-04-80-60
High Commission for the Republic of Nigeria   0171 839 1244
Royal Norwegian Embassy   0171 591 5500

O

Embassy of the Sultanate of Oman   0171 225 0001

P

High Commission for the Islamic Republic of
  Pakistan   0171 664 9200
Embassy of the Republic of Panama   0171 493 4646

Papua New Guinea High Commission	0171 930 0922/7
Embassy of Paraguay	0171 9377 1253/ 6629
Embassy of Peru	0171 235 1917/2545/ 3802
Embassy of the Republic of the Philippines	0171 937 1600
Embassy of the Republic of Poland	0171 580 4324/9
Portuguese Embassy	0171 235 5331

R

Embassy of Romania	0171 937 9666
Embassy of the Russian Federation	0171 229 2666
Embassy of the Republic of Rwanda	0171 930 2570

S

Embassy of the Independent State of Samoa (based in Brussels)	660-84-54
Royal Embassy of Saudi Arabia	0171 917 3000
Embassy of the Republic of Senegal	0171 937 7237
High Commission for Seychelles	0171 224 1660
Sierra Leone High Commission	0171 636 6483/6
High Commission for the Republic of Singapore	0171 235 8315
Embassy of the Slovak Republic	0171 243 0803
Embassy of the Republic of Slovenia	0171 495 7775
High Commission for the Republic of South Africa	0171 451 7299
Spanish Embassy	0171 235 5555
High Commission for the Democratic Socialist Republic of Sri Lanka	0171 262 1841/7
Embassy of the Republic of the Sudan	0171 839 8080
Kingdom of Swaziland High Commission	0171 630 6611
Embassy of Sweden	0171 917 6400
Embassy of Switzerland	0171 616 6000
Embassy of the Syrian Arab Republic	0171 245 9012

T

High Commission for the United Republic of Tanzania	0171 499 8951/4
Royal Thai Embassy	0171 589 0173/2944

Tonga High Commission	0171 724 5828
Office of the High Commissioner for the Republic of Trinidad and Tobago	0171 245 9351
Tunisian Embassy	0171 584 8117
Turkish Embassy	0171 393 0202

U

Uganda High Commission	0171 839 5783
Embassy of Ukraine	0171 727 6312
Embassy of the United Arab Emirates	0171 581 1281
United States of America (American) Embassy	0171 499 9000
Embassy of the Oriental Republic of Uruguay	0171 584 8192

V

Venezuelan Embassy	0171 584 4206/7
Embassy of the Socialist Republic of Vietnam	0171 937 1912

Y

Embassy of the Republic of Yemen	0171 584 6607
Embassy of the Federal Republic of Yugoslavia (Serbia and Montenegro)	0171 370 6105

Z

High Commission for the Republic of Zambia	0171 589 6655
High Commission for the Republic of Zimbabwe	0171 836 7755

LAW: ENGLAND AND WALES

Lord Chancellor

The Lord High Chancellor of Great Britain, colloquially called 'the Lord Chancellor', is the chief judicial officer in England, and receives a peerage on appointment. He is also a member of the Privy Council and of the Cabinet. He is Speaker of the House of Lords, where he sits on the Woolsack, President of the House of Lords sitting in its judicial capacity as the highest Court of Appeal in the United Kingdom, and President of the Court of Appeal and of the Chancery Division of the High Court. He vacates office with the government.

A letter concerning his department should be addressed to the Rt Hon the Lord Chancellor.

Beginning of Letter

Formal	My Lord
Social	Dear Lord Chancellor

Otherwise according to his rank in the peerage. The letters QC do not appear after his name.

Lord Chief Justice of England

He is the head of the judges of the Queen's Bench Division and takes precedence over all other judges of this Division. He also presides in the Court of Appeal (Criminal Division). He is a Privy Counsellor, and on appointment is raised to the peerage.

A letter concerning his office may be addressed to the Rt Hon the Lord Chief Justice of England.

Beginning of Letter

Formal	My Lord
Social	Dear Lord Chief Justice

Otherwise according to his rank in the peerage. The letters QC do not appear after his name.

Master of the Rolls

The Master of the Rolls sits on and presides over the Court of Appeal (Civil Division) and has third place in legal seniority after the Lord Chancellor and the Lord Chief Justice.

He is knighted on appointment, and is a member of the Privy Council.

He is addressed according to his judicial rank. A letter concerning his office may be addressed to the Rt Hon the Master of the Rolls.

President of the Family Division

The President presides over the Family Division of the High Court. In legal precedence his place is next after the Master of the Rolls.

He is knighted on appointment, and is a member of the Privy Council. He is addressed according to his judicial rank.

Lords of Appeal in Ordinary

Lords of Appeal in Ordinary, who are always members of the Privy Council, are created peers for life. They preside over appeals in the House of Lords in its judicial capacity.

The letters QC are not used after the name of a Lord of Appeal in Ordinary.

A Lord of Appeal in Ordinary is appointed a peer under Section 6 of the Appellate Jurisdiction Act 1876, by virtue of which he is entitled during his life to rank as a Baron. That he is not in law a Baron is demonstrated by the fact that it required a Royal Warrant, which was not issued until 1897, to give his children precedence next after the children of a Baron.

Lord Justice of the Court of Appeal

Sixteen Lord Justices are appointed to sit in the Court of Appeal with the Master of the Rolls. Such a judge is admitted to the Privy Council as a member of the Judicial Committee, and normally will have been created a Knight or a Dame as a Judge of the High Court of Justice.

The forename is not used as a form of address except where there is more than one Lord Justice with the same surname. Then the senior is not referred to by his forename, but the first name of a junior is used on all occasions (for example, Rt Hon Lord Justice Davies

162

and Rt Hon Lord Justice Edmund Davies).
    The letters QC do not appear after the name.
    A retired Lord Justice is addressed 'the Rt Hon Sir John Blank'.

Beginning of Letter
        Formal   My Lord or My Lady
        Social   Dear Lord or Lady Justice

Envelope
The Rt Hon Lord or Lady Justice Smith

Verbal Address
        Formal   My Lord or My Lady
        Social   Lord or Lady Justice

Description in Conversation
        Formal and Social The Lord Justice or Lord Justice Brown
        Judicial Matters   His Lordship or Her Ladyship
        especially on the Bench

Judge of High Court

The High Court of Justice is the part of the Supreme Court of Judicature
which does not comprise the Court of Appeal or the Crown Court, and
is divided into three Divisions: Queen's Bench, Chancery and Family.
High Court Judges are styled 'the Hon Mr Justice' and are known as
Puisne (pronounced 'pju:ni') Judges, which literally means 'younger'.
    High Court Judges are knighted on appointment or made Dame of
the Most Excellent Order of the British Empire.
    The letters QC do not appear after their names.

Beginning of Letter: Men
        Formal: Dear Sir
        Judicial Matters   My Lord or Sir
        Social   Dear Judge (excluding the surname)

Envelope: Men
        Formal and Judicial
            Matters   The Hon Mr Justice Smith (excluding the
                                 first name). If there is more than one Judge

163

of the High Court with the same surname, the senior Judge is referred to by his surname alone, and the forename of the junior Judge is used on all occasions, as in Mrs Justice Lane and Mr Justice Geoffrey Lane.

Social   Sir John Smith ('the Honourable' is not used in conjunction with 'Sir John Smith')

Verbal Address: Men

Judicial Matters and
     on the Bench   My (or His) Lord or Your (or His) Lordship
Social   Mr Justice Smith or Sir John (Smith): for example, Sir John and Lady Smith
Members of the Bar may address a High Court Judge as 'judge'

Beginning of Letter: Women

Formal   Dear Madam
Social   Dear Dame Elizabeth (Lane)

Envelope: Women

Formal and Judicial
     Matters   The Hon Mrs Justice Lane (regardless of marital status)
Social   The Hon Dame Elizabeth Lane

Verbal Address: Women

Judicial Matters and
     on the Bench   My (or Her) Lady or Your (or Her) Ladyship
Social   Mrs Justice Lane or Dame Elizabeth (Lane)
Members of the Bar may address her as 'Judge'

Judge of High Court (Retired)

High Court Judges retire when they are seventy-five.

The prefix 'the Honourable' and style 'the Hon Mr (or Mrs) Justice' are dropped on retirement.

Circuit Judge
If he or she was a Queen's Counsel when at the Bar, the letters QC should follow the name in correspondence.

Beginning of Letter
Formal and Judicial
    Matters   Dear Sir or Dear Madam
  Social   Dear Judge

Envelope
Formal and Social His or Her Honour Judge Smith (excluding forename). If more than one Circuit Judge of the same surname are assembled together at the same address, the forename may be added in brackets.
If a Knight:
Formal   His Honour Judge Sir John Smith
Social   Sir John Smith

Verbal Address
Formal   Sir or Madam or the Judge or Judge (Surname)
Judicial Matters and
  on the Bench   Your Honour or His or Her Honour
Social   Judge (excluding surname). If he is a Knight, he may also be called privately Sir John (Smith)

Retired Circuit Judges
The prefix 'His (or Her) Honour' is retained on retirement, but the word judge is replaced with forename or initials, so Judge Smith becomes on an envelope His Honour John Smith.

Attorney-General and Solicitor-General
They are Law Officers of the Crown, advise the government on legal matters, and represent the Crown in Court in the more serious or important cases. Both are political appointments.

The Attorney-General is head of the Bar in England and takes precedence over all barristers. The Solicitor-General is junior in precedence to the Attorney-General and is a Queen's Counsel.

A Solicitor-General is also appointed for Scotland.

They can be addressed in letters or on envelopes by name or rank.

Queen's Counsel and Barristers

Barristers are divided into Queen's Counsel and Junior Counsel. When a barrister becomes a QC, he or she is said to 'take silk' from the silk gown that they wear.

The letters QC are placed after the name of Queen's Counsel while they are at the Bar or after appointment to the Circuit Bench. Those who were appointed King's Counsel changed the letters KC to QC at the beginning of the present reign.

A QC appointed a Circuit Judge continues to use the initials, but High Court Judges cease to use them.

Recorders

Recorders are barristers or solicitors. The correct address is the same as that for an Esquire or female equivalent, or according to rank.

On the Bench they are addressed as 'Your Honour'.

If the Recorder is Queen's Counsel, then QC should be added after his or her name.

Beginning of Letter
    Formal   Dear Sir or Madam
    Official Business   Dear Mr or Miss/Mrs/Ms Recorder
    Social   As for an Esquire or female equivalent, or
                    applicable rank

Envelope
    Formal and Social   As for an Esquire or female equivalent

Justice of the Peace and Magistrate

Justices of the Peace are appointed by the Crown for every metropolitan and non-metropolitan county. On the Bench he or she is addressed as 'Your Worship' and described as 'His or Her Worship'; otherwise as an Esquire or a female equivalent. He or she may use the letters JP after his or her name. The letters JP precede DL (Deputy Lieutenant), as the former is a Crown appointment and the latter a Lord-Lieutenant's appointment.

If a Justice of the Peace has been transferred to the Supplemental List at the age of seventy, he or she may still have the letters JP placed after their name.

Stipendiary Magistrate

These are full-time paid appointments, held by barristers or solicitors.

While on the Bench he or she is addressed as a Magistrate, otherwise as an Esquire, followed by the appointment.

A Stipendiary Magistrate is not accorded JP after his or her name.

Coroner

He or she is addressed as an Esquire or equivalent and is known as 'Sir' or 'Ma'am' in court.

Diocesan Chancellor: Men

The Bishop of the Diocese usually appoints the Diocesan Chancellor for life. He acts as the legal adviser to the Bishop and is Judge of the Consistory Court.

The following instructions are for writing to the Diocesan Chancellor in his official capacity only.

Beginning of Letter
Formal	Dear Chancellor or Dear Sir
Social	Dear Chancellor

Envelope
The Worshipful Chancellor Peter (or P) Smith
If in Holy Orders: the Reverend Chancellor Peter Smith

Verbal Address
Formal	Mr Chancellor
Social	Chancellor
In Court	Sir or Worshipful Sir (not Your Worship)

Description in Conversation
The Chancellor (or if necessary the Diocesan Chancellor)

Diocesan Chancellor: Women
As above, with the following exceptions:

Beginning of Letter
Formal	Dear Chancellor or Dear Madam
Social	Dear Chancellor

Envelope
The Worshipful Chancellor Miss Sheila Cameron

Verbal Address
Formal	Madam Chancellor
Social	Chancellor
In Court	Madam or Worshipful Madam (not Your Worship)

LAW: SCOTLAND

Lord of Session

A Senator (Judge) of the College of Justice in Scotland is known as a Lord of Session. On taking his seat on the Bench he is given a Judicial title by which he is known both in office and on retirement.

The Lord Justice General and the Lord Justice Clerk are addressed for all purposes by their appointments and not by the Judicial Titles with which they take their seats on the Bench.

Beginning of Letter

Formal	My Lord
Social	Dear Lord Cameron

Envelope

The Hon Lord Cameron
  If a Privy Counsellor, the Rt Hon Lord Wylie

Verbal Address

Formal	My Lord
Social	Lord Cameron

Description in Conversation

By their judicial title: for example, Lord Cameron. The Lord Justice General and the Lord Justice Clerk are known by their appointments.

Retirement

As in office.

Lord Justice General

The Lord Justice General and the Lord Justice Clerk are always addressed by their appointments and not by the judicial titles with which they take their seats on the Bench.

They are Lords of Session and Privy Counsellors.

Beginning of Letter

| Formal | My Lord |
| Social | Dear Lord Justice General |

Envelope
The Rt Hon the Lord Justice General

Description in Conversation
Lord Justice General

Retirement
When retired from office, they are known by the judicial title with the prefix 'the Right Honourable'.

Lord Justice Clerk

On taking his seat on the Bench he receives a judicial title but is always described by his office.

Beginning of Letter

| Formal | My Lord |
| Social | Dear Lord Justice Clerk |

Envelope
The Rt Hon the Lord Justice Clerk if a Privy Counsellor; otherwise the Hon the Lord Justice Clerk.

Verbal Address

| Formal | My Lord |
| Social | Lord Justice Clerk |

Description in Conversation
Lord Justice Clerk

Retirement
If he retires from office, he is known by his judicial title with the prefix 'the Right Hon' if a Privy Counsellor; otherwise 'the Hon'.

Wife or Widow of Lord Justice Clerk
As for the wife or widow of a Lord of Session (see below).

Chairman of Scottish Land Court
On appointment as Chairman he receives a judicial title by which he is always known, both in office and on retirement. He is treated as a Lord of Session.

Wife or Widow of a Lord of Session and of the Chairman of Scottish Land Court
A wife or widow of a Lord of Session (including Lord Justice General and Lord Justice Clerk) and of the Chairman of the Scottish Land Court is addressed by her husband's judicial title preceded by 'Lady'

She has no prefix before 'Lady', but in other respects she is addressed as the wife of a Baron.

Children of a Lord of Session and of the Chairman of Scottish Land Court
They receive no courtesy rank or style.

Lord Advocate
The Lord Advocate is the principal Law Officer of the Crown in Scotland, corresponding to the Attorney-General in England. He is one of the four Law Officers of the Crown, and as such a Minister of the Crown.

He may be either a Member of Parliament or a member of the House of Lords, but need not necessarily be either. He is invariably admitted to the Privy Council on taking office, as he is a member of the Scottish Universities Committee of the Council.

Beginning of Letter

Formal	My Lord (if a peer)
Otherwise	Dear Sir
Social	By name but, if connected with his department, 'Dear Lord Advocate'

Envelope
The Rt Hon the Lord Advocate, QC, MP or the Rt Hon John Smith, QC, MP

Sheriff
The office of Sheriff in Scotland is now principally a judicial one. The Sheriff Courts have a very wide criminal and civil jurisdiction, considerably wider than the jurisdiction of the Crown Courts and the County Courts in England.

The holder of the office of Sheriff Principal is, however, the direct descendant of the king's peace-keeping officer of feudal times and continues to exercise administrative and executive functions within his Sheriffdom.

Scotland is divided into six Sheriffdoms, each having its own Sheriff Principal. Most Sheriffdoms are divided into Sheriff Court districts, each having one or more Sheriff(s). Within his own Sheriffdom, the Sheriff Principal takes precedence immediately after the Lord-Lieutenant.

The Sheriffs Principal are all senior Queen's Counsel and are appointed on a full-time basis. All the Sheriffs are either advocates or solicitors and are also appointed on a full-time basis.

All Sheriffs Principal and Sheriffs are addressed as 'My Lord' or 'My Lady' on the Bench, and as 'Sheriff Smith' formally and socially.

LAW: NORTHERN IRELAND

The Lord Chief Justice, if a Knight, is addressed by his forename and surname, as in 'the Right Honourable Sir Robert Lowry, Lord Chief Justice of Northern Ireland'.

The remainder of the judiciary is addressed as in England and Wales.

Summary Table

Name	Envelope	Letter	Verbal Address
The Lord Chancellor	The Rt Hon the Lord Chancellor	Dear Lord Chancellor	Lord Chancellor
The Lord Chief Justice of England	The Rt Hon the Lord Chief Justice of England	Dear Lord Chief Justice	Lord Chief Justice
Master of the Rolls	The Rt Hon the Master of the Rolls	Dear Master of the Rolls or Dear John Smith	Master of the Rolls or by name
The President of the Family Division	The Rt Hon the President of the Family Division	Dear President or Dear John Smith	President or by name
Lords of Appeal (in Ordinary)	The Rt Hon the Lord Roch	Dear Lord Roch	Lord Roch
Lord Justice of the Court of Appeal	The Rt Hon Lord Justice Kirkwood	Dear Lord Justice	Lord Justice
High Court Judge	The Hon Mr Justice Simpson	Dear Judge	Mr Simpson
Female High Court Judge Elizabeth	The Hon Mrs Justice Acton, DBE	Dear Judge or Dear Dame	Dame Elizabeth
Circuit Judge	His Honour Judge Reeves/His Honour Sir Donald Reeves (if he or she was a Queen's Counsel when at the Bar, then QC should follow name)	Dear Judge	Judge
Queen's Counsel	Donald Reeves, Esq, QC	Dear Mr Reeves	Mr Reeves

LOCAL GOVERNMENT

Lord-Lieutenant
The Crown appoints a Lord-Lieutenant (the two words should be
hyphenated) for each of the following regions:

England

Bedfordshire
Bristol
Berkshire
Buckinghamshire
Cambridgeshire
Cheshire
Cornwall
Cumbria
Derbyshire
Devon
Dorset
Durham
East Riding of Yorkshire
East Sussex
Essex
Gloucestershire
Greater London
Greater Manchester
Hampshire
Hereford and Worcester
Hertfordshire
Isle of Wight (Lord-Lieutenant
    and Governor)

Kent
Lancashire
Leicestershire
Lincolnshire
Merseyside
Norfolk
Northamptonshire
Northumberland
North Yorkshire
Nottinghamshire
Oxfordshire
Rutland
Somerset
South Yorkshire
Staffordshire
Suffolk
Surrey
Tyne and Wear
Warwickshire
West Midlands
West Sussex
West Yorkshire
Wiltshire

Wales

Clwyd
Dyfed
Gwent
Gwynedd

Mid Glamorgan
Powys
South Glamorgan
West Glamorgan

Scotland
Scotland has thirty-one Lord-Lieutenants appointed by Her Majesty the Queen. In addition, the Lord Provosts of the cities of Aberdeen, Dundee, Edinburgh and Glasgow are ex officio Lord-Lieutenants for those cities.

Aberdeenshire	Morayshire
Angus	Nairn
Argyll and Bute	Orkney
Ayrshire and Arran	Perth and Kinross
Banffshire	Renfrewshire
Berwickshire	Ross and Cromarty
Caithness	Roxburgh, Ettrick and Lauderdale
Clackmannan	Shetland
Dumfries	Stewartry of Kirkcudbright
Dunbartonshire	Stirling and Falkirk
East Lothian	Sutherland
Fife	Tweeddale
Inverness	West Lothian
Kincardineshire	Western Isles
Lanarkshire	Wigtown
Midlothian	

Northern Ireland
The Crown appoints a Lord-Lieutenant for each of the following:

Co Antrim	Co Fermanagh
Co Armagh	Co Londonderry
Belfast city	Londonderry city
Co Down	Co Tyrone

A Lord-Lieutenant is the Sovereign's representative in each county etc. Officially, he or she is appointed 'Her Majesty's Lord-Lieutenant of and in the County of . . .', but the usual style is the Lord-Lieutenant of Blankshire.

Form of Address
There is no specific form of address for a Lord-Lieutenant, nor are letters appended after his or her name. Correspondence may be addressed:

Formal	Colonel Sir John Brown, KCB, DSO, HM Lord-Lieutenant of Blankshire
Otherwise	Colonel Sir John Brown, KCB, DSO, Lord-Lieutenant of Blankshire

In speech a Lord-Lieutenant is referred to as 'Lord-Lieutenant' or 'the Lord-Lieutenant'. The plural form of Lord-Lieutenant is Lord-Lieutenants.

HM Lieutenant

For the following counties the Crown also appoints one or more Lieutenants, styled Her Majesty's Lieutenant for Blankshire, who also represent the Sovereign.

Yorkshire (five)
Sussex (two)
Lothian (two)
Glamorgan (three)
Londonderry (two)

There is no specific form of address for a Lieutenant, nor are there any letters for this appointment appended after the name.

Official correspondence is addressed:

Formal	Mrs Catherine Catsby, HM Lieutenant of Blankshire
Otherwise	Mrs Catherine Catsby, Lieutenant of Blankshire

In speech a Lieutenant is referred to as 'Her Majesty's Lieutenant'.

Vice Lord-Lieutenant

For the period of office, a Lord-Lieutenant appoints a Vice Lord-Lieutenant from among the Deputy Lieutenants.

There is no recognised abbreviation for a Vice Lord-Lieutenant: he or she continues to use the letters DL after their name.

Official correspondence is addressed:

Edward Green, Esq, DL
Vice Lord-Lieutenant of Blankshire

Deputy Lieutenant

For the period of office, the Lord-Lieutenant of Greater London also appoints thirty-two 'designated Deputy Lieutenants' (one for each London borough) from among the Deputy Lieutenants, for whom there is likewise no recognised abbreviation, and to whom official correspondence should be addressed:
Robert White, Esq, DL, Assistant Lieutenant of Greater London.

These guidelines apply for Lord-Lieutenants and their deputies in Scotland, Northern Ireland and Wales.

High Sheriff

The Crown, on the advice of the Privy Council, appoints a High Sheriff annually in March for each of the regions listed above in England. The Duke of Cornwall (the Prince of Wales) appoints the High Sheriff of Cornwall, and The Queen, in right of her Duchy of Lancaster, appoints the High Sheriffs for Lancashire, Greater Manchester and Merseyside.

High Sheriffs of regions and cities in Northern Ireland and regions in Wales are appointed as listed above, except in Wales, where three are appointed for, respectively, Mid Glamorgan, South Glamorgan and West Glamorgan.

Official correspondence may be addressed:
Mrs Jane Edwards,
High Sheriff of Loamshire.

Sheriff: England, Wales and Northern Ireland

City of London
Two Sheriffs are elected annually by the City Guilds (the Livery Companies). It is customary for an Alderman who has not served the office of Lord Mayor to be elected as one of them.

The Sheriff who is also an Alderman is addressed according to rank, or simply as 'Sheriff', but when writing in official capacity the following forms may be used.

Beginning of Letter
Dear Alderman and Sheriff (omitting the name)

Envelope: Men
Mr Alderman and Sheriff Smith

177

Alderman and Sheriff Sir John Brown
Alderman and Sheriff the Rt Hon Lord Portsdown
Lieutenant-Colonel, Alderman and Sheriff Jones

Envelope: Women
Miss/Mrs/Ms Alderman and Sheriff White
Alderman and Sheriff Lady Green (being the wife of a Baronet or Knight)
Alderman and Sheriff the Lady Loamshire (being the wife of a peer)

Verbal Address
Sheriff, or by name. The Sheriff who is not an Alderman is addressed
as above, but omitting all reference to Alderman.

Sheriff: Other Cities etc.
The City of Oxford has the right to elect a Sheriff annually, as have the
following, which were anciently counties in themselves, or were
'counties corporate':

Berwick-upon-Tweed	Lichfield
Bristol	Lincoln
Canterbury	Newcastle upon Tyne
Carmarthen	Norwich
Chester	Nottingham
Durham	Poole
Exeter	Southampton
Gloucester	Worcester
Kingston upon Hull	York

These Sheriffs, whose duties are chiefly of a ceremonial kind, are not to
be confused with High Sheriffs of counties.

There is no special form of address for these Sheriffs, although the
appointment may follow the name in official correspondence.

Under-Sheriff
One (or occasionally more than one) Under-Sheriff may be appointed
to assist each High Sheriff or to act in his or her absence.

One or two Under-Sheriffs are also appointed to assist the Sheriffs
for the City of London.

There is no specific form of address, but in official correspondence the appointment is included after the name, as in
Brigadier John Jones, CBE,
Under-Sheriff of Cheshire

Chairman of a County Council
Each of the regions in England listed above under Lord-Lieutenant has a County Council which elects a Chairman, a Vice-Chairman and in some cases a Deputy Chairman.

So, too, with the regions in Wales, except that there are separate County Councils for Mid Glamorgan, South Glamorgan and West Glamorgan.

Beginning of Letter
Dear Chairman (even though the office be held by a woman)

Envelope
Formal	The Chairman of Cheshire County Council
Social	By name: that is Mr Smith or Mrs Jones

Verbal Address
Chairman (even though the office be held by a woman) or by name: that is, Mr Smith or Mrs Jones

Description in Conversation
The Chairman or by name.

For Vice-Chairman and Deputy Chairman the above rules apply.

In Scotland each of the following regions has a Regional or Islands Council:

Those that elect a Convenor and Vice-Convenor	*Those that elect a Chairman and Vice-Chairman*
Borders	Central
Dumfries and Galloway	Fife
Lothian	Grampian
Western Isles	Highland
	Orkney
	Shetland

Strathclyde
Tayside

A Convenor is addressed as for a Chairman, omitting 'Mr'.

A Vice-Convenor is addressed as for a Vice-Chairman, omitting 'Mr'.

Civic Heads, England and Wales

New Mayor and Assembly for London

Plans for a new elected Mayor and Assembly could reach fruition by the year 2000. Many details are yet to be confirmed, but the following is the proposed general structure of the new system.

EU and Commonwealth citizens living in London will elect a Mayor by the supplementary voting system.

The new Assembly will comprise twenty-five members, fourteen representing a voting area and a further eleven London-wide members.

The Greater London Authority (GLA) will have some 250 staff to run committees and implement policy, and for administration.

Two new executive bodies, Transport for London (TFL) and the London Development Agency, together with two new Authorities, the Metropolitan Police Authority (MPA) and the London Fire and Emergency Planning Authority (LFEPA), will give the Mayor sweeping powers over transport and economic development.

The MPA will consist of twenty-three members appointed by the Mayor, including the Deputy Mayor.

The LFEPA will be made up of seventeen representatives appointed by the Mayor, including nine GLA members and eight members nominated by the boroughs, which will represent the thirty-three local authorities.

The Mayor will be responsible for designing an economic development strategy which is to be implemented by the new executive London Development Agency (LDA) under his or her guidance.

The Mayor will address the key issues in the capital, which will include transport, 'spatial development', the environment, housing, and the development and preservation of culture and international recognition and status.

Etiquette and protocol for the new Mayor and Assembly are as yet ambiguous. However, the inference is that it will be a modern and less rigid system, with the emphasis very much on representation as opposed to tradition.

Existing Structure
Greater London
These are:

> The Lord Mayor of London
> The Lord Mayor of Westminster
> The Mayor of the Royal Borough of Kensington and Chelsea
> The Mayor of the Royal Borough of Kingston-upon-Thames
> The Mayors of the twenty-nine other boroughs into which the area is divided

Northern Ireland has neither County nor Regional Councils.

Cities Elsewhere
The following elect Lord Mayors:

Birmingham	Newcastle upon Tyne
Bradford	Norwich
Bristol	Nottingham
Cardiff	Oxford
Coventry	Plymouth
Kingston upon Hull	Portsmouth
Leeds	Sheffield
Leicester	Stoke-on-Trent
Liverpool	York
Manchester	

The following elect Mayors:

Bath	Lancaster
Cambridge	Lincoln
Canterbury	Peterborough
Carlisle	St Albans
Chester	Salford
Derby	Southampton
Durham	Swansea

Exeter
Gloucester
Hereford

Wakefield
Winchester
Worcester

The following elect Chairmen:

Bangor
Chichester
Ely
Lichfield
Ripon

Rochester
Salisbury
Truro
Wells

Metropolitan District and District Councils
For a full list of these, see *The Municipal Year Book*. Each of these granted borough status elects a Mayor; the others elect a Chairman.

Parish Councils (England only) and Community Councils (Wales only)
Those that have adopted the style of City or Town Council elect a City Mayor or Town Mayor. For a full list, see *The Municipal Year Book*. The remainder elect a Chairman.

Civic Heads, Northern Ireland

Cities
Belfast elects a Lord Mayor.
Londonderry elects a Mayor.

District Councils
For a full list of these, see *The Municipal Year Book*. Some elect a Mayor, others a Chairman.

Lord Mayor

The Lord Mayor of London, Westminster and York have been styled 'the Right Honourable' since time immemorial. Other Lord Mayors are so styled only when granted this privilege by the Sovereign: these are Belfast and Cardiff. The remainder are usually styled 'the Right Worshipful'.

There is no difference in the form of address for a female Lord Mayor.

Beginning of Letter

Formal	My Lord Mayor
Social	Dear Lord Mayor

Envelope

Formal and Social The Right Honourable the Lord Mayor
of . . .

The Right Worshipful the Lord Mayor of . . .

If desired, the name, preceded by Councillor, may follow the office, but 'the Right Honourable' or 'the Right Worshipful' should always be placed before 'the Lord Mayor'.

Verbal Address

My Lord Mayor, or Lord Mayor

Description in Conversation

The Lord Mayor, or The Lord Mayor of . . .

Lady Mayoress

A Lady Mayoress (that is, the wife or other chosen female consort, such as a daughter, of a Lord Mayor) is not styled 'the Right Honourable' or 'the Right Worshipful'.

Beginning of Letter

Formal	My Lady Mayoress
Social	Dear Lady Mayoress

Envelope

The Lady Mayoress of . . .

If desired, the name, preceded by Councillor, where applicable, may follow the office.

Verbal Address
My Lady Mayoress or Lady Mayoress

Description in Conversation
The Lady Mayoress or
The Lady Mayoress of . . .

Lord Mayor's Consort
A lady Lord Mayor's husband is so styled but is addressed by his name.

Deputy Lord Mayor
The rules for addressing a Lord Mayor apply, except that he or she is styled neither 'Right Honourable' nor 'Right Worshipful', and the verbal address is 'Deputy Lord Mayor'.

There is no Deputy Lord Mayor of (the City of) London. An Alderman deputising for the Lord Mayor of London is styled Lord Mayor *locum tenens*.

Deputy Lady Mayoress
The rules for addressing a Lady Mayoress apply, except that the verbal address is 'Deputy Lady Mayoress'.

Mayor
The Mayor of a city is styled 'the Right Worshipful'. The Mayors of Hastings, Hythe, new Romney and Rye, the ancient Cinque Ports, are also styled in this way. All other Mayors (including town Mayors) are styled 'the Worshipful'.

Beginning of Letter
    Formal   Mr or Madam Mayor
    Social   Dear Mr or Madam Mayor
  These forms are used even if the Mayor is a peer.

Envelope
The Right Worshipful the Mayor of (the City of) . . .
The Worshipful the Mayor of the Royal Borough of . . .

The Worshipful the Mayor of . . .

If desired, the Mayor's name, preceded by Councillor, may follow the office, but 'the Right Worshipful' or 'the Worshipful' should precede 'the Mayor'.

Verbal Address
Mr or Madam Mayor
or Mayor

'Your Worship' is archaic, except when the Mayor is sitting as a magistrate (to do this, he or she must also be a Justice of the Peace).

If, however, more than one Mayor is present, 'Your Worships' must be used because there is no acceptable plural form of 'Mr or Madam Mayor'.

Description in Conversation
The Mayor or
The Mayor of . . .

Mayoress

A Mayoress (that is, the wife or other chosen female consort, such as a daughter, of a Mayor) is so styled, not 'the Right Worshipful' or 'the Worshipful'.

Beginning of Letter
> Formal   Madam Mayoress
> Social   Dear Mayoress

These forms are used even if the Mayoress is a peeress.

Envelope
The Mayoress of . . .

If desired, the Mayoress's name, preceded by Councillor (where applicable), may follow the office.

Verbal Address
Mayoress

Description in Conversation
The Mayoress or the Mayoress of . . .

Mayor's Consort
A lady Mayor's husband is so styled, but for all purposes he should be addressed by name.

Deputy Mayor
A Deputy Mayor is so styled, not 'the Right Worshipful' or 'the Worshipful'. Otherwise the above rules for addressing a Mayor apply.

Deputy Mayoress
As above for a Mayoress, with the addition of 'Deputy'.

Chairman of District Council or Parish Council
As for the Chairman of a County Council, (see page 179).

Alderman (Corporation of London only)
Beginning of Letter

Formal	Dear Alderman
Social	By name

Envelope: Men

Formal	Mr Alderman (followed by his name)
	Alderman Sir (followed by his name etc. for a Baronet or Knight)
	Alderman the Right Hon Lord (followed by his title etc. for a peer)
	Lieutenant Colonel and Alderman (followed by his title, name etc. for one holding a rank in the Armed Forces)

Envelope: Women

Formal	Mrs or Miss Alderman (followed by her name)
	Alderman Lady (followed by her name for the wife of a Baronet or Knight)
	Alderman the Lady (followed by her title for the wife of a peer)
Social	By name

Verbal Address
As for Description in Conversation, below.

Description in Conversation: Men
Alderman, which may be followed by his name and, where applicable, his title.

Description in Conversation: Women
Alderman, which may be followed by her name, preceded by Mrs or Miss or, where applicable, her title.

Honorary Alderman
Councils may elect Honorary Aldermen for life. They are addressed as for an Esquire, or appropriate rank, except that on the envelope 'Honorary Alderman' may follow the name.

Common Councilman (Corporation of London only)
As for an Esquire, or appropriate rank. For a woman, her correct style.
   On the envelope the letters CC should follow the name after any orders or decorations. Members of the Court of Common Council are not styled 'Councillor'.

Deputy (Corporation of London only)
A Common Councilman in each ward is appointed Deputy to the Alderman of the ward. He or she is addressed at the beginning of a letter as 'Dear Deputy' and on the envelope as for an Esquire, or appropriate rank, or in the case of a woman, her correct style followed by the word 'Deputy'.

City, Borough or District Councillor
Beginning of Letter

Formal	Dear Councillor, which may be followed by his or her name, preceded, where applicable, by rank and title or, in the case of a woman, by 'Mrs' or 'Miss' ('Mr' is not used)
Social	By name

Envelope

Formal	Councillor, followed by his or her name preceded, where applicable, by rank and title and, in the case of a woman, by 'Mrs' or 'Miss'
Social	By name

Verbal Address
Councillor, which may be followed by his or her name and, where applicable, rank, title and, in the case of a woman, 'Mrs' or 'Miss' ('Mr' is not used)

Description in Conversation
As for Verbal Address.

Corporation and Municipal Officers

These are normally addressed by their appointment: for example, at the beginning of a letter 'Dear Chief Executive' and on the envelope 'the Chief Executive (of . . .)'.

Similarly, 'Dear Town Clerk', 'Dear Chamberlain', 'Dear City Engineer'. Formal letters may, however, begin 'Dear Sir or Madam'.

Civic Heads, Scotland

The District Councils of the cities of Aberdeen, Dundee, Edinburgh and Glasgow elect Lord Provosts. The Lord Provosts of Edinburgh and Glasgow are styled 'the Right Honourable'.

Other District Councils elect a Provost, a Chairman or a Convenor. For a full list see *The Municipal Year Book*.

Beginning of Letter

Formal	My Lord Provost
	Dear Provost
	Dear (Mr or Madam) Chairman
	Dear Convenor
Social	Dear Lord Provost. Otherwise as above

There is no difference in the form of address for a lady Lord Provost.

Envelope
The Rt Hon the Lord Provost of Edinburgh or Glasgow

188

The Lord Provost of Aberdeen or Dundee
The Provost of . . .
The Chairman of . . .
The Convenor of . . .

Description in Conversation
The Lord Provost (of . . .)
The Provost (of . . .)
The Chairman (of . . .)
The Convenor (of . . .)

Verbal Address
My Lord Provost
Provost
Chairman
Convenor

Lady Provost
The wife (or other chosen lady consort, such as a daughter) of a Lord Provost is styled 'the Lady Provost', but the Lady Provosts of Edinburgh and Glasgow are not styled 'the Right Honourable'.

Beginning of Letter

Formal	My Lady Provost
Social	Dear Lady Provost

Envelope
The Lady Provost of . . .
  If desired, this may be followed by her name.

Description in Conversation
The Lady Provost (of . . .)

Verbal Address
My Lady Provost or Lady Provost

Wife of a Provost, Chairman or Convenor

The wife of a Provost, Chairman or Convenor has no style comparable with Mayoress. She is addressed by name.

Councillor

The form of address follows English practice (see page 187).

Municipal Officers

The form of address follows English practice except for the use of Depute in lieu of Deputy, as in Depute Chief Executive.

Republic of Ireland

Dublin and Cork elect Lord Mayors who are styled 'the Right Honourable'. Other cities and towns elect Mayors who are styled 'the Worshipful'. Forms of address are as in England.

Space precludes inclusion of the rules distinguishing cities from towns since these vary from country to country. In general terms, however, the smaller municipalities are towns, the larger ones cities.

Summary Table

Name & Place Card	Envelope	Letter	Verbal Address
Lord (and Lady) Mayor *Place Card:* Lord Mayor	The Right Honourable Lord Mayor of Coventry (Some lord mayors are styled the Right Worshipful instead of the Right Honourable. Always check individual circumstances)	Dear Lord Mayor	My Lord Mayor or Lord Mayor
Lady Mayoress (usually wife or daughter of Mayor) *Place Card:* Lady Mayoress	The Lady Mayoress of Coventry	Dear Lady Mayoress	Lady Mayoress

Consort of Lady Mayor is called the Lord Mayor's Consort, but is addressed by his name. *Place Card:* Mr David Howden	David Howden, Esq	Dear Mr Howden	Mr Howden
Mayor *Place Card:* Mayor of Manchester	Generally, Mayors of cities and particular historical towns are styled 'the Right Worshipful the Mayor of Manchester'. Other town Mayors are usually styled 'the Worshipful Mayor of Dunlop'	Dear Mr Mayor	Mr Mayor
Alderman *Place Card:* Alderman Wade	Mr Alderman Wade/ Alderman Sir Michael Wade/Alderman the Rt Hon the Lord Wade/Major and Alderman Wade (this is also correct for women)	Dear Alderman or Dear Name	Alderman Wade
City, Borough or District Councillor *Place Card:* Councillor Hanson	Councillor Hanson	Dear Councillor	Councillor

MEDICINE

There are two distinct forms of address for the broad disciplines of **medicine** and **surgery**.

Medicine (Including General Practice)

A Doctor of Medicine who practises *medicine* is known as 'Doctor'.

A Physician who holds other medical degrees or diplomas (including those that are both medical and surgical, for example MRCS, LRCP, MB and BS, is known by courtesy as 'Doctor' in speech. Where one has qualifications in more than one discipline, he or she is usually addressed according to that which he or she practises.

Where one progresses in the same degree, qualification etc., only the higher is shown. Thus, if a Bachelor of Medicine becomes a Doctor of Medicine, he or she is shown only as MD or DM (according to the university); similarly, if a MRCP becomes a FRCP, only the latter is shown. An Anaesthetist (FFA, RCS), a Pathologist (FRCPath) and a Radiologist (FRCR) are all called 'Doctor'.

Beginning of Letter

Formal	Dear Sir or Dear Madam
Social	Dear Doctor Smith
	Dear Sir John

Envelope

Margaret Smith, MD, FRCP or Dr Margaret Smith
Dame Margaret Smith, MD, FRCP
John Brown, Esq, BM, BS or Dr John Brown
William Robinson, Esq, MRCS, LRCP or Dr William Robinson

Note: Those with doctorates, masterships and fellowships should be addressed on the envelope with the appropriate letters. Others who practise medicine, as in the second and third examples, may be addressed on the envelope as Dr William Robinson if the exact qualifying diplomas (such as MB or BM, BS, BChi or ChB) are not known.

Verbal Address and Description in Conversation
Dr Smith

Surgery (including Gynaecology)

A Surgeon (usually with a Mastership or Fellowship in Surgery) is known as 'Mr or Miss/Mrs/Ms Smith' in speech.

A Doctor of Medicine who practises surgery is known as 'Mr or Miss/Mrs/Ms Smith' in speech. Where a doctor has qualifications in more than one discipline, it is usual for him or her to be addressed according to that which he or she practises.

Beginning of Letter

Formal	Dear Sir or Madam
Social	Dear Mr or Miss/Mrs/Ms Smith
	Dear Sir John

Envelope
John Smith, Esq, MS, FRCS
William Jones, Esq, DM, MS, FRCS
Dame Jennifer Smith, MS, FRCS

An Obstetrician or a Gynaecologist (usually MRCOG or FRCOG) is addressed as a Surgeon in England and Wales. In Scotland and Northern Ireland it is the custom for him or her to be called 'Doctor'.

Verbal Address and Description in Conversation
Mr Smith

Dental Practitioner

A Dental Surgeon is referred to as a Surgeon – that is, Mr John Jones – with the appropriate post-nominal letters signifying his degrees or qualifications.

In general practice, he may be referred to as a Doctor if he has a medical degree or qualification in addition to a dental qualification, but not otherwise.

Letters after the Name

By custom, those denoting medicine follow those of orders, decorations and medals bestowed by the Crown. They are usually placed in the following order:

Doctorates
Masterships
Baccalaureates (degrees of Bachelor)
Postgraduate diplomas (for example, fellowships and memberships except MRCS)
Qualifying diplomas (MRCS, LRCP etc.)

It is the custom for letters indicating doctorates, masterships and fellowships to be given in correspondence. Baccalaureates, memberships and qualifying diplomas may be shown if no higher qualifications are held.

It is sufficient for a maximum of three series of letters to be shown: for example, MD, FRCS, FRCOG. If required for formal lists, the following is the complete list of letters commonly used in medicine in the UK.

Doctorates
Style: 'Doctor of . . .':

DM   Medicine
MD   Medicine
DCh   Surgery
DChD Dental Surgery

Masterships
Style: 'Master of . . .':

MC or MCh	Surgery
MChir	Surgery
MS	Surgery
CM or ChM	Surgery
MDS	Dental Surgery
MAO	Art of Obstetrics
MCB	Clinical Biochemistry
MChOrth	Orthopaedic Surgery

MCHOtol	Otology
MClinPsychol	Clinical Psychology
MCommH	Community Health

Baccalaureates
Style: 'Bachelor of . . .':

BM	Medicine
MB	Medicine
BCh or Chb	Surgery
BChir	Surgery
BS	Surgery
ChB	Surgery
BDS	Dental Surgery
BAO	Art of Obstetrics
BAc	Acupuncture
BASc	Applied Science
BDSc	Dental Science
BHy or BHyg	Hygiene
BPharm	Pharmacy

Postgraduate Diplomas: Fellowships
Style: 'Fellow of the Royal College of . . .':

FRCP	Physicians
FRCP	Physicians of Edinburgh
FRCPI	Physicians of Ireland
FRCP (Glasg)	Fellow (*qua* physician) of the Royal College of Physicians and Surgeons of Glasgow
FRCS	Surgeons
FRCS Ed	Surgeons of Edinburgh
FRCSI	Surgeons of Ireland
FRCS (Glasg)	Fellow (*qua* surgeon) of the Royal College of Physicians and Surgeons of Glasgow
FRCOG	Obstetricians and Gynaecologists
FRCGP	General Practitioners
FRCPath	Pathologists
FRCPsych	Psychiatrists
FRCR	Radiologists

Postgraduate Diplomas: Memberships
Style: 'Member of the Royal College of . . .':

MRCP	Physicians
MRCP Ed	Physicians of Edinburgh
MRCPI	Physicians of Ireland
MRCP (Glasg)	Physicians and Surgeons of Glasgow
MRCP (UK)	Physicians and Surgeons of UK
MRCOG	Obstetricians and Gynaecologists
MRCGP	General Practitioners
MRCPath	Pathologists
MRCPsych	Psychiatrists
FFA RCS	Fellow of the Faculty of Anaesthetists, the Royal College of Surgeons
FDS RCS	Fellow in Dental Surgery, the Royal College of Surgeons
FFCM	Fellow of the Faculty of Community Medicine
MFCM	Member of the Faculty of Community Medicine

Postgraduate Diplomas: Qualifying Diplomas

MRCS, LRCP	Member of the Royal College of Surgeons and Licentiate of the Royal College of Physicians
LRCP, LRCS, LRFPS	Licentiate of the Royal College of Physicians of Edinburgh, Licentiate of the Royal College of Surgeons of Edinburgh, Licentiate of the Royal Faculty of Physicians and Surgeons of Glasgow
LRCP, LRCS, LRCPS	Licentiate of the first two Royal Colleges, Licentiate of the Royal College of Physicians and Surgeons of Glasgow
LRCPI and LM	Licentiate of the Royal College of Physicians of Ireland and Licentiate in Midwifery
LRCSI and LM	Licentiate of the Royal College of Surgeons in Ireland and Licentiate in Midwifery

| LSA | Licentiate of the Society of Apothecaries |
| LMSSA | Licentiate in Medicine and Surgery, the Society of Apothecaries |

Other Postgraduate Diplomas

MMSA	Master of Midwifery, the Society of Apothecaries
DPH	Diploma in Public Health
DO	Diploma in Ophthalmology
DOMS	Diploma in Ophthalmic Medicine and Surgery
DPM	Diploma in Psychological Medicine
DCP	Diploma in Clinical Pathology
Dip Bact	Diploma in Bacteriology
DMRD	Diploma in Medical Radio-Diagnosis
DMRT	Diploma in Medical Radio-Therapy
DMRE	Diploma in Medical Radiology and Electrology
DPhysMed	Diploma in Physical Medicine
DA	Diploma in Anaesthesia
DCH	Diploma in Child Health
DIH	Diploma in Industrial Health
DLO	Diploma in Laryngology and Orology
DObstRCOG	Diploma in Obstetrics, the Royal College of Obstetricians and Gynaecologists
DTM and H	Diploma in Tropical Medicine and Hygiene
DMJ	Diploma in Medical Jurisprudence
Dip Soc Med Edin	Diploma in Social Medicine of the University of Edinburgh

Nursing, Midwifery and Health Visiting

As nursing and society changes, so do the titles by which nurses prefer to be addressed. Nurses in clinical practice will often address each other by first names. More senior (and older) nurses may wish to be addressed in a more formal way, and official correspondence should always be addressed using the official title.

In the interests of public protection, nurses, midwives and health

197

visitors are 'licensed' to practise by the United Kingdom Central Council for Nursing, Midwifery and Health Visiting (UKCC). The UKCC – established by Act of Parliament – is responsible for maintaining a professional register. It is illegal to claim to be a registered nurse, midwife or health visitor in the absence of an appropriate entry on the register.

Preregistration training leads to eligibility to register on one of five parts of the (fifteen-part) register.

> Adult (General Nurse)
> Mental Health Nurse
> Learning Disability Nurse
> Children's Nurse
> Midwife

A midwife may also be a nurse, but many are not. Confusing the titles can cause offence to some midwives.

The Prime Minister announced in summer 1998 that a new appointment of 'Consultant Nurse' is to be developed by 2000. Consultant Nurses will be of equivalent status to general medical consultants and head large teams of nursing staff.

Department of Health
Chief Nursing Officer and Director of Nursing
Assistant Chief Nursing Officer
Nursing Officer
Midwifery Officer
Regional Nurse Director

NHS Trusts
Nurse Executive Director (or Director of Nursing). Nurses in management may be known by several different titles, depending on the trust: for example, Nurse Manager, Clinical Nurse Manager, Clinical Manager, Senior Nurse.

Senior Clinical Nurses (that is, experienced and expert nurses in a specialist clinical field) may be titled Clinical Nurse Specialist.

NHS Trust Hospitals

Wards and departments will be managed by a Charge Nurse (male), Ward Manager (male or female) or Ward Sister (female).

A Senior Staff Nurse or Staff Nurse will be a qualified nurse working in a ward or department.

NHS Trusts: Community

District Nurse or Community Nurse
Health Visitor
School Nurse
Community Psychiatric Nurse
Community Paediatric Nurse
General Practitioners often employ a Practice Nurse in their surgeries.

Universities

All nursing, midwifery and health visiting education takes place in higher education institutions. Nurse educators are usually referred to as lecturers: for example, Lecturer in Nursing Studies. A Lecturer-Practitioner will be a nurse educator who is dually employed by a university and NHS Trust.

Summary Table

Name	Envelope	Letter	Verbal Address
Doctor	Dr Petra Faulks, MD, FRCP Sir Peter Baucher, MD, FRCP	Dear Dr Faulks Dear Sir Peter (if a Knight)	Dr Faulks Sir Peter (if a Knight)
Surgeon	William Forde, Esq, MS, FRCS Sir William Forde, MS, FRCS (if a Knight)	Dear Mr Forde or Dear Sir William (if a Knight)	Mr Forde or Sir Willian (if a Knight)
Dentist	Dentists are correctly addressed as surgeons, i.e. Mr/Mrs/Miss/Ms, unless additional qualifications allow their title to be Dr		

MERCHANT NAVY AND AIRLINE OFFICERS

Merchant Navy

The Master of the ship always ranks as Captain (that is, he holds a Master's Certificate and commands, or has commanded, a ship) and is referred to as Captain or Master.

In some companies, for example at Trinity House, the senior Captain holds the rank of Commodore, of which there is one per company. Unlike the military, a Captain does not usually use his or her title when not on board.

In large ships (mostly passenger) there is a Staff Captain, one step below the Captain. Other deck officers are as follows:

> Chief Officer
> Second Officer
> Third Officer
> Fourth Officer

The old names of First Mate (for Chief Officer), Second Mate (for Second Officer) etc. are still used, mostly in coastal ships.

On small craft, for example fishing vessels, the Captain is often referred to as Skipper. However, Captains of larger vessels should never be called so.

In the engineering department, the Chief Engineer is sometimes known as Commodore Chief Engineer, otherwise Chief.

Some ships carry a Junior Chief Officer. In large ships there can be as many as three First Officers, three Second Officers and three Third Officers. In this case each is known as 'Senior', 'Intermediate' and 'Junior'.

The other ranks are Second Engineer Officer, Third Engineer Officer etc., occasionally down to Eighth Engineer Officer.

Other ships' officers include the Surgeon, Purser, Assistant Purser, Catering Officer (and occasionally Assistant Catering Officer) and Radio Officer.

Further information may be obtained from the General Secretary, Mercantile Marine Service Association, Nautilus House, Mariners Park, Wallasey, Merseyside L45 7PH.

Forms of Address
The Commodore and Captain are addressed and referred to by these ranks.
The Staff Captain is addressed and referred to as Captain Jones.
These ranks are retained in retirement, but without the word '(retired)' after the name.
All other officers (including the Commodore Chief Engineer) are referred to as Mr Jones, except the Surgeon, who is known by his medical status: for example, Dr Johnson.

Beginning of Letter

Formal	Dear Sir
Social	Dear Commodore Jones
	Dear Captain Brown
	Dear Mr Smith

Envelope
Letters signifying Orders etc. are followed by those indicating the Service (such as RNR):

Commodore John Jones, OBE, RNR
Captain William Smith, MBE
Captain William Brown
Staff Captain, ss *Bengal*
John Robinson, Esq
Third Officer, ss *Bengal*

As with the deck officers, in large ships there can also be more than one Second Engineer Officer, Third Engineer Officer etc., as in Edward Black, Esq, Second Engineer Officer, ss *Bengal*.

Verbal Address
Commodore Jones
Captain Smith
Mr Robinson

Description in Conversation
As for Verbal Address.

Airline Officers

The Captain is referred to as Captain Smith and addressed as Captain John (or J) Smith. Other officers vary according to the company, but in the main they are Senior First Officer, First Officer and Second Officer. They are addressed as John Jones, Esq, and referred to as Mr Jones.

POLICE

The ranks of Deputy Chief Constable, Chief Superintendent and Deputy Assistant Commissioner (Metropolitan Police) are now obsolete. However, there are still some officers in service who hold these ranks.

CID officers add the prefix 'Detective' in the ranks from Constable to Chief Superintendent, as in Detective Sergeant Robert Smith, Esq.

There is no longer any differentiation between male and female officers. All are able to progress as far as their abilities allow.

These guidelines do not differ in Scotland and Northern Ireland.

Metropolitan Police and City of London Police

Commissioner

Beginning of Letter

Formal	Dear Sir or Madam
Social	
If a Knight or Dame	Dear Sir John or Dame Elizabeth (Smith)
Otherwise	Dear Mr or Miss/Mrs/Ms Smith or Commissioner

Envelope
Sir John Jones (followed by decorations)
John Jones, Esq (followed by decorations)
Commissioner of Police of the Metropolis, or for the City of London

Verbal Address
Commissioner or by name

Deputy or Assistant Commissioner
Beginning of Letter
As for Commissioner, but if by his or her appointment then Dear Deputy Commissioner (or Assistant Commissioner).

Envelope
Sir John Smith (followed by decorations) or John Smith, Esq (followed by decorations). Deputy Commissioner of Police of the Metropolis, or Assistant Commissioner of Police for the City of London

Verbal Address
By appointment or by name

Deputy Assistant Commissioner
Beginning of Letter

Formal	Dear Sir or Madam
Social	Dear Mr or Miss/Mrs/Ms Smith
	Dear Deputy Assistant Commissioner

Envelope
John Smith, Esq (followed by decorations),
Deputy Assistant Commissioner, Metropolitan Police

Verbal Address
By appointment or by name

Commander and Superintendent
Beginning of Letter

Formal	Dear Sir or Madam
Social	Dear Commander Smith (or appropriate rank)
	or Dear Mr or Miss/Mrs/Ms Smith

Envelope
With rank before name followed by 'Metropolitan Police' or 'City of London Police', as in Commander J W Johnson, MBE, Metropolitan Police
or by name followed by appointment, as in
John W Johnson, Esq, MBE, Chief Superintendent, Metropolitan Police

For the CID, 'Detective' is added before Chief Superintendent or Superintendent.

Verbal Address
By appointment or by name

Chief Inspector, Inspector, Police Sergeant and Police Constable

At the beginning of a letter the appropriate rank is placed before the name: that is, Dear Chief Inspector (Inspector, Sergeant or Constable) Smith, with the prefix 'Detective' if a member of CID.

The rank is placed on the envelope before the name. Police Sergeant is often abbreviated to PS, Police Constable to PC, Detective Sergeant to DS and Detective Constable to DC.

Other Police Forces

Chief Constable

Beginning of Letter
By name, or 'Dear Chief Constable'

Envelope
Sir John Smith or John Smith, Esq, as appropriate (followed by decorations), Chief Constable, Blankshire Constabulary

Verbal Address
Chief Constable or by name

Description in Conversation
The Chief Constable or by name

Deputy or Assistant Chief Constable

As for Chief Constable, with the substitution of the appropriate appointment.

Chief Superintendent or Superintendent

As for Metropolitan Police, with the substitution of the appropriate force.

Chief Inspector and Other Ranks

Chief Inspector, Inspector, Police Sergeant and Police Constable as for Metropolitan Police, above, with the substitution of the appropriate force.

Summary Table

Name	Envelope	Letter	Verbal Address
Police Commissioner (of Metropolitan forces)	Sir Charles Maxwell (followed by any decorations), Commissioner of Police of the Metropolis/for the City of Birmingham	Dear Sir Charles or Dear Commissioner	Commissioner or Sir Charles
Deputy or Assistant Commissioner	Thomas Fitzgerald, Esq, Deputy Commissioner of Police of the Metropolis for the City of Birmingham	Dear Mr Fitzgerald or Dear Deputy	Deputy Commissioner or Mr Fitzgerald
Chief Inspector, Inspector, Police Sergeant or Police Constable	Police Sergeant Deborah Bennett (abbreviations, e.g. PS, are often used on envelopes)	Dear Police Sergeant Bennett or Dear Miss Bennett	Police Sergeant Bennett or Miss Bennett
Chief Constable (other police forces). Assistant Chief Constables have the same form	Angus Howe, Esq, followed by any decorations, Chief Constable, Hampshire Constabulary	Dear Chief Constable	Chief Constable

GOVERNMENT AND CIVIL SERVICE

All Cabinet Ministers of the United Kingdom Parliament are members of the Privy Council. Other Ministers outside the Cabinet may also be admitted to the Privy Council. They accordingly have the prefix 'the Rt Hon' before their names. (*Note:* The Rt Hon takes the place of Mrs or Miss before a woman's name.)

All Members of the House of Commons of the United Kingdom have the letters MP following their names.

There is no special form of address for the partner of either a Privy Counsellor or a Member of Parliament

Several junior Ministers of an administration are not admitted to the Privy Council. Most of these are Members of Parliament, but a few may have seats in the House of Lords.

Member of HM Government
Beginning of Letter

Formal	Dear Sir or Madam
Social	Dear Mr or Miss/Mrs/Ms Blake or appropriate rank

If the writer knows the Minister concerned, and the subject of the letter broadly concerns his or her department, it is permissible to write to him or her by appointment, as in:

> Dear Prime Minister
> Lord Chancellor etc.

Or by name

> Dear Mr Blair
> Lord Irvine etc.

When writing to a Minister by appointment (as in Dear Minister), the letter is ended 'Yours sincerely'.

Although now very rare, for a very formal letter the following ending may be used:
I have the honour to be,
Sir or Madam,
Yours faithfully
'Your obedient servant' has become obsolete and is inappropriate.

Envelope
Personal Letter
A letter to a Minister sent to his or her department normally includes both name and appointment. For example:
The Rt Hon Sir Michael Blank, KBE, MP,
Secretary of State for Foreign Affairs

Ministerial Letter
A letter sent to a Minister as the head of department is addressed by appointment only, as in the Secretary of State for Foreign Affairs.

Verbal Address and Description in Conversation
By appointment or name

The Speaker of the House of Commons
'Mr or Madam Speaker' is the customary designation on parliamentary matters; otherwise according to his or her rank.

Government Departments (Civil Service)
Beginning of Letter
He or she is addressed as for an Esquire or the feminine equivalent:

Formal	Dear Sir or Madam
Social	Dear Mr or Miss/Mrs/Ms Byron or appropriate rank

The alternative style of writing by appointment is not normally employed when this is cumbersome: for example, Dear Permanent Under-Secretary.
    The very formal style of 'Sir' or 'Madam' is used within the Civil Service on specific official matters but only very occasionally outside.
    When writing to a member of the Civil Service by appointment (as in Dear Under-Secretary), the letter is ended 'Yours sincerely'.

For a very formal letter, use the following:

I have the honour to be,
Sir or Madam,
Yours faithfully
   'Your obedient servant' has become obsolete.

Envelope
Personal Letter
A letter to a member of the Civil Service sent to his or her department normally includes both name and appointment.
Official Letter
This is addressed by appointment only.

   If a letter relates only to a minor matter, it can be addressed to 'the Secretary' of the appropriate department rather than to its ministerial head (although it is still appropriate to address the letter to the ministerial head).

Verbal Address and Description in Conversation
By appointment or name.

Summary Table

Name	Envelope	Letter	Verbal Address
The Prime Minister	The Rt Hon Margaret Chamberlain, MP, the Prime Minister	Dear Prime Minister	Prime Minister
The Deputy Prime Minister	The Rt Hon Thomas Keenan, the Deputy Prime Minister	Dear Deputy Prime Minister	Deputy Prime Minister
The Chancellor of the Exchequer	The Rt Hon Charles Finnigan, the Chancellor of the Exchequer	Dear Chancellor	Chancellor
Lord Privy Seal	The Rt Hon the Earl of Annandale, the Lord Privy Seal	Dear Lord Privy Seal	Lord Privy Seal
The President of the Board of Trade	The Rt Hon the President of the Board of Trade	Dear President	President

Minister	The Rt Hon Anthony Gordon, MP, Secretary of State for the Environment	Dear Minister	Minister
Backbencher	Richard Williamson Esq, MP	Dear Mr Williamson	Mr Williamson

THE CHURCH AND RELIGION

Women have been ordained into the Churches of England (1994), Scotland (1969), Wales (1996) and Ireland (1990), but cannot realise office above and including that of Bishop.

Church of England and Associated Churches in the Anglican Communion

Ordained clergymen of the Church of England, and other Churches within the Anglican Communion, do not receive the accolade of knighthood, though the letters signifying an order of knighthood are placed after the name, as in the Right Reverend the Lord Bishop of Brompton, KCVO.

Doctorate degrees should be added on the envelope where appropriate.

If a clergyman succeeds to a title, or has a courtesy title or style, the ecclesiastical style precedes the temporal.

When it is desired to show that a clergyman has served in the Armed Forces – for example, in a list of retired officers – the following form is used: the Reverend John Smith, Commander, Royal Navy.

'The Reverend' is often abbreviated to 'the Rev', although some clergymen prefer it to be written in full; others prefer the abbreviation 'the Revd', but 'the Rev' is most usual.

Partners of the clergy do not have any special form of address.

Unless otherwise stated, Deans, Provosts, Archdeacons, Canons and Prebendaries should be addressed formally in writing as 'Very Reverend Sir (or Madam)', and the letter concluded 'I have the honour to remain, Very Reverend Sir (or Madam), your obedient servant' or 'Yours sincerely'.

Archbishops of Canterbury and York

They are Privy Counsellors and accordingly are addressed 'the Most Reverend and Right Honourable . . .' and have seats in the House of Lords. The Archbishop of Canterbury is Primate of all England and

Metropolitan. The Archbishop of York is Primate of England and Metropolitan.

Beginning of Letter

Formal	My Lord Archbishop or Your Grace
Social	Dear Lord Archbishop or Dear Archbishop

Envelope
The Most Reverend and Right Hon the Lord Archbishop of Canterbury/ York

Verbal Address

Formal	Your Grace
Social	Archbishop

Description in Conversation
The Archbishop (of York)

Archbishops of the Church of Ireland and Other Provinces
There are two Archbishops of the Church of Ireland: Armagh (Primate of all Ireland) and Dublin (Primate of Ireland).

Beginning of Letter

Formal	My Lord Archbishop or Your Grace
Social	Dear Lord Archbishop or Dear Archbishop

Envelope
The Most Reverend the Lord Archbishop of Blank

Verbal Address

Formal	Your Grace
Social	Archbishop

Description in Conversation
The Archbishop (of Blank)

Retired Archbishops
On retirement, Archbishops revert to the status of a Bishop. The former Archbishop of Canterbury is usually created a peer.

The correct way to address retired Archbishops is the same as that for retired Bishops (see page 214).

Bishop of London
He is always a Privy Counsellor and accordingly is addressed as Right Reverend and Right Honourable.

Beginning of Letter
Dear Bishop

Ending of Letter
Yours sincerely

Envelope
The Right Reverend and Right Hon the Lord Bishop of London

Verbal Address
Bishop

Description in Conversation
The Bishop (of London)

Bishops, Diocesan and Suffragan, Church of England and the Church in Wales
The Bishops of London, Durham and Winchester have seats in the House of Lords. When a vacancy arises, the senior Diocesan Bishop without a seat fills it, and the vacated See is then placed at the foot of the list of those awaiting seats. Translation of a Bishop from one See to another does not affect the right to sit in the House of Lords. The Bishop of Sodor and Man is an ex officio member of the Legislative Council of the Isle of Man.

In each diocese of the Church of England, Suffragan Bishops are appointed on the recommendation of the Bishop to assist him. These are styled by the name of some ancient town within the See. While enjoying full episcopal rights, they do not qualify for membership of the House of Lords.

A Suffragan Bishop is usually given by custom or courtesy the style of 'Lord' Bishop (that is, whether this title is ecclesiastical or temporal), but is not so styled in an official document.

The Church in Wales became a separate Province of the Anglican Communion as a result of disestablishment in 1920. The office of Archbishop of Wales is held by one of their six Diocesan Bishops.

Beginning of Letter
Dear Bishop

Envelope
The Right Reverend the Lord Bishop of Blank or the Right Reverend the Bishop of Blank

Verbal Address
Bishop

Description in Conversation
The Bishop (of Blank)

Assistant and Retired Bishops
Beginning of Letter
Dear Bishop

Envelope
The Right Rev John Smith
    If a Privy Counsellor (for example, a retired Bishop of London), the Right Rev and Right Hon John Smith

Verbal Address
Bishop

Description in Conversation
The Bishop or by name: Bishop Smith, for example.

Bishops, Episcopal Church in Scotland

Since the Episcopal Church is not the State Church of Scotland, a Bishop has no official precedence and recognition and is therefore addressed as 'the Right Rev John Smith, Bishop of X', and not as 'the Right Rev the Bishop of X'.

Socially, the style is as for a Diocesan Bishop of the Church of England (see page 213), except for the Primus of Scotland who acts as the Presiding Bishop who is elected by the other bishops and has no Metropolitan power. The style is the Most Reverend the Primus.

The following is the form of address for the Primus.

Beginning of Letter
Dear Primus

Envelope
The Most Reverend the Primus

Verbal Address
Primus

Description in Conversation
The Primus

Bishops, Church of Ireland

Bishops are styled as Diocesan Bishops in the Church of England, with the following exception: the Bishop of Meath (Premier Bishop of the Church of Ireland) is styled 'the Most Reverend' instead of 'the Right Reverend'.

Dean

A Dean is the incumbent of a cathedral or collegiate church, except when he or she is a Provost; the style is also used in certain colleges.

Beginning of Letter
    Social   Dear Dean

Envelope
The Very Reverend the Dean of Ely

215

Verbal Address
Dean or Mr or Miss/Mrs/Ms Dean

Description in Conversation
The Dean (of Ely)

Retired Dean

After retirement, he or she is addressed as are other clergy – that is, 'the Reverend' instead of 'the Very Reverend', as above – unless he or she remains an Archdeacon, Canon or Prebendary or is appointed to emeritus rank, when the address is according to the appropriate rank. The word 'emeritus' is used only in official documents.

Provost

The incumbent of a cathedral which has been so created out of a parish church and whose responsibilities in consequence carry additionally something in the nature of Rector or Vicar is usually appointed a Provost and not a Dean.

Where a cathedral has a Provost rather than a Dean, the freehold and the patronage is normally vested in the Provost for the time being, and not in the Chapter as would be normal where the appointment of Dean existed. In other respects duties are the same as a Dean's.

The style is also used in certain non-ecclesiastical appointments, such as the heads of certain colleges.

Beginning of Letter
    Social   Dear Provost

Envelope
The Very Reverend the Provost of Coventry

Verbal Address
Provost

Description in Conversation
The Provost (of Coventry)

Retired Provost

After retirement he or she is addressed as other clergy – that is, 'the Reverend' instead of 'the Very Reverend' – unless he or she remains an Archdeacon, Canon or Prebendary or is appointed to emeritus rank, when the address is as such. The word 'emeritus' is used only in official documents.

Archdeacon

An Archdeacon is a senior clergyman whose duty it is to supervise the clergy and to administer part of a diocese, hence the territorial designation. As well as visitation duties, he or she is in charge of the fabric of parish churches and their contents.

Beginning of Letter
    Social   Dear Archdeacon

Envelope
The Venerable the Archdeacon of Exeter

Verbal Address
Archdeacon

Description in Conversation
The Archdeacon (of Exeter)

Retired Archdeacon

After retirement, the address is as for other clergy – that is, 'the Reverend' in place of 'the Venerable', as above – unless he or she remains a Canon or Prebendary or is appointed to emeritus rank, when he or she is addressed accordingly. The word 'emeritus' is used only in official documents.

Canon

A Canon is either residentiary, with duties in a cathedral, or honorary. The latter is usually given to incumbents with a record of honourable service in the diocese.

    A Minor Canon is a cleric attached to a cathedral or collegiate church to assist in the daily services. The address is as other clergy.

Beginning of Letter
    Social   Dear Canon or Dear Canon Smith

Envelope
The Reverend Canon John Smith

Verbal Address
Canon or Canon Smith

Description in Conversation
The Canon or Canon Smith

Retired Canon
After retirement, the address is as for other clergy unless appointed a Canon Emeritus, when addressed as previously. The word 'emeritus' is used only in official documents.
    Honorary Canons usually retain their title unless they specifically resign it on leaving the diocese or retiring from the Church.

Prebendary
Prebendaries have a Prebendal Stall in certain cathedrals or collegiate churches. The appointment is similar to a non-residentiary Canon.

Beginning of Letter
    Social   Dear Prebendary or Dear Prebendary Smith

Envelope
The Reverend Prebendary John Smith

Verbal Address
Prebendary or Prebendary Smith

Description in Conversation
Prebendary or Prebendary Smith

Retired Prebendary

After retirement, the address is as for other clergy unless appointed to emeritus rank. In this case, the address continues as that for Prebendary. The word 'emeritus' is used only in official documents.

Rural Dean

No special form of address, but he or she is often an honorary Canon.

Other Clergy

Beginning of Letter

Social	Dear Mr Smith or Dear Father Smith, according to personal preference. When writing to beneficed clergy, the form 'Dear Rector' or 'Dear Vicar' may be used.

Envelope

The Reverend John Smith

The form 'the Reverend Smith' or 'Reverend Smith' is incorrect and should never be used.

Verbal Address

'Mr Smith' or 'Father Smith', according to personal preference.

Description in Conversation

'Mr Smith' or 'Father Smith', according to personal preference, or 'the Rector' or 'the Vicar', if applicable.

Religious Communities, Church of England: Men

Ordained members of Religious Orders are addressed as Father and lay members as Brother, except in the case of the Society of St Francis, all of whose members are called Brother.

The Head of a Community may be:

The Right Reverend the Abbot
The Reverend the Prior
The Reverend Superior General
The Reverend Pro Superior

The Reverend Superior

Beginning of Letter

Superior
By his office:
Dear Father Abbot
Dear Father Prior
Dear Father Superior (including Superior General and Pro Superior)

Other Ordained Members
Dear Reverend Father (this covers all ordained members); alternatively, the name may be used, as in
Dear Father Smith
Dear Father David (for Orders where surnames are not used)
Dear Dom Andrew (Benedictine)
Dear Brother John (Franciscan)
Dear Father (all Orders where the name is not known)

Lay Members
Dear Brother Andrew
Dear Brother (all Orders where the name is not known)
Dear Dom Andrew (Benedictine)

Envelope
Superior
By his office, followed by the letters to denote his Order. For example:
The Right Reverend the Lord Abbot, OSB
The Reverend the Prior, CGA
    A few communities do not have letters.

Other Ordained Members
The Reverend Andrew Thompson, OGS or the Reverend Fr Andrew Thompson, OGS
The Reverend Fr Andrew CGA (if the surname is not used)
The Reverend Dom John Smith, OSB (Benedictine)
Brother George, SSF (Franciscan)

Lay Members
Brother John (with his surname, if used by his Order), Dom John Smith, OSB (Benedictine)

Verbal Address
Superior
Father Abbot
Father Prior
Father Superior (including Superior General and Pro Superior)

Other Ordained Members
Father David (with his surname, if used by his Order)
Dom John Smith, Dom John or Father Smith (Benedictine)
Brother George (Franciscan)

Lay Members
Brother John or Brother
Dom John (Benedictine)
   The surname or religious name may be used if distinction is necessary or on introduction.

Description in Conversation
Superior
The Abbot
The Prior (or appropriate office)

Other Ordained Members
Father Smith, Father David, Dom Andrew Smith (Benedictine), Brother Philip (Franciscan)

Lay Members
Brother Andrew (and his surname if used by his Order), Dom John Smith

Religious Communities, Church of England: Women

Beginning of Letter
Superiors by their office. For example:

Dear Mother Superior (including an Abbess)
Dear Prioress
Dear Reverend Mother
Dear Sister Superior
Other Sisters
Dear Sister Agnes
Dear Dame Mary (Benedictine, having taken final vows)
Dear Sister Mary (Benedictine)

Envelope
Superiors
By office, followed by the letters of their Order (a few communities do not have letters), such as:

The Right Reverend the Abbess, OSB
The Reverend the Prioress
The Reverend Mother Superior
The Reverend Mother
The Reverend Mother General
The Reverend Sister Superior
The Reverend Mother Audrey Mary

Other Sisters
Sister Agnes, followed by the letters of her Order
The Reverend Dame Mary Smith, OSB (Benedictine, having taken final vows)
Sister Mary Smith, OSB (Benedictine)

Verbal Address
Superiors by office:
Reverend Mother (in some communities 'Mother')

Other Sisters
Sister Agnes (in some communities 'Sister')

Description in Conversation
Superiors by office:
The Lady Abbess

Other Sisters
Sister Agnes
Dame Mary Smith (Benedictine, if final vows have been taken)
Sister Mary Smith (Benedictine)

Chaplains to HM Forces

A chaplain serving with HM Forces is addressed by ecclesiastical rank and never in speech by relative Service rank, which is only for administrative purposes. It is not necessary or usual to write the Service rank, but when used formally it must appear in brackets after the ecclesiastical title and before the chaplain's forename or initials.

The Chaplain of the Fleet, the Chaplain General to the Forces, Army, and the Chaplain-in-Chief, Royal Air Force, are Archdeacons and therefore 'the Venerable' is placed before the name. Letters begin with the appointment or name, as in 'Dear Chaplain General' or 'Dear Archdeacon Smith'.

Envelopes are addressed accordingly – for example, 'the Chaplain of the Fleet', 'the Chaplain General', 'Chaplain-in-Chief' or 'the Venerable John Smith' – followed by his appointment. Verbally, they are addressed by their appointment or as Archdeacon, as may be appropriate.

The Deputy Chaplain General to the Forces, Army, the Principal Chaplain, Church of Scotland and Free Churches, Royal Navy, or Royal Air Force, and the Principal Roman Catholic Chaplain, Royal Navy, Army or Royal Air Force, are addressed in correspondence by name or by appointment. Principal Roman Catholic Chaplains are Monsignori, and are addressed accordingly.

Other chaplains are addressed by name or by appointment in correspondence as may be appropriate: for example, 'Dear Canon Jones', 'Dear Mr Jones', 'Dear Assistant Chaplain General' etc. When the name is used, the appointment held should be placed after the name, as in the Reverend John Jones, OBE, MA, CF and Assistant Chaplain General, HQ, Blankshire Command.

The letters RN and RAF are placed after the names of chaplains to these Services, following any letters for decorations etc. Army chaplains have the letters 'CF' after the name, following any letters for decorations etc. Verbally, a chaplain may be addressed by name, by appointment or by ecclesiastical title or, informally, as 'Padre'.

When the chaplain's name is not known, correspondence should be addressed to, for example, the Church of England Chaplain, RAF Station, Blanktown, or the Roman Catholic Chaplain, HMS *Blankshire*, etc.

Correspondence to a Jewish Chaplain is addressed to, for example, the Reverend David Smith, CF, Senior Jewish Chaplain, Blanktown Garrison, etc. Verbally he is addressed as 'Rabbi', as 'Minister' or 'Padre' as may be appropriate.

Archbishops' and Bishops' Signatures: Church of England

Archbishops and Bishops sign, after a cross, their forenames followed by their Province or See, sometimes in Latin, or a Latin abbreviation. For example:

+ Donald Cantuar
+ Robin Worcester

The following sign, after their forenames, as below. Other Sees are accorded the usual spelling.

Archbishops

| Canterbury | Cantuar |
| York | Ebor |

Bishops

Carlisle	Carliol
Chester	Cestr
Chichester	Cicestr
Durham	Dunelm
Ely	Elien
Gloucester	Gloucestr
London	Londin
Norwich	Norvic
Oxford	Oxon
Peterborough	Petriburg
Rochester	Roffen
Salisbury	Sarum
Truro	Truron
Winchester	Winton

Retired Bishops
They sign their name after a cross, followed by Bishop.

Archbishops' and Bishops' Signatures: Church in Wales
The Archbishop and Metropolitan signs, after a cross, the forename followed by 'Canibrensis'. A Bishop signs, after a cross, the forename and diocese. The Bishop of Llandaff signs as 'Landav', and others by the usual spelling of the diocese.

Archbishops' and Bishops' Signatures: Episcopal Church in Scotland
Bishops (including the Primus) sign, after a cross, their forename followed by their diocese, except that the Bishop of Moray, Ross and Caithness signs 'Moray' and the Bishop of St Andrews, Dunkeld and Dunblane signs 'St Andrews' – without the other dioceses.

The Bishop of Edinburgh signs by his forename followed by 'Edenburgen'.

Archbishops' and Bishops' Signatures: Church of Ireland
Archbishops sign, after a cross, their forename followed by their Province. Bishops sign, after a cross, their forename followed by the first diocese in their title.

Church of Scotland
This is the Established Church in Scotland, and is Presbyterian by constitution. The Supreme Court of the Church is the General Assembly that meets annually in May and is presided over by a Moderator, who is appointed each year by the Assembly.

The Sovereign either attends in person or is represented by the Lord High Commissioner to the General Assembly, who is appointed by the Crown.

Lord High Commissioner to the General Assembly
The same styles are used whether a man or woman is appointed to this office.

Beginning of Letter
Your Grace
This form of address is adhered to even when the Lord High Commissioner is a member of the Royal Family, with the sole exception of The Duke of Edinburgh, who would be referred to as His Royal Highness in all references, having senior precedence to the Lord High Commissioner.

Ending of Letter
I have the honour to remain, Your Grace's most devoted and obedient servant

Envelope
His or Her Grace the Lord High Commissioner

Verbal Address
Your Grace

Description in Conversation
The Lord High Commissioner

Moderator of the General Assembly
Beginning of Letter

Formal	Dear Sir or Madam or Dear Moderator
Social	Dear Mr or Miss/Mrs/Ms Smith or Dear Moderator

Envelope
The Rt Rev the Moderator of the General Assembly of the Church of Scotland, or The Rt Rev John Smith

Verbal Address
Moderator

Description in Conversation
The Moderator

Former Moderators

After his year of office, a former Moderator is styled the Very Reverend John Smith. Otherwise as for Other Clergy, Church of Scotland, below.

Dean of the Chapel Royal and Dean of the Thistle

They are styled 'the Very Reverend'. Sometimes one person holds both appointments.

Other Clergy

Beginning of Letter

Formal	Dear Sir or
	Dear Minister
Social	Dear Mr or Miss/Mrs/Ms Smith or
	Dear Minister

Envelope
The Reverend John Smith
The Minister of Blanktown (if a Minister of a Parish)
   If a lady were ordained, she would be styled 'the Reverend Mary Smith.' Miss/Mrs/Ms should not be used.

Verbal Address
Mr Smith or Minister

Description in Conversation
Mr Smith or The Minister

Methodist Church, Baptist Union of Great Britain and Ireland, and Free Churches of Other Denominations. Ministers

Beginning of Letter

Formal	Dear Sir or Madam
Social	Dear Mr or Miss/Mrs/Ms Smith

Envelope
The Reverend John Smith (the Reverend Dr John Smith, or with the appropriate letters signifying a doctor's degree). Lady Ministers are

addressed as the Reverend Mary Smith. Miss/Mrs/Ms should not be used.

Verbal Address
Mr or Miss/Mrs/Ms Smith
   On the platform the President of the Methodist Church, the Methodist Church in Ireland etc., and the President of the Baptist Union of Great Britain and Ireland (who may be a layman) are referred to as Mr or Madam President.

The Congregational Federation consists of those members of the Congregational Church in England and Wales who did not join the United Reformed Church.
   The Chairman of the Congregational Union in Scotland is referred to as Mr or Madam Chairman.

Description in Conversation
Dr or Mr or Miss/Mrs/Ms Smith or the Minister, the Pastor, the President etc.

Deaconess of the Methodist Church
She is referred to as Sister Jane Smith and is known in her community as Sister Jane, but in a written description she may be referred to as Deaconess Jane Smith, which distinguishes her from a nursing sister.

United Reformed Church of England and Wales
The United Reformed Church came into being in October 1972 by the Union of the Presbyterian Church of England with the Congregational Church in England and Wales.

Moderator of the General Assembly of the United Reformed Church in England and Wales

Beginning of Letter
Formal	Dear Moderator or Mr/Madam Moderator
Social	Dear Moderator or Mr/Madam Moderator

Envelope
The Rt Rev John Smith

Verbal Address
Moderator (or Mr/Madam Moderator)

Description in Conversation
The Moderator

Former Moderators
After his or her year of office, a Moderator reverts to 'the Rev'.

Ministers
As for Other Clergy; (see page 227), except that the form 'Dear Minister' is not used. Verbal address is Mr or Miss/Mrs/Ms Smith.

If a lady, she is styled the Rev Mary Smith (Mrs or Miss is not used).

Presbyterian Church of Wales
Moderators of the General Assembly of the Presbyterian (or Calvinist Methodist) Church of Wales continue to be styled 'the Reverend'.

It is not customary to address the Moderator of this Church by name.

Beginning of Letter
    Social   Dear Moderator
Ministers are styled as for the United Reformed Church (see page 228).

Presbyterian Church in Ireland
Moderators of the General Assembly of the Presbyterian Church in Ireland are addressed as for the United Reform Church of England and Wales, viz. the Right Reverend.

Former Moderators are styled 'the Very Reverend'.

229

Beginning of Letter
Dear Dr Smith or Dear Moderator

Ministers are styled as for the United Reformed Church (see page 228).

Salvation Army

After a two-year residential course as a cadet, a student is commissioned as an officer (as the Movement terms its Ministers). Ranks are as follows:

General
Chief of the Staff
Commissioner
Colonel
Lieutenant-Colonel
Major
Captain
Lieutenant

One Commissioner is appointed to be Chief of the Staff of the Salvation Army. The senior officer of the Movement within other countries is the territorial commander, or officer commanding in smaller territories, who holds the rank of Commissioner, Colonel or Lieutenant-Colonel.

The senior officer of the whole Movement is the General of the Salvation Army, who is elected by the High Council.

Married Officers

Commissioned officers marry within the commissioned ranks of the Salvation Army. If they marry outside these ranks, they opt out of officership of the Salvation Army, though they may continue as lay members.

Beginning of Letter
According to their rank, as follows:

Dear General
Dear Chief (that is, Chief of the Staff)
Dear Commissioner

Dear Colonel (includes Lieutenant-Colonel)
Dear Major
Dear Captain
Dear Lieutenant

An officer's wife may be referred to by her name (Mrs Smith, say) or by her husband's rank: for example, Mrs Major Smith.

Envelope
According to the exact rank held (Major John Jones or Captain Mary Brown, say), except for married ladies who may take their husband's rank on marriage: for example, the wife of Major Frank Briggs is addressed on the envelope 'Mrs Major Frank Briggs'.

Moravian Church in Great Britain and Ireland
Within this Church the term 'Brother' (including a Bishop) or 'Sister' may be used in general correspondence.

Roman Catholic Church
The territorial designation and the term 'My Lord' are not officially recognised within the United Kingdom, and accordingly are not used in official communications and documents. Hence, in these communications Archbishops, Bishops, Abbots and Priors are addressed by name and not by their Province, diocese, etc.

The Pope
Beginning of Letter
Your Holiness or Most Holy Father

Ending of Letter

For Roman Catholics	I have the honour to be, Your Holiness's most devoted and obedient child (or most humble child)
For non-Roman Catholics	I have the honour to be (or to remain), Your Holiness's obedient servant

Envelope
His Holiness the Pope

Verbal Address
Your Holiness

Description in Conversation
His Holiness or the Pope

Cardinal

If appointed to a See, the address may be by appointment: for example, 'His Eminence Cardinal Smith'. The territorial designation is not officially used when such letters are addressed to the person and not territorially to the Province or diocese.

Beginning of Letter

Formal	Your Eminence or My Lord Cardinal
Officially Recognised	Your Eminence
Social	Dear Cardinal Smith

Ending of Letter

Very Formal:

For Roman Catholics	I have the honour to be (or to remain), My Lord Cardinal, Your Eminence's devoted and obedient child Roman Catholics in Holy Orders write 'servant' instead of 'child'
Formal	I remain, Your Eminence (My Lord Cardinal is sometimes used in place of Your Eminence), Yours faithfully
Officially Recognised	I have the honour to be (or to remain), Your Eminence's obedient servant
Social	Yours sincerely

Envelope

Formal and Social (if an Archbishop)	His Eminence the Cardinal Archbishop of Westminster

| (if not an Archbishop) | His Eminence Cardinal Smith |
| Officially Recognised | His Eminence Cardinal Smith |

Verbal Address

| Formal | Your Eminence |
| Social | Cardinal (Smith) |

Description in Conversation

| Formal | His Eminence |
| Social | Cardinal (Smith) |

Archbishop

On retirement from office, a Roman Catholic Archbishop is appointed to a titular See and is then normally addressed by name.

Beginning of Letter

Formal	My Lord Archbishop
Officially Recognised	Most Reverend Sir
Social	Dear Archbishop

Ending of Letter

Very Formal: For Roman Catholics	I have the honour to be (or to remain), Your Grace's devoted and obedient child Roman Catholics in Holy Orders write 'servant' instead of 'child'
Formal	I remain, Your Grace, Yours faithfully or Yours faithfully
Officially Recognised	I have the honour to be, Most Reverend Sir, Your obedient servant
Social	Yours sincerely

Envelope

Formal and Social	His Grace the Archbishop of Sydney
Officially Recognised	The Most Reverend Archbishop Smith
Titular Archbishop	The Most Reverend Archbishop Smith

Verbal Address

Formal	Your Grace
Social	Archbishop

Description in Conversation

Formal	His Grace
Social	The Archbishop (of Blank)

Bishop

Roman Catholic Bishops are styled 'Right Reverend', except in Ireland where they are styled 'Most Reverend'.

In lists prepared by non-Roman Catholic organisations, a Roman Catholic Bishop should be mentioned by name: for example, the Right Reverend Bishop Brown. If the territorial designation is given, and there is an Anglican Bishop whose See has the same name, it should be stated, as in 'Roman Catholic Bishop of Lancaster'.

Letter endings now tend to be more informal than they were in the past.

On retirement from his See or office, a Bishop is appointed to a titular See, and addressed by name. Though it is not the usual practice, the titular See may be appended on the envelope after the name if desired.

Beginning of Letter

Formal	My Lord (usual) or My Lord Bishop
Officially Recognised	Right Reverend Sir (*Note:* 'Most Reverend Sir' for an Irish Bishop)
Social	Dear Bishop or Dear Bishop Smith

Ending of Letter

Very Formal:

For Roman Catholics	I have the honour to be, Your Lordship's obedient child. Roman Catholics in Holy Orders write 'servant' instead of child'
Formal	I remain, My Lord, Yours faithfully (My Lord Bishop may be used in place of My Lord) or Yours faithfully
Officially	I have the honour to be (or to remain), Right

| Recognised | Reverend Sir, Your obedient servant (*Note:* 'Most Reverend Sir' for an Irish Bishop) |
| Social | Yours sincerely |

Envelope

| Formal and Social | His Lordship the Bishop of Blank or the Right Reverend John Smith, Bishop of Bramber (*Note:*) 'Most Reverend' for an Irish Bishop) The Right Reverend John Smith Auxiliary Bishop of . . . |
| Officially Recognised | The Right Reverend Bishop Smith |

In Ireland the abbreviation 'Dr' is included on the envelope before the name, as in 'the Most Reverend Dr John Smith, Bishop of Kildare'.

Verbal Address

| Formal | My Lord (usual) or My Lord Bishop |
| Social | Bishop |

Description in Conversation

| Formal | His Lordship |
| Social | The Bishop |

Abbot
Beginning of Letter

Formal	My Lord Abbot or Right Reverend and Dear Father Abbot
Officially Recognised	Right Reverend Sir
Social	Dear Father Abbot

Ending of Letter

Very Formal: For Roman Catholics	I beg to remain, My Lord Abbot, Your devoted and obedient servant,
Formal	Yours faithfully
Social	Yours sincerely

Envelope

Formal and Social	The Right Reverend the Abbot of Blank (followed by the initials of his Order)
Officially Recognised	The Right Reverend John Smith (followed by the initials of his Order)

Verbal Address

Formal	Father Abbot
Social	Abbot

Description in Conversation
The Abbot (of Blank)

Monsignor

This title is held by virtue of a particular office, a Protonotary Apostolic, a Prelate of Honour or a Chaplain to His Holiness the Pope.

Monsignori are addressed as the Reverend instead of the Right Reverend or the Very Reverend.

Beginning of Letter

Formal	Reverend Sir
Social	Dear Monsignor Smith (usual) or Dear Monsignore

Envelope
The Reverend Monsignor John Smith or
The Reverend Monsignore
   If he is a Canon:

The Very Reverend Monsignor (Canon) John Smith

Verbal Address
Monsignor Smith (usually adopted) or Monsignore
   If he is a Canon, he is usually known as 'Monsignor Smith'

Description in Conversation
Monsignor Smith

Provincial

The Provincial is the Superior of a Province in a Religious Order, such as the Dominicans, the Franciscans or the Jesuits.

Beginning of Letter
Formal	Very Reverend Father Provincial or Very Reverend Father
Social	Dear Father Provincial or Dear Father Smith

Envelope
The Very Reverend Father Provincial (followed by the letters of his Order) or the Very Reverend Father Smith (followed by the letters of his Order)

Verbal Address
Father Provincial

Description in Conversation
Father Provincial

Prior

Beginning of Letter
Very Formal	Very Reverend and Dear Father Prior
Formal and Social	Dear Father Prior

Envelope
The Very Reverend the Prior of Blank or the Very Reverend John Smith (followed by the initials of his Order)

Verbal Address
Father Prior

Description in Conversation
The Prior (of Blank)

Provost

The form of address is as for a Canon (see below), with the substitution of Provost for Canon.

Canon

If he is a Monsignor, see Monsignor, page 236.

Beginning of Letter

Formal	Very Reverend Sir
Social	Dear Canon Smith or Dear Canon

Envelope
The Very Reverend Canon John Smith

Verbal Address
Canon Smith

Description in Conversation
Canon Smith

Priest

Beginning of Letter

Formal	Dear Reverend Father
Social	Dear Father Smith

Envelope
The Reverend John Smith (usual) or
The Reverend Fr Smith
   If a Regular, the initials of the Order should be added after the name.

Verbal Address
Father
   The surname may be used if distinction is necessary, or on introduction, or Father John (for Regulars where only the Christian or
religious name is used).

Description in Conversation
Father Smith, or Father John (for Regulars where only the Christian or
religious name is used).

Lay Brothers

They are verbally addressed as 'Brother' and referred to as 'Brother John'.

Religious Communities: Women

The appropriate letters of the orders are placed after the name.

Although previously a religious name was usually adopted on taking vows, and the forename and surname not used, it is becoming the practice in some orders to retain both forename and surname.

An Abbess is addressed 'The Lady Abbess' and in some orders 'the Right Reverend and Lady Abbess'.

Reverend Mother or Reverend Sister Superior

Beginning of Letter
According to office:
Dear Reverend Mother or
Dear Sister Superior

Envelope
According to office:
The Reverend Mother Prioress
The Reverend Mother
The Sister Superior

Verbal Address
According to office:
Reverend Mother
The Sister Superior

Description in Conversation
According to office:
The Mother Prioress
The Reverend Mother
The Sister Superior

Sister of Orders
Beginning of Letter
Dear Sister Mary

Envelope
The Reverend Sister Mary, DC
The Reverend Sister Mary O'Brien, with the letters of her Order

Verbal Address
Sister Mary

Description in Conversation
Sister Mary (O'Brien)

Benedictine Nuns
The following refers principally to the practice of the English Benedictine Congregation. In other Benedictine monasteries of nuns there is considerable diversity of practice.

Abbess
She is formally referred to as Lady Abbess, though in some monasteries 'Mother Abbess' has replaced this.

Beginning of Letter
Dear Lady Abbess or Mother Abbess

Envelope
The Lady Abbess or Mother Abbess, X Abbey
    The courtesy style of 'the Right Reverend' is not normally used.

Verbal Address
Lady Abbess or Mother Abbess

Description in Conversation
The Lady Abbess or Mother Abbess

Prioress

A Prioress may be either a Conventual Prioress or a Claustral Prioress (corresponding to Conventual or Claustral Priors), though at present there are no Conventual Prioresses in the English Congregation.

Prioresses are addressed and referred to as 'Mother Prioress'.

Nun in Final Vows

The formal style of address and reference is 'Dame' (corresponding to 'Dom' for a monk), but in ordinary use 'Sister' is common.

Beginning of Letter
Dear Dame Jane

Envelope
Dame Jane Smith

Verbal Address
Dame Jane or Sister Jane

Description in Conversation
Dame Jane or Sister Jane

Novices, Juniors and Extern Sisters

They are addressed as Sisters.
The envelope is addressed:
Sister Jane Smith
X Abbey

Religious Communities: Men
Order of St Benedict

Custom varies considerably from Congregation to Congregation and even from monastery to monastery.

The following notes are intended as a guide for use in Great Britain. American Benedictines of the two American Congregations do not use 'Dom' but are styled 'the Reverend John Smith, OSB'.

Lay Brothers are referred to as Claustral Brothers.

The form of addressing 'Juniors' (or 'Clerics', as they are called in some monasteries) – that is, monks studying for the priesthood – varies according to the monastery.

Monks who are priests could be addressed verbally and in informal letters as 'Father'; those who are not priests as 'Brother'. In formal letters and usage, 'Dom' may be applied to all. Many Benedictines are content not to have OSB appended to the name, 'Dom' being sufficient distinction.

Benedictine Abbot

Benedictine Abbots in Great Britain are not 'Lord' Abbots. The head of a Benedictine Congregation is generally referred to as the Abbot President.

Beginning of Letter

To the Abbot President	Dear Father President
To other Abbots	Dear Father Abbot

Envelope

To the Abbot President	The Right Reverend the Abbot President, X Abbey
To other Abbots	The Right Reverend the Abbot of Y or the Right Reverend Father Abbot, or by name: the Right Reverend Dom AS, Abbot of Y

Verbal Address

The Abbot President	Father President
Other Abbots	Father Abbot

Description in Conversation

The Abbot President	As such
Other Abbots	The Abbot (of Buckfast)

Titular Abbots

It is customary, though not invariably so, for a retired Abbot to take the title of an extinct Abbey. Titular Abbacies may also be conferred on individual monks. Such Abbots, if they have a local title, may be addressed as 'the Right Reverend the Abbot of X', but by practice and custom in the English Congregation they are usually addressed 'the Right Reverend Dom John Smith'.

Letters may begin 'Dear Father Abbot', 'Dear Father John' or even 'Dear Abbot John'.

Abbot Visitor or Abbot General
Where these offices exist, they are so addressed.

Verbal Address
Father Abbot

Prior
Priors, whether Conventual Priors (superiors of independent monasteries) or Claustral Priors (second in command to the Abbot in an Abbey), have the style Very Reverend. A Conventual Prior is thus addressed on the envelope:
The Very Reverend the Prior, X Priory or The Very Reverend the Prior of X

A Claustral Prior is addressed on the envelope:
The Very Reverend the Prior, X Abbey

Letters begin 'Dear Father Prior' and the address in conversation is 'Father Prior'.

Titular Priors
In the English Benedictine Congregation there are a number of titular Priors bearing the titles of ancient cathedral monasteries. They are formally addressed or referred to as 'the Very Reverend the Prior of X', but by practice and custom in the Congregation 'the Very Reverend Dom John Smith' is most usual.

Letters begin 'Dear Father Prior' or 'Dear Father John'.

Priests
Beginning of Letter

Formal	Dear Dom Julian
Social	Dear Father Julian

Dear Father, if the name is not known

Envelope
The Reverend Dom Julian Smith, OSB
The use of 'the Reverend' and 'OSB' is optional.

Verbal Address
Formal   Dom John
Social   Father
If distinction is necessary or on introduction, 'Father Smith'.
'Dom' is treated as an official style, such as in official occasions and notices, title pages of books etc, but in ordinary conversation 'Padre' is used.

Description in Conversation
Dom John Smith
Parochially, he is often referred to as 'Father Smith'.

Monks Who Are Not Priests
This includes both monks who are preparing for priesthood and those who are not going to take Orders.
Novices should always be addressed as 'Brother', and it is usual in the English Congregation for this style to be used for those not yet in solemn or final vows.

Envelope
The Reverend Brother Julian Smith, OSB
The use of 'the Reverend' and 'OSB' is optional.
'Dom' may be used as appropriate in these cases, as for Priests.

Description in Conversation
Brother Julian

Friar
Members of certain Religious Orders, especially the Mendicant Orders of Franciscans (Grey Friars), Dominicans (Black Friars), Augustinians (Austin Friars) and Carmelites (White Friars), are known as Friars and not Monks, primarily due to their flexibility of movement within the Order.

Each order is organised with a Father Provincial for each Province, and a Father Prior (or Father Guardian in the case of the Franciscan Order) for each House. Though 'friar' means 'brother', the term covers all priests and lay brothers.

Forms of address are as for those of other religious orders.

Society of Jesus

Jesuits do not normally accept ecclesiastical dignities. To do so would be contrary to the views expressed by their founder, St Ignatius Loyola. The General, Provincials, Vice-Provincials and Major Superiors (normally those in charge of a mission area) are entitled to the prefix 'the Very Reverend'. All others are addressed as 'the Reverend'.

An exception to the above is when a Jesuit receives an episcopal appointment in special circumstances: for example, as an Archbishop or Bishop. He then takes the appropriate ecclesiastical style for such office.

Members of the Order append SJ after their names. The Order is restricted to men.

The Jewish Community

Orthodox Synagogues

They include the United Synagogue.

The Chief Rabbi

His appointment is Chief Rabbi of the United Hebrew Congregation of the British Commonwealth of Nations.

Beginning of Letter

Formal	Dear Sir or
	Dear Chief Rabbi
Social	Dear Chief Rabbi

Envelope

The Chief Rabbi Dr Mark Bernstein

The prefix 'the Very Reverend' is formally correct but not always preferred.

Verbal Address
Chief Rabbi

Description in Conversation
The Chief Rabbi

The Chief Rabbi Emeritus

As for the Chief Rabbi, but with the addition of 'Emeritus'.
The prefix 'the Very Reverend' is formally correct but is not normally used.

Envelope
Chief Rabbi Emeritus Sir Mark Bernstein, KBE

Rabbi

Beginning of Letter

Formal	Dear Sir or Madam
Social	Dear Rabbi Wiseman
	Dear Dr Wiseman (if a doctor)

Envelope
Rabbi J Wiseman
Rabbi Dr J Wiseman (if a doctor)
'The Reverend' before Rabbi is not used.

Verbal Address
Rabbi Wiseman
Dr Wiseman (if a doctor)

Description in Conversation
Rabbi Wiseman
Dr Wiseman (if a doctor)

Minister

Readers and Cantors also use the title 'the Reverend'.

Beginning of Letter

Formal	Dear Sir or Reverend Sir
Social	Dear Mr Wiseman
	Dear Dr Wiseman (if a doctor)

Envelope
The Reverend David Wiseman
The Reverend Dr David Wiseman (if a doctor)

Verbal Address
Mr Wiseman
Dr Wiseman (if a doctor)

Description in conversation
Mr Wiseman
Dr Wiseman (if a doctor)

Reform and Liberal Synagogues
The Reform Synagogues of Great Britain and the Union of Liberal and Progressive Synagogues are separate organisations. However, they have a Council of Reform and Liberal Rabbis whose chairman is their Ecclesiastical Representative.

The Ecclesiastical Representative and other Rabbis are addressed identically as Rabbis.

For further information regarding the correct forms of address in Judaism, contact: Chief Rabbinate, 735 High Road, London N12 0US. Tel: 0181 343 6301.

Other Major Faiths in the UK

Buddhism
There are approximately 25,000 adherents in Britain with up to 20 temples or monasteries in the UK, and 300 million Buddhists worldwide in more than 500 groups and centres.

There is no supreme governing body for Buddhism.

Contact: The Buddhist Society, 58 Eccleston Square, London SW1V 1PH. Tel: 0171 834 5858. General Secretary: R C Maddox.

Hinduism
There are approximately 360,000 adherents in Britain with up to 150 temples in the UK, and 800 million Hindus worldwide. The main ethnic languages are Gujarati, Hindi, Punjabi, Tamil, Bengali and Marathi.

Those styled Mr (Smith) should be addressed 'Shri' (Smith), and Mrs (Jones) 'Shri-Madee' (Jones).

There is no centrally trained and ordained priesthood.

Contact: Arya Pratinidhi Sabha (UK) and Arya Samaj London, 69a Argyle Road, London W13 0LY. Tel: 0181 991 1732. President: Prof. S N Bharadwaj.

Islam
There are approximately one million adherents in Britain with up to 900 mosques in the UK, and 1,000 million Muslims worldwide.

There is no central organisation or authority for Islam.

Contact: Union of Muslim Organisations of the UK and Eire, 109 Campden Hill Road, London W8 7TL. Tel: 0171 229 0538. General Secretary: Dr S A Pasha.

Summary Table

Name	Envelope	Letter	Verbal Address
Church of England			
Archbishop	The Most Reverend and Right Honourable the Lord Archbishop of York	Dear Archbishop or By name	Archbishop
Bishop	The Right Reverend the Bishop of Bath and Wells	Dear Bishop	Bishop
Bishop of London (always a Privy Counsellor)	The Right Reverend and Right Honourable the Lord Bishop of London	Dear Bishop	Bishop
Diocesan Bishop	The Right Reverend the Lord Bishop of Chichester	Dear Lord Bishop	Lord Bishop
Dean and Provost	The Very Reverend the	Dear Dean	Dean

248

	Dean of Hallam		
Archdeacon	The Venerable Archdeacon of Lincoln	Dear Archdeacon	Archdeacon
Canon	The Reverend Canon Edward Downes	Dear Canon or Dear Canon Downes	Canon
Other clergy	The Reverend Jemima Patrick	Dear Miss Patrick	Miss Patrick or Vicar or Rector (if the cleric so addressed is the incumbent of parish where you live or worship)

Roman Catholic Church

The Pope	His Holiness the Pope	Your Holiness or Most Holy Father	Your Holiness
Apostolic Nuncio	His Excellency Archbishop Victorio Varinnthia, the Apostolic Nuncio	Your Excellency	Your Excellency
Cardinal	His Eminence the Cardinal. Archbishop of Glasgow/His Eminence Lawrence Moore, Cardinal Archbishop of Glasgow/ His Eminence Lawrence Moore (if not an Archbishop)	Your Eminence or Dear Cardinal Moore	Your Eminence or Cardinal Moore
Archbishop	His Grace the Archbishop of Salford	Your Grace or Dear Archbishop	Your Grace or Bishop
Bishop	The Right Reverend Philip Bayswater, Bishop of Penrith	My Lord Bishop or Dear Bishop	My Lord or Bishop Bayswater
Monsignor	The Right Reverend/ The Very Reverend (if Canon) Monsignor Bartlett	Dear Monsignor Bartlett	Monsignor Bartlett
Other priests	The Reverend Father Cooper	Dear Father Cooper	Father
Abbot	The Right Reverend the Abbot of Arlington (followed by the initials of his Order)	Dear Father Abbott or Dear Abbot Arlington	Father Abbott

The Jewish Community

The Chief Rabbi	The Chief Rabbi	Dear Chief Rabbi	Chief Rabbi
Rabbi	Rabbi Daniel Bernstein or Rabbi Dr Bernstein	Dear Rabbi Bernstein or Dr Bernstein (if a doctor)	Rabbi Bernstein or Dr Bernstein (if a doctor)
Ministers	The Reverend Jacob Goldstein or The Reverend Dr Jacob Goldstein (if a doctor)	Dear Mr Goldstein or Dr Goldstein (if a doctor)	Mr Goldstein or Dr Goldstein (if a doctor)

THE UNITED NATIONS

The United Nations is comprised of six principal organs, as follows.

Secretariat

The other organs of the UN are serviced by the Secretariat, which also administers the programmes and policies laid down by them. The Secretary-General is at its head and is appointed by the General Assembly on the recommendation of the Security Council.

The United Nations Charter describes the Secretary-General's role as the chief administrative officer of the entire organisation.

An official letter concerning his or her office should be addressed to His Excellency Mr Henry White, Secretary-General of the United Nations, or Her Excellency Mrs Elizabeth Green, Secretary-General of the United Nations.

Beginning of Letter
Formal	Dear Sir or Madam
Social	Dear Mr White or Mrs Green

Verbal Address
Formal	Your Excellency
Social	Mr White or Mrs Green

Under-Secretaries-General may be addressed Dear Mr or Mrs Under-Secretary-General etc., but it is more common to write Dear Mr White or Mrs Green etc.

General Assembly

The General Assembly is the main deliberative organ and is composed of representatives of all Member States, each of which has one vote.

The General Assembly's regular sessions begin each year on the third Tuesday in September. At the start of each regular session, the Assembly elects a new President, twenty-one Vice-Presidents and seven Chairmen for the seven main committees of the Assembly.

The presidency of the Assembly rotates each year among five groups of States: African, Asian, Eastern European, Latin American and Western European and other States.

Security Council
The Security Council has primary responsibility for the maintenance of international peace and security. The council consists of fifteen members: five permanent members – China, France, the Russian Federation, the United Kingdom and the United States – with ten more elected by the General Assembly for terms of two years.

The Security Council recommends to the General Assembly the appointment of the Secretary-General and, together with the Assembly, elects the Judges of the International Court.

Economic and Social Council
The Economic and Social Council is the principal organ that coordinates the economic and social work of the UN and the specialised agencies and institutions, known as the 'United Nations Family' of organisations.

Trusteeship Council
The Trusteeship Council supervises the administration of Trust Territories placed under the Trusteeship System.

International Court of Justice
The International Court of Justice is the principal judicial organ of the UN.

The jurisdiction of the court covers all questions that States refer to it and all matters provided for in the UN Charter.

The court consists of fifteen Judges elected by the General Assembly and the Security Council. No two Judges can be nationals of the same State. The Judges serve for a term of nine years but can be elected for more than one term.

An official letter should be addressed to: the Honourable Mr Justice White or the Honourable Mrs Justice Green.

Any committee or sub-committee of the UN that has a chairman uses the standard form of address.

It is common to differentiate between male and female chairmen by the terms 'Mr Chairman' and 'Madam Chairman'. The term 'Chair' is not used.

OFFICIAL AND SOCIAL
OCCASIONS

ROYAL INVITATIONS

The Sovereign

Her Majesty's invitations are sent by:

- The Lord Steward of the Household to a State Banquet.

- The Lord Chamberlain to all major Court functions, such as a Garden Party, Wedding, Funeral or Memorial Service.

- The Master of the Household to all domestic functions given by The Queen at Buckingham Palace, or where The Queen is resident.

It is customary for invitations from The Queen to be considered as commands. Replies should be worded with this in mind, and addressed to the member of Her Majesty's Household who has issued the invitation.

An invitation to a Garden Party comes with an admission card. This states that an acknowledgement is not required unless the guest is unable to attend. In this case the admission card must be returned.

An invitation may be worded something like,

> The Master of the Household
> is Commanded by Her Majesty to invite
> Mr and Mrs John Brown
> to an Afternoon Party at Sandringham House
> on Thursday, 16 January from 4 to 6.30 p.m.

Acceptance

Suitable wording might be:

Mr and Mrs John Brown present their compliments to the Master of the Household, and have the honour to obey Her Majesty's Command to luncheon on 10 May at 12.30 o'clock.

Non-Acceptance

It is important to state the reason for non-acceptance. Bearing in mind that the invitation is a command, 'a prior engagement' is not considered to be a sufficient reason for failing to obey.

Suitable wording might be:
Mr and Mrs John Brown present their compliments to the Master of the Household, and much regret that they will be unable to obey Her Majesty's Command to . . . on . . . owing to the illness of Mrs John Brown.

A Letter of Thanks
When appropriate, such as after a State Banquet, but not after a Garden Party, this is addressed to the member of the Household who forwarded the invitation. The writer should ask him to convey his thanks to Her Majesty for . . . etc.

Queen Elizabeth The Queen Mother
Invitations are sent by the Comptroller of the Household to Queen Elizabeth The Queen Mother, except on very formal occasions, such as the wedding of The Princess Margaret, when they were sent by the Lord Chamberlain.

Invitations from The Queen Mother are also considered to be commands, and answers should reflect this tradition.

Acceptance and Non-Acceptance
As for The Sovereign, above.

Other Members of the Royal Family
Invitations from other members of the Royal Family are not 'commands'. They will usually be forwarded by a Member of their Household, to whom the reply should be addressed.

In other respects, as for The Sovereign, above.

Invitations to Members of The Royal Family
An invitation to a member of the Royal Family – that is, those with the titles of 'His (or Her) Royal Highness' – is extended via a letter to the appropriate Private Secretary. The title of a Royal guest is shown in full, as in:

Her Majesty The Queen
His Royal Highness The Prince Philip, Duke of Edinburgh

Their Royal Highnesses the Duke and Duchess of Kent

A member of a branch of the Royal Family, other than a Royal peer or peeress, is likewise given the full appropriate description in all written communications, as in:

His Royal Highness Prince Michael of Kent

A married Princess is shown with her husband's title or name on an invitation and the envelope, as in:

Her Royal Highness Princess Alexandra, the Hon Lady Angus Ogilvy

If the invitation includes her husband, she is still described as above, as in:

Her Royal Highness Princess Alexandra, the Hon Lady Angus Ogilvy, and the Hon Sir Angus Ogilvy

In these cases the Princess appears before her husband.

The word 'The' before 'Prince' or 'Princess' is restricted to The Prince Philip, Duke of Edinburgh, and the children of a Sovereign. Other members of the Royal Family without peerages are described as His (or Her) Royal Highness Prince (or Princess) . . .

INVITATIONS TO OFFICIAL FUNCTIONS

For a function given by an organisation, society etc., the invitation is usually issued on a card, which may be engraved in script from a copper plate or printed (in script or Roman type). It should make clear the following:

(a) The nature of the function: for example, 'For the Opening of . . . by . . .'; 'To mark the Centenary of . . .'; 'For a Dinner' etc.

(b) Where the function is to be held: for example, at The Splendide, Park Lane, W1, Ballroom entrance.

(c) The date of the function.

(d) The time of the function: for example, 12.45 for 1 p.m. (for a lunch); 6 to 8 p.m. (for a reception); 7.30 for 8 p.m. (for a dinner). When it is desired to indicate the time at which a function will end, there are two alternatives: '8 p.m. to Midnight' or '8 p.m. Cars (or carriages) at Midnight'. For a formal ceremony, such as the laying of a foundation stone, unveiling a statue etc., for which an invitation gives only the starting time – for example, at 3 p.m. – the card should also bear some such phrase as: 'Guests are requested to be seated by 2.45 p.m.'.

(e) The dress. For a day function (including a cocktail-hour reception) this need be specified only if it is to be other than lounge suit: for example, morning dress, academic robes etc. For an evening function it should always be specified: for example, evening dress, dinner jacket, lounge suit, uniform etc. 'Decorations' should also be specified when appropriate. See Dress Codes, page 302.

To indicate that a member of the Royal Family will be present, one of the following is engraved or printed at the top of the card:

In the gracious presence of Her Majesty The Queen
In the gracious presence of Her Majesty Queen Elizabeth The
Queen Mother
In the presence of His (or Her) Royal Highness (the) Prince (or
(the) Princess) . . .

Note: The word 'gracious' is included only for The Queen and The
Queen Mother. The word 'The' is included only for children of the
Sovereign.

If desired, the presence of an important non-royal guest may be
indicated using a formulation along the lines of: 'To meet (or in honour
of) the Right Honourable the Lord Mayor of London and the Lady
Mayoress'.

> The President, Sir John Blank, KBE
> and
> Council of The National Society of
> request the pleasure of the company of
>
> Sir Charles and Lady Colville
>
> at their Twenty-First Annual Banquet
> to be held at the Hotel Magnificent, Manchester, (Oak Suite)
> on Saturday, 27th February
> at 7.30 for 8 pm
>
> R.S.V.P.
> The Secretary
> 123, Piccadilly
> Manchester
>
> Evening Dress
> or Dinner Jacket
> Decorations

Admission Cards

To assist the Toastmaster (announcer), or to prevent gatecrashers, 'Please
bring this invitation with you' may be added at the bottom of the
invitation card. Alternatively (especially for an evening function for
which a large card cannot be carried easily in a pocket or handbag), the
following wording may be added: 'An admission card will be sent on
receipt of your acceptance'.

261

Admission cards should be printed in roman type and should not exceed 4.5 × 3.5 inches (11.5 × 9 centimetres) in size.

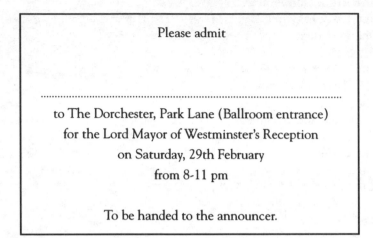

Please admit

....

to The Dorchester, Park Lane (Ballroom entrance)
for the Lord Mayor of Westminster's Reception
on Saturday, 29th February
from 8-11 pm

To be handed to the announcer.

An admission card to a ceremony may be used to allocate a specific seat. Separate admission cards should be sent for husband and wife, even though they have both been included on the same invitation card.

Additional information or instructions, such as about car parking, are best given on a separate sheet sent with the invitation or with the admission card.

Name on Admission Cards

The guest is shown on an admission card by office or by name, in the form in which he is to be announced to the host and hostess. If by name, this is limited to his title, rank and name, except that the following prefixes should be included:

- His Grace – for the Archbishops of Canterbury and York

- His Eminence – for a Cardinal

- His Excellency – for Ambassadors and High Commissioners

- The Right Honourable, the Right Worshipful, The Worshipful etc. – for Civic Heads who are so styled

Examples are:

The Prime Minister
Mrs Head (the Prime Minister's wife)
The Right Honourable the Lord Mayor (of London)
The Lady Mayoress (of London)
The President of the Royal Society
His Excellency* the Swedish Ambassador
Madame Blank
The Duke of Loamshire
The Duchess of Loamshire
His Grace the Archbishop of Canterbury
His Eminence the Cardinal Archbishop of Westminster
The Bishop of Hereford
The Earl of Wessex
The Countess of Wessex
General Sir John Cannon
Lady Cannon
Lord Russell
Judge Mace
Miss Single
Mr Neville
Mrs Neville
Dr James

*'His Excellency' may be abbreviated to HE on admission cards – but not by the announcer.

Members of the Royal Family

An invitation to a member of the Royal Family is always extended by letter, either through the Lord-Lieutenant of the county or to the Private Secretary. The latter is the general rule in London, the former elsewhere. A printed invitation is not sent, though a specimen may be forwarded to the Private Secretary, if desired.

It may be both prudent and diplomatic to make an informal enquiry, to the Private Secretary, as to the possibility of a favourable response prior to extending a formal invitation. The approach should include an outline of the nature and purpose of the function.

Whether the consort (husband or wife) of a member of the Royal Family should be included in the invitation depends on the nature of the function. This point can be raised with the Lord-Lieutenant or

Private Secretary in the informal enquiry.

Only in exceptional circumstances should two or more members of the Royal Family (other than consorts) be invited to the same function. If an invitation to a member of the Royal Family is declined, it may subsequently be extended to a more junior member, but never to a more senior one.

Once an invitation to a member of the Royal Family has been accepted, the organisers of the function should discuss with the Private Secretary, or with another member of the Royal Household nominated by him, the detailed arrangements in so far as they concern the royal guest (time of their arrival, by whom they will be accompanied, dress, which of the guests are to be presented and when etc.).

Names on Invitations

Invitations to official functions give the host by their office and/or name. This is engraved or printed, with their full title, rank etc. followed by decorations etc. (*Note:* Invitations to private functions are treated differently. See page 268.)

Prefixes such as His Grace, His Excellency, the Right Worshipful are, however, omitted, except that 'the Right Honourable' is included for a Privy Counsellor who is not a peer.

The prefix 'The Honourable (Hon)' and the suffix 'Esquire' are never used. (In both cases a gentleman is shown as Mr John Smith).

The younger sons of a Duke or Marquess are shown as, for example, Lord John Russell, and the daughters of a Duke, Marquess or Earl as, for example, Lady Jane Gilbert.

An invitation to a clergyman with the rank of the Reverend should be in the form 'the Reverend John and Mrs Henderson.'

An invitation to a pair of guests of some relationship other than husband and wife takes one of the following forms:

- Brother and sister: Mr John Brown and Miss Elizabeth Brown.

- Mother and son: Mrs George Carruthers and Mr William Carruthers. (*Note:* Invitations to adult offspring are usually sent separately from those to their parent/s).

- Unmarried couple: Mr Rick Blaine and Miss Ilsa Bond.

Examples are:

The Right Hon the Prime Minister and Mrs Head
The Duke and Duchess of Loamshire
The Lord Mayor and Lady Mayoress of Blanktown
The President of the Royal Academy, Sir John Brown, KBE, and
    Lady Brown
The President of the Royal Society and Lady Smith
The French Ambassador and Madame Pompadour
Rear-Admiral the Earl of Nonsuch, CB, DSO, and the Countess of
    Nonsuch
Colonel Sir John Bayonet, Bt, MVO, and Lady Bayonet
The Master of the Worshipful Company of Holeborers and Mrs
    White
The Right Honourable William Black, LLD, QC, MP
The Archbishop of Canterbury and Mrs Church
The Cardinal Archbishop of Westminster
The Earl of Ludlow, OBE, MC, and the Countess of Ludlow
The Dean of Westminster, the Very Reverend James D Brown,
    KCVO, MA, DD (and Mrs Brown)
Professor Albert Blossom, FRS, MA, and Mrs Blossom
Lord and Lady John Russell
Mr Justice Wig and Mrs Wig
Mr and Mrs Paul Neville
Dr and Mrs Henry James
Miss Dorothy Trubshaw and Guest

The Envelope

An invitation to an official function should be addressed only to the guest invited in their own right if sent to their official address, even if their partner is also invited. They are given their full prefix, title, rank, decorations etc., as for a formal letter.

If the invitation is sent to the home address, it is traditional for only the wife's name to appear on the envelope. See page 269.)

Replies

These, which should be on headed paper to show the sender's address, are best illustrated by examples:

(a) Mr and Mrs William Brown thank the President and Council of the National Society of . . . for their kind invitation for Saturday, 29 February, which they accept with much pleasure (or which they have the honour to accept).

(b) Lord and Lady White thank the Master of the Worshipful Company of Holeborers for his kind invitation for Saturday 29 February, which they much regret being unable to accept. (A reason may be given: for examples, owing to a previous engagement, because of absence abroad etc.)

(c) The Reverend John and Mrs White thank the Dean and Chapter of . . . for their kind invitation for Saturday, 29 February. They accept with much pleasure for the service in the Abbey but regret that they are unable to accept for the subsequent reception.

The date is placed underneath.

Reply Cards

The organisation of a large function is greatly facilitated by the use of reply cards (printed in Roman type), which are sent out with the invitations. These should be of small postcard size and may be numbered serially for ready reference to the invitation list, which it is seldom practicable to draw up in alphabetical order.

An example is:

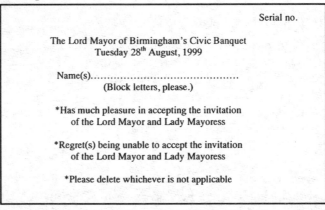

A reply card may also be used to obtain other information, such as 'I shall/I shall not require car parking facilities'.

Guests should always use the printed card for their reply. Should they wish to add anything, such as an explanation for their inability to accept, this should be done in a separate letter.

The reply to an invitation which takes the form '. . . and Lady' or '. . . and Guest' should always give the name of the chosen lady or guest.

Because postage is now so expensive, the considerate host or organiser of an official function for which it is only necessary to know the approximate number who will be attending (for example, an afternoon party or an evening reception) will request replies only from those able to accept: that is, by adding to the specimen invitation cards below the words requesting an answer, 'only if able to accept', and also by deleting the asterisks, the line beginning 'Regrets' and the footnote on the reply card.

INVITATIONS TO PRIVATE FUNCTIONS

There are two kinds of invitations to formal functions, which (unless time is short) are prepared on cards engraved in script from a copper plate:

- For formal luncheon and dinner parties.

- 'At Home' invitations for all other parties, such as dances, receptions, garden parties, luncheons, dinners and suppers.

Invitations to informal functions may be extended by letter, telephone etc. and will not be dealt with here. Suffice to say that it is up to the hosts to decide and make clear to guests the appropriate level of formality and all the other relevant details and arrangements. The level of formality of the invitation should accord with that of the occasion.

Invitations to Formal Luncheon and Dinner Parties

These are engraved on a card of good texture, usually about 6 × 4.5 inches (15 × 11.5 centimetres) in size (or slightly larger if necessary), and are prepared in the name of both the host and hostess (see example above). If time is short, they may be printed or thermography used, which gives an engraved look (both cheaper and acceptable options). They contain some of the information as for an official function but with certain important exceptions, which are given in the appropriate section.

Alternatively, the more old-fashioned style of 'request the pleasure of the company of' may be adopted, the guests' names being added on the next line, in place of the top left-hand corner.

If the lunch or dinner is to take place at an address other than that to which the replies are to be sent – at an hotel – for example, this is stated on a line after the date. The time may be placed either after the date or at the bottom right-hand corner before, or in place of, the address.

Those given to regular formal entertaining may keep a stock of invitation cards. The occasion, date, time and also place (if away from home) are then added by hand. This card may also be prepared with the wording 'request the pleasure of the company of', the guests' names being added thereafter.

Mr and Mrs Crispin Smith

Sir John and Lady Brent
request the pleasure of your company
at Dinner
on Tuesday, 29ᵗʰ February
at 8 for 8.30 o'clock

R.S.V.P.
23 Cadogan Square
London SW1

If the luncheon or dinner is not a very formal one, an 'At Home' card may be used. The time, such as 12.45 for 1.15 o'clock (or p.m.), or '8 for 8.30 o'clock (or p.m.), is usually sufficient indication of the occasion.

At Home Invitations

These invitations, which for formal occasions are usually engraved on a card of good texture about 6 × 4.5 inches (15 × 11.5 centimetres) in size (or slightly larger if necessary), are prepared in the name of the hostess only, in the case of married couples. If the time of the function is not a sufficient indication as to its nature, the latter may be stated on the card: for example, 'Dancing 10 o'clock'. If the invitation extends from, say, 6 o'clock to 8.30, the description 'cocktails', 'wine', 'sherry' etc. is unnecessary, though it is often included.

For many 'At Home' functions except dances, a smaller card may be used, usually 4.5 × 3.5 inches (11.5 × 9 centimetres), which shows the

Mr Edward Shaw

Lady Elizabeth Berkeley

at Home

Monday, 1st June

R.S.V.P.
Faversham Hall
Tinbury   Dancing
Essex   10.30 pm

Mr and Mrs Edward Shaw

Mrs Hugh Harrington

at Home

Wednesday, 30th June

Mercers' Hall, Ironmonger Lane, EC2

R.S.V.P.
25 Cumberland Terrace
London NW1   6.45 pm
Please bring this card with you

hostess's name, 'At Home', RSVP and her address. A stock of these cards can be purchased for various functions. Other details are completed by the hostess.

Miss Barbara Worth

Mrs *Richard Greene*
at Home

R.S.V.P.
16 Argyll Lane
London W8 8JK

Monday, May 12th
6.30 pm

For small informal parties a basic stock of 'At Home' cards may be purchased, which merely have 'At Home' and 'RSVP' engraved (or printed) on them. They would usually be 4.5 × 3.5 inches (11.5 × 9 centimetres). The hostess then adds her name, address, date, time, name of guests and other necessary information.

Host and Hostess

The exact rank in the peerage of the host and/or hostess is given on all types of invitation. The word 'the' before a title is usually omitted for the ranks of Marquess and Earl, and always for those of Viscount and Baron (Marchioness of Flintshire, Viscountess Longhurst, for example).

No prefixes appear before the name, such as 'the Right Honourable', 'the Honourable', 'His Excellency', 'the Worshipful'.

No letters are placed after the name, such as those that signify decorations or degrees, or the letters 'Bt'.

271

Joint Hostesses.

If there is more than one hostess, their names are placed one under the other. The first name corresponds to the address to which the replies are to be sent. If a joint party is to be held at a hostess's house and the replies are to be sent to her, her name is placed first on the invitation, irrespective of any title held.

Miss Sally Brown

Mr Henry Waterhouse, Lady Black,
Mr Sebastian Jones
at Home
for Elizabeth, Henrietta and Fiona
Wednesday, 6ᵗʰ June
The Hyde Park Hotel

R.S.V.P.
757, Bedford Square
London WC1

Dancing
10 o'clock

If the hostesses are to deal with replies separately, their addresses are placed from left to right at the foot of the card, in the same order as their names.

Other Information on the Invitation

'Decorations' on a private invitation implies that a member of the Royal Family is expected to be present. (*Note:* The word does not have this meaning on an official invitation.)

For functions where the hostess considers it necessary to indicate the dress expected to be worn, 'White Tie' may be added for evening dress,

'Black Tie' for dinner jackets, or 'Afternoon Dress' or 'Informal' for lounge suits. Otherwise she is content to leave this to the discretion of her guests. Whenever possible, many hostesses will try to indicate more specifically the level of dressiness expected, either verbally or in a letter if one is being sent with the invitation. See Dress Codes, page 302.

If it is necessary to keep out gatecrashers, 'Please bring this invitation with you' may be added at the foot of the card.

If there is no information to the contrary, it is understood that the function is to be held at the address to which a reply is requested.

If the function takes place in the country, it is often useful if a map is placed on the back of the card or on a separate sheet.

Enclosures

A separate slip is often sent, with times of trains and such requests as 'Are you coming by road or rail?' or 'Do you want to be included in a dinner party, or a dinner party and house party?'

Sending Out Invitations

It is wise, unless part of a ruse to discourage particular guests from coming, to send invitations as early as possible. While a quiet, intimate dinner among close friends may be arranged over the phone with little notice, the more formal a gathering, and the more people being invited, the more advance warning is advisable. A minimum of six weeks should mean that most people are not booked up, will give guests ample time to reply, and provide the hosts with preparation time in abundance.

If an invitation is extended and accepted verbally – for example, by telephone – it should be confirmed by an invitation card on which 'RSVP' has been deleted, and 'To remind' or 'Pour mémoire' substituted. In this case there is no need for acknowledgement.

Names of Guests

These are written in the top left corner, except for formal luncheon/ dinner invitations designed to include them in the middle of the card. See also invitations to Official Functions, page 260. The following should be noted:

(a) No prefixes, such as 'the Right Honourable', 'the Honourable', 'His Excellency', 'the Worshipful' are employed.

(b) No letters after the name, such as those that signify decorations or degrees, or the letters 'Bt' are given.

(c) All peers and peeresses, apart from Dukes and Duchesses, who are referred to by these titles, are given in the form of 'Lord and Lady Blank'. This is the established custom for all private functions except the very important, when the exact rank in the peerage may be given.

(d) Grown-up sons and daughters are usually sent separate invitations even when they live at home. However, when their exact names, or their availability, are not known, it is permissible to add 'and Family' after their parents' names.

(e) The addition 'and Guest' or 'and Partner' (not 'and Friend') may be added to allow a guest to bring an unspecified guest or partner with him/her.

(f) During Ascot week and other similar occasions and festivals for which house parties are given, invitations may show after the names of the guests 'and House Party'.

Examples are:

The Lord Mayor (and Lady Mayoress) of London
The Swedish Ambassador (and Madame Blank)
The Duke (and Duchess) of Loamshire
The Archbishop of Canterbury (and Mrs Jones)
Lord (and Lady) Wessex
General Sir John (and Lady) Cannon
Air Commodore (and Mrs) John Plane
Professor (and Mrs) Albert Blossom
The Dean of Rochester (and Mrs Proudie)
The Archdeacon of Exeter (and Mrs Pugh)
Canon (and Mrs) John Porter
The Reverend John (and Mrs) Henderson
Dr (and Mrs) John Homer
Mr (and Mrs) John Brown
Miss Dorothy Brown

Envelope
It is still customary to address an invitation to both husband and wife to the wife only. Guests are given their full prefix, title, rank, decorations etc., as for a formal letter.

Replies
These are sent on writing paper with the address, as for official functions. They are addressed to the hostess even when the invitation is a joint one from the host and hostess.

When invitations are extended to unnamed guests such as 'and Partner' or 'and Family', the reply should contain the names of those who will attend. A named invitee should be substituted with another guest only with the hostess's express permission.

WEDDING INVITATIONS

Weddings have not been immune to the changing times. Long-standing conventions have been affected both by the general relaxation of attitudes to formal procedure and by the increasing complexity of modern family arrangements.

Nevertheless, many people still relish and value a decidedly traditional approach as a way of emphasising the special nature of the occasion. The other benefit of tradition is that it provides a tried and tested procedure to follow, and therefore can never be faulted.

The most traditional and elegant wedding invitations combine quality of material with simplicity of style. They consist of four pages and are engraved from copper plate on heavy card (around 600 grammes), usually in black copperplate script, on a white or cream matt background. Flat printing should be avoided if economically possible, but thermography or raised printing provide less costly alternatives.

In keeping with the era's predisposition towards excess, the usual dimensions have stretched from 7 × 5.5 inches (17.8 × 14 centimetres) to 8 × 6 (20.3 × 15.2 centimetres), and cards have become heavier. Further growth is cautioned against in the name of humility, simplicity and aesthetics. For similar reasons, flourishes such as rounded corners and gold edges should be used only with restraint, if at all.

Whether conservative or radical, a wedding invitation must contain certain key elements of essential information, above all: who is to be married, the name of the hosts, and their relationship to the former, locations of ceremony and/or reception, date, time and details of where to send a reply. Above all, be sure to check the proof with care, as mistakes may prove costly or, worse, embarrassing.

The most common variations from the norm arise because of the particular relationship between host(s) and bride. In the examples that follow, the possible variants are treated in turn.

Other variations are a matter of taste and custom. For instance, if desired, 'honour' can be used in place of 'pleasure' in all the examples – a format that is still popular in the US but is rarely used now in Britain, being thought of as old-fashioned.

Similarly, it is acceptable to place a dotted line after 'requests the

---

Miss Rosemary Carrington

Lieutenant-Colonel and Mrs *John Standish*
request the pleasure of
your company at the marriage
of their daughter
Caroline
to
Mr *Christopher Henry Herbert*
at St. Paul's Church, Knightsbridge
on Wednesday, 14th *March*
at 3 o'clock
and afterwards at
The Hyde Park Hotel

R.S.V.P.
Charford Manor,
Washington,
Sussex.

---

pleasure of the company of' and fill in the guest's name thereafter, but this also tends to be considered outdated. More commonly, the names of guests are written by hand, preferably with a fountain pen, on the top left of the invitation, as for other invitations.

Names are styled as for official functions (see page 268). For the ranks of officers in the Services, see the relevant section under The

Armed Forces, page 121. For titles of Host, hostess, and bridegroom, see Host and Hostess, page 271. 'The Honourable' is never used.

1. Overleaf is a specimen invitation where both parents of the bride are the host and hostess.

The following examples show alternative wording.

2. The bride's mother is the only hostess:

Mrs John Standish
requests the pleasure of
your company at the marriage
of her daughter
Caroline etc.

3. The bride's father is the only host:

Mr John Standish
requests the pleasure of
your company at the marriage
of his daughter
Caroline etc.

4. The bride's mother and stepfather are the host and hostess:

Mr and Mrs John Forsyte
request the pleasure of
your company at the marriage
of her daughter
Caroline etc.
    The bride's surname may be included if desired if she has not adopted her stepfather's.

5. The bride's father and stepmother are the host and hostess:

Mr and Mrs John Standish
request the pleasure of
your company at the marriage
of her daughter
Caroline etc.

6. The bride's stepmother is the hostess:

   Mrs John Standish
   requests the pleasure of
   your company at the marriage
   of her stepdaughter
   Caroline etc.

7. The bride's parents have been divorced, but they are the joint host and hostess:

   Mr John King and
   Mrs George Tremayne*
   request the pleasure of
   your company at the marriage
   of their daughter
   Sybil etc.
   *'Mrs Frances King' if she has not remarried.
      If the bride's parents have married again, the subsequent husband and wife do not play a prominent part at the wedding.

8. The bride's relatives, guardians or god-parent(s) are the host and hostess:

   Admiral Sir John and Lady Fortescue
   request the pleasure of
   your company at the marriage
   of their niece/ward/his (her) god-daughter
   Alexandra etc.
      The bride's surname may be added if it is different from the host's and hostess's.

9. The bride's relatives, for example, who are not husband and wife are the host and hostess or joint hostesses (for example, brother and sister, brother and sister-in-law, or sisters): As in Example 8, but the surname should be repeated. For example:

   Captain John Buckfast and Lady Buckfast
   Mr John Buckfast and Mrs Henry Lowndes
   Mr John Buckfast and Mrs Edward Buckfast
   Miss Maria Buckfast and Mrs William Bagshot

10. The bride is the hostess:

Miss Emily Grattan
requests the pleasure of your company
at her marriage to Mr John Anderson

11. The bride and groom are joint hosts:

Mr John Brown and Miss Emily Grattan
request the pleasure of your company
at their marriage . . .

12. Second and subsequent marriages: As in Examples 1 to 9, as applicable, but when the bride is a widow she is described as, for instance, 'Fleur, widow of Mr Michael Mont'; if her marriage has been dissolved, as 'Mrs Fleur Mont'. If she has reverted to her maiden name, only her first name is necessary.

     If the bride is hostess, then as in Example 10, with her name as Mrs John Smith or Mrs Mary Smith, as applicable.

13. Invitation to the reception only: If the church is too small to accommodate all the guests, the invitation should read:

. . . request(s) the pleasure of your company
at the reception following the marriage
of their daughter Ann to . . . at . . . on . . .

If the bride is hostess, the wording should read:

. . . at the reception following her marriage
to . . . at . . . on . . .

In either case a leaflet should be placed inside the envelope with the invitation to give the reason. For example:

Owing to the small size of Little Wotton Church it is possible to ask only very few guests to the Service. We hope you will forgive this invitation being to the Reception only.

In no circumstances is a guest invited to the wedding but not to the reception.

Invitations may come with a variety of enclosures. Some hosts include reply cards, whether for ease of response or as a spur to the lazier or more impolite invitees. These are usually printed, with a space for guests to fill in their names, and measure 3.5 × 5.5 inches (9 × 14 centimetres).

It may sometimes be wise to include a map on a separate sheet of paper, as well as any extraordinary details, such as transport arrangements, where relevant.

Postponements and Cancellations

In the unhappy event of either eventuality, a card, generally 4.5 × 3 or 5.5 × 3.5 inches (11.5 × 7.6 or 14 × 9, centimetres), printed on white or cream card, is usually sent, worded along the following lines:

1. Indefinite postponement:

    Owing to the recent death of Colonel Samuel Braithwaite, Mr and Mrs John Blank deeply regret that they are obliged to cancel the invitations to the marriage of their daughter Elizabeth to Mr Mark Braithwaite on . . .

    Invitations are then sent out again when the new date is fixed.

2. Postponement to a later date:

    Owing to the illness of Mrs Victor Scott, Mr and Mrs John Blank deeply regret that they are obliged to postpone the invitations to the marriage of their daughter Anne to Mr John Scott at St Margaret's Church, Westminster, from Thursday, 14 December 1997 to Wednesday, 2 February 1998.

3. Cancellation of invitations because the wedding is to take place quietly:

    Owing to the recent death of her husband, Mrs John Black much regrets that she is obliged to cancel the invitations to the marriage of her daughter Elizabeth to Captain Jonathan Trelawny, which will now take place very quietly on Wednesday 10 October 1998.

Invitations are then sent out by letter to near relations and close friends only.
    Note that, barring the breaking off of the engagement, it is the 'invitations' that are postponed or cancelled, rather than the wedding.

4.   Cancellation of the wedding – engagement broken off:

Sir John and Lady Hopley announce that the marriage of their daughter Emma to Mr Christopher Camberley, which was arranged for Wednesday 4 June 1999, will not now take place.

Envelopes and Replies
These are as described under Invitations to Private Functions (see page 268).

LIST OF NAMES ON PROGRAMMES, BROCHURES ETC.

Names were traditionally listed in order of precedence. However, this procedure is now falling into disuse as both too complicated and old-fashioned. It may even give offence if important patrons, guests or benefactors are not given the prominence they deserve for want of a hereditary title.

An acceptable solution is to list names in alphabetical order, the sole exception being that the Sovereign and other members of the Royal Family must come first. Members of the Royal Family are always shown with the royal style, usually in full (for example, 'Her Royal Highness . . .'). Others should be treated consistently, either in the formal or social style, whichever is adopted. For example:

Formal Style
>His Grace the Duke of Blank
>Her Grace the Duchess of Blank
>Her Grace Mary, Duchess of Blank
>The Rt Hon the Earl of Blank
>The Rt Hon the Lord Blank
>His Grace the Archbishop of Blank, or the Most Reverend the Lord Archbishop of Blank
>The Right Reverend the Lord Bishop of Blank
>The Very Reverend the Dean of Blank
>The Reverend John Smith
>The Rt Hon John Brown

There is no rule for the position of 'the' in lists of peers. 'Rt Hon the Earl of Blank', 'the Rt Hon Viscount Blank' or 'Rt Hon Lord Blank' are not wrong, but the above usage is recommended. Similarly, it is not laid down whether one should use upper or lower case for the first letter of 'the' within a sentence, except that the former must always be accorded to The Queen and to Queen Elizabeth The Queen Mother and to the children of the Sovereign, as in The Prince Edward.

Social Style
The Duke of Blank
The Duchess of Blank
Mary, Duchess of Blank
The Earl of Blank
The Lord Blank
The Lord Archbishop of Blank
The Lord Bishop of Blank
The Dean of Blank
The Reverend John Smith
The Rt Hon John Brown

Peers and peeresses are given the territorial designation only if it forms an integral part of the title (for example, Viscount Montgomery of Alamein).

Peers and peeresses by courtesy and former wives of peers are not accorded 'the' or the formal prefix of Most Hon or Rt Hon.

Untitled men are either consistently shown as 'John Smith, Esq' or as 'Mr John Smith', and doctors (holders of academic degrees) as 'John Smith, Esq, DSc' or 'Dr John Smith' (not 'Dr John Smith, DSc').

For the position of letters after the name, see appropriate section.

JOINT FORMS OF ADDRESS

There are occasions when it may be fitting to use a joint form of address for husband and wife when addressing an envelope. Christmas cards and letters to close relatives or friends are the most obvious cases in point.

The use of the joint form for invitations to both public and private functions is also becoming common, although potentially complicated. When life was more straightforward, the former were addressed to the husband (if sent to his official address) and the latter to the wife at the home address. However, these clear waters of tradition have been muddied by the sexual revolution, with women now being guests in their own right on a more regular basis. Clearly, if the female partner in a relationship is being invited in her official capacity, while her husband is included as a courtesy, then the invitation should not be addressed to him alone. Equally, many people may well feel that to address an invitation to a private function solely to a wife is somewhat old-fashioned and formal.

Other than this, the chief difficulty in using a joint form arises where husband and wife are differently styled. The following is a guide (initials may, of course, be used instead of first names if desired):

> Lieutenant-Colonel the Hon John and Mrs Smith
> Major John and the Hon Mrs Smith
> The Reverend John and Mrs Smith
> The Hon Guy and Lady Moira Black
> The Hon Guy and Mrs White
> Mr Donald Home and the Countess of Blackadder
> Mr John and Lady Barbara Jones
> Mr John and the Hon Mrs Green
> Mr and Mrs Thomas Brown

To which one must now add the possibility (verging on probability) of the need to address unmarried couples, whether heterosexual or homosexual, in the joint form. The only mildly awkward consideration here might be the order in which to list the names. If applicable, it seems sensible in such cases to name first whichever partner is the 'official' invitee. In other cases discretion and common sense must be the host's guides.

A couple who are both doctors, when the wife practises under her maiden name, should still be addressed in the traditional social style of Dr and Mrs Cross. In a professional capacity, however, they would of course be listed under their individual names.

CHRISTMAS CARDS

The practice of sending these is evolving along with all other social activities. Alongside their traditional function as vessels of goodwill and remembrance between family and friends, Christmas cards have been adopted by the business world as a professional courtesy. As is the way with such things, when one firm starts to do something, the rest feel obliged to follow suit. As a result, an avalanche of cards now cascades from the postbox from businesses grateful for custom, professionals reminding clients of their existence, and all manner of bodies on to whose mailing list the hapless receiver of glad tidings may have strayed.

It is worth noting that the nature of Christmas celebration has also undergone transformation. In parallel with the traditional Christian festivity, there have developed secular, multicultural and ecumenical variations on the Christmas theme. For many people, Christmas is now a festival of goodwill, rather than a Christian, or even a religious, event.

At the same time it is good to remember that others still place great store in the Christian aspect of the occasion, and their claims on the tradition should certainly be taken into account. The sender should, where possible, attempt to tailor cards with the recipients in mind.

In any case, catch-all solutions are nowadays always at hand. Cards can easily be found that are traditional, without being overtly religious, and 'Season's Greetings' provides a useful form of universal greeting that should avoid offending anyone.

It should also be borne in mind that subtlety and understatement are in keeping with the spirit of the occasion. The proliferation of cards for the reasons expressed above provides a further good reason for keeping them small.

It is customary for the husband's name to be given before his wife's, but this is a matter of personal choice. The wife's forename is, however, retained. Therefore, a card should be inscribed from 'John and Mary Smith', rather than from 'Mr and Mrs John Smith'. If the names are printed, the surname should be crossed through on cards sent to those on first-name terms. See also Joint Forms of Address, page 285.

It is permissible to include a short personal letter when the card is to friends or relatives who are rarely seen. However, a general newsletter is not considered an acceptable inclusion.

Cards should be sent in envelopes with diagonal flaps and left unsealed.

PROFESSIONAL AND BUSINESS CARDS

These used to be only for professional or business purposes, but with the decline of the visiting card they have taken on some of its social functions and will often be handed out indiscriminately for any number of reasons.

The most common dimensions are 3.5×2 inches (9×5 centimetres). The particular style, design and detailing, such as the inclusion of a logo, may be a matter of personal taste or may follow a strict corporate policy. Either way, an effort should be made to design cards in keeping with the type of business concerned.

Cards are usually printed, but may be engraved if a grander impression is desired, or thought appropriate. Thermography, as previously mentioned, provides another option.

The name and professional title should be centred, in large characters, with the name of the firm (if not in a logo at the top), its address, and telephone, fax and e-mail numbers in smaller characters in the bottom left-and right-hand corners, or spread across the bottom.

A home address and telephone number would, in the past, have been added only if absolutely necessary. However, with the ever-growing army of the self-employed, and the legions of those on flexitime or who work from home, this is becoming an increasingly useful, indeed vital, practice for many. It also reflects the crossover between the business and social functions of the new breed of cards. Nevertheless, many people would prefer not to give out such personal information quite so readily, and they may console themselves, as they refrain from doing so, that they have tradition on their side.

A business card being intended to show the bearer's qualifications, the appropriate letters may be suffixed to the name: for example, FRIBA.

It is not necessary to prefix the name with any title, rank, Mr, Mrs or Miss, but this is sometimes done, especially if the card is engraved, to be similar in appearance to a visiting card. If a retired officer from one of the Armed Forces gives his rank, 'Retd', 'Ret' or 'Rtd' should be added to the right of and slightly below his name (or, where applicable, after Royal Navy etc.)

289

Punctuation may be included or omitted as desired.

It may be useful to use the reverse of the card to provide the same details in a second language.

TABLE PLANS

Seating arrangements remain for many people something of a logistical nightmare. There are clear guidelines, but these, as with all things, have been thrown into disarray by the relaxation of the rules of precedence and by the spread of sexual equality.

It remains essential to accord pre-eminence to senior members of the Royal Family and to respect tradition where their retinues are concerned but, other than this, common sense should be employed to juggle all claims to precedence, including those based on aristocratic lineage. Whereas in some situations social rank may still be deemed to be of utmost importance, at the majority of functions considerations such as professional status and age are now treated as equally or more powerful determining factors.

The nature of the occasion provides the most telling guide, and should offer indications as to the relative significance of guests. Clearly, a guest of honour must be seated so as to reflect his or her status and, by way of example, the chairman of a host company, the MP of the constituency in which a function is held, a foreign dignitary whose country is being honoured, or a benefactor who made the whole thing possible should all be recognised and seated appropriately.

Royal Guests

When The Queen attends a function, the host surrenders his place to her and takes up the seat on her right.

Other members of the Royal Family (that is, The Queen Mother and those entitled to the prefix Royal Highness) are given special precedence. The husband of a lady member of the Royal Family is accorded precedence immediately after her when both attend a function. If he attends alone, he retains his own precedence, unless he is the principal guest. See Invitations to Official Functions, page 260.

The Suite in attendance on a member of the Royal Family should be placed reasonably near to him or her.

No guest should leave a function before a member of the Royal

Family, except in special circumstances, when prior permission should be obtained.

This rule may be honoured in the breach rather than in the observance at charity balls etc. which continue after midnight. Equally, the organiser of an evening function may seek (through the Private Secretary) 'blanket' permission for guests who may have transport difficulties if they do not leave by a certain hour (to catch the last train, for example) to do so before the member of the Royal Family leaves.

A guest holding an official position whose duties require him to leave a function before the member of the Royal Family in order to keep another engagement should seek permission to do so (through the Private Secretary) in advance of the function.

Official Functions

The principal guest is placed on the host's right (except for The Queen, for whom see above). Traditionally, the principal guest's wife would be placed on the host's left, the host's wife being placed on the right of the principal guest. If wives were not present the second most important guest would be placed on the host's left.

In this day and age it is almost as likely for the host, or for that matter the principal guest, to be a woman, in which case the same basic principles may be extrapolated to their logical conclusion, and judicious juggling employed to achieve the desired balance.

When the principal guest is The Queen (or other Head of State), a member of the Royal Family, a Prime Minister, a member of the Cabinet, or someone of comparable importance, the need to invite some or all of the following, and their partners, should be considered. Bear in mind that those who accept (and their partners) would customarily be placed in this order of precedence after such principal guest:

1. The Lord-Lieutenant of the county

2. The Lord Mayor, Lord Provost, Mayor or Provost of the city, borough etc.

3. The High Sheriff of the county

4. The Chairman of the County Council

Note: The Lord Mayor of London has precedence throughout his City immediately after the Sovereign, and elsewhere immediately after Earls.

Other Lord Mayors and Mayors (Provosts and Lord Provosts in Scotland), as well as Council chairmen, have precedence immediately after the Royal Family on their own civic premises, and after the Lord-Lieutenant elsewhere in their city or borough. On relevant occasions these guests may, as a courtesy, yield their prime places to a 'guest of honour', or, for example, to an Archbishop at a Church function, to the Lord Chancellor and the Speaker of the House of Commons at a Parliamentary function, to the Lord Chief Justice or Master of the Rolls at a legal function and so on. Outside their areas of jurisdiction, all except the Lord Mayor of London have no precedence other than that which courtesy, or the occasion, may demand.

Ambassadors, High Commissioners and Chargés d'Affaires should be placed at the top table, their relative precedence being strictly observed (see Diplomatic Service, page 147). As a general rule, diplomatic representatives from countries that do not enjoy diplomatic relations with each other should not be invited to the same function. When, as sometimes happens, it is necessary to invite them, care should be taken to avoid placing them near each other.

Ministers of the Crown and Privy Counsellors should be placed at the top table.

Important dignitaries of the Established Church are placed high among the guests. High dignitaries of other Churches should, as a courtesy, be accorded status immediately succeeding those of the same rank from the Established Church.

When a function takes place within premises belonging to some organisation other than the host's, a senior representative of that organisation should be invited and placed high among the guests.

Other important guests are placed in order of precedence and importance, subject to the following general rules:

(a) Important members of the inviting body should be interspersed among the principal guests.

(b) Guests' partners should be placed according to the precedence of the guest invited in their own right.

(c) It is up to the host to decide whether husbands and wives are to be seated together or apart. The former is easier to arrange; the latter (which is always followed at private functions) gives both husband and wife a chance to meet new faces.

293

Semi-Official Functions

The host must decide whether a semi-official function, such as a society or firm's annual dinner, is to be a formal one, with precedence observed (as at an official function), or whether, as tends to be the case today, it should be a less formal one with less regard for precedence. Even so, the members of the host organisation (and their partners) should be interspersed among the other guests; on no account should the former be seated in one block and the latter in another.

Guests' Lists

Guests may be shown where they are placed at table in various ways:

(a) For a party not exceeding thirty, a seating plan may be displayed on a table or board.

(b) For a larger party of up to a hundred, a numbered drawing of the table may be displayed with a list of the guests alongside it in alphabetical order, each with a seat number.

(c) For parties larger than (b), each guest should be provided with a printed table plan, with the names listed in alphabetical order, or with a table diagram with the seat ringed or arrowed.

The following rules are customarily observed (where an alternative is shown, this is at the host's discretion, subject to observing consistency throughout the list).

- Any guest invited by virtue of office should be so indicated: for example, Fenchurch, Sir William, KBE, President of the Society of . . .

- Peers and peeresses are shown by their exact rank in the peerage: for example, Middlesex, The Earl of, KBE; Flintshire, The Countess of, etc. The word 'the' is optional for Viscounts, Barons, their wives and widows. They must all be treated identically, except for peers by courtesy who do not have the prefix 'the' (see below). The prefix appropriate to the grade of peer may be shown if desired.

    His or Her Grace – Duke or Duchess

The Most Hon – Marquess or Marchioness
The Right Hon – other peers and peeresses
Again, a decision has to be taken whether this prefix is to be used.
If it is, all peers and peeresses, apart from those by courtesy (see
below), should be treated similarly.

- Peers and peeresses by courtesy, and former wives of peers, have
  no peerage prefix: that is, neither 'the Right Hon' etc. nor 'the'.
  courtesy styles: those with the prefix 'Lord' or 'Lady' before their
  first names do not have the prefix 'the'; the courtesy style of 'the
  Hon' is shown.

- Privy Counsellors are given the prefix 'the Right Hon' but not the
  suffix 'PC' (except for peers and peeresses, when these letters are
  shown).

- Baronets are shown with the suffix of 'Bt'.

- Honours and decorations (and degrees when appropriate) should
  be included; also the principal other awards, such as fellowships of
  learned societies. Male guests without title or rank should be styled
  'Mr'. This is especially true when both husbands and wives are
  invited: the solecism of mixing the styles – for example, John
  Brown, Esq, and Mrs John Brown – must be avoided.

Place Cards

These should be brief, honours, decorations, degrees etc. being omitted.
So too is the formal prefix for peers, who are shown as, for example,
'The Earl of Blank' or 'Lord Blank'. 'The Right Hon' is retained for
Privy Counsellors who are not peers, and the suffixes RN, QC and MP
for those so entitled.

Any office held should be omitted, except that important guests
should be indicated by their office instead of their name: for example,
the Swiss Ambassador, the Lord Mayor etc.

'The Hon' is usually shown before the name at a public function but
omitted at a private party.

'Mr' invariably takes the place of 'Esq'. Other rules are as for Guests,
Lists, above.

Grace

Grace is usually said before a meal, and sometimes afterwards, in which case it precedes the Loyal Toast(s).

There is no Preamble to Grace. The Toastmaster announces only, 'Pray silence for Grace by your President' or 'by Canon John Jones', 'the Reverend John Jones' etc.

A Bishop may be asked to say Grace except that, if his Chaplain is present, it is customary for him to do so.

The Loyal Toasts

The first and principal Loyal Toast, as approved by The Queen, is: 'The Queen'. It is incorrect to use such forms as: 'I give you the Loyal Toast of Her Majesty The Queen'. To obtain the necessary silence, the Toastmaster may say, without Preamble: 'Pray silence for your President', for example.

The second Loyal Toast, which, if given, immediately follows the first, is likewise limited to: 'Queen Elizabeth The Queen Mother, The Prince Philip, Duke of Edinburgh, The Prince of Wales, and the other members of the Royal Family'.

Guests do not smoke until after the Loyal Toast(s). The announcement 'Ladies and Gentlemen, you may now smoke' is superfluous unless The Queen or The Queen Mother be present. In this case it is necessary to announce: 'Ladies and Gentlemen, you have Her Majesty's permission to smoke'.

The Loyal Toast in Lancashire, Greater Manchester and Merseyside follows the traditional wording used in the old county of Lancaster. The Queen intimated on the reorganisation of the county boundaries in 1974 that she hoped that those who wished to do so would feel free to continue to give the Loyal Toast in the traditional form – 'The Queen, Duke of Lancaster' – throughout the north-west of England or at Lancastrian organisations elsewhere. In Jersey, the toast of 'The Queen, our Duke' (that is, Duke of Normandy) is local and unofficial, and used when only islanders are present. This toast is not used in the other Channel Islands.

Table Plans for Private Functions

The host is customarily seated at one end of the table, the hostess at the other end. Alternatively, the host may be seated in the centre of one side of the table, and the hostess immediately opposite to him*. The latter follows the custom at Court and invariably on the Continent.

The principal male guest is placed on the right of the hostess, and his wife on the right of the host. The other seating is largely a matter for the hostess to decide according to the mutual interests of the guests. Strict order of precedence need not be observed, but should not be ignored. Nevertheless, the days of guests feeling slighted at being seated below their perceived ranks and turning over their plates to indicate their displeasure are, one hopes, long gone. However, care should still be taken to ensure that the diplomatic precedence of High Commissioners and Ambassadors is observed. See page 147.

*Exceptionally, if the party numbers eight, the hostess may give up her place to the chief male guest: otherwise it is impracticable to preserve the rule of seating the sexes alternately. If a party numbers six or ten (that is, in multiples of four in addition to the host and hostess), the table is easier to arrange, by placing men and women alternately, but today this custom is not too rigidly applied.

SPEECHES

The Preamble

It is impossible to give a list of those who should be mentioned in the Preamble of a speech, since this depends so much on those present at a particular function. In general, however, the list should be kept as short as possible, subject to avoiding any omission that would cause justifiable offence.

The speaker does not, of course, include himself in his preamble.

The Queen and Queen Elizabeth The Queen Mother

Should The Queen or Queen Elizabeth The Queen Mother be present, a Preamble begins: 'May it please Your Majesty'.

The Host

With the above exception, a Preamble begins with the host, who is referred to by his office. For example:

> Mr President
> Mr Chairman
> Mr Vice-Chancellor
> Master
> Mr Prime Warden etc.

President

If a member of the Royal Family, he or she is referred to as 'Your Royal Highness and President'.

If a non-Royal Duke or Duchess, as 'Your Grace and President'.

If a peer other than a Duke, as 'My Lord and President'. ('My Lord President' is incorrect, except for the Lord President of the Privy Council.)

If a lady, either titled or untitled, with the exception of a member of the Royal Family or a Duchess, as 'Madam President'.

If a gentleman below the rank of peer, as 'Mr President'.

Vice-President

When a Vice-President takes the chair, he or she may be referred to as 'Mr Vice-President' or 'Madam Vice-President' (with the relevant prefix mentioned under President), but he or she is more usually referred to as 'Mr Chairman' or 'Madam Chairman'.

Chairman

A chairman is called 'Mr Chairman' or 'Madam Chairman' irrespective of his or her rank, with the exception of a member of the Royal Family, who is referred to as 'Your Royal Highness'. A peer should not be called 'My Lord Chairman'.

If a vice-chairman, managing director or other officer of the organisation takes the chair, he or she is still referred to as 'Mr Chairman' or 'Madam Chairman': that is, the use of these expressions is not restricted to the actual chairman of the organisation.

Other Important Guests

The following list gives the form in which various persons should be included in a Preamble in order of precedence, after those already mentioned above.

> Your Royal Highness
> My Lord Mayor (My Lord Provost, Mr Mayor, Provost etc.).
>   See Note 1, below
> Mr Recorder (outside London)
> Mr Chairman of the ... County Council (outside Greater
>   London)
> My Lord Chancellor
> Prime Minister (or, more formally, 'Mr Prime Minister'). See
>   Note 2, below
> Your Excellency(ies). See Note 3, below
> Your Grace(s). See Note 4, below
> My Lord(s). See Note 5, below
> Ladies and Gentlemen. See Note 6, below

Note 1: This applies only to the Civic Head of the city, borough etc. in which the function takes place. If desired to mention a Civic Head from elsewhere who is present, this should be done after 'My Lords'. More than one Lord Mayor (or Lord Provost) may be covered either by 'My Lord Mayors' (or 'My Lord Provosts') or by naming each (for example,

'My Lord Mayor of York, My Lord Mayor of Plymouth, My Lord Provost of Aberdeen'). There is no plural for 'Mr Mayor': the form 'Your Worships' should be used, although 'Your Worship' is archaic.

Note 2: Also:
> My Lord President (that is, of the Privy Council)
> My Lord Privy Seal
> Mr Chancellor (of the Exchequer or of the Duchy of Lancaster)
> Minister(s) (of, more formally, Mr Minister). (This covers a Secretary of State. The terms 'Mr Secretary of State' and 'Mr Secretary' are archaic. Other Ministers are not mentioned in a Preamble when the Prime Minister attends a function).

Note 3: High Commissioners and Ambassadors.

Note 4: This covers Dukes and Duchesses. Should the Archbishop of Canterbury be present, 'Your Grace' (or 'Your Graces' if a Duke or Duchess is also attending) should be mentioned before 'My Lord Chancellor'. Similarly, the Archbishop of York is covered by including 'Your Grace' immediately after 'My Lord Chancellor': that is, both Archbishops rank before 'Your Excellencies'.

Note 5: For peers other than Dukes, peers by courtesy, for diocesan Bishops by right, and for other Bishops by courtesy. In the absence of any peers, the form 'My Lord Bishops' may be used.

Note 6: When, as sometimes happens, only one lady is present, the form should be 'Lady ('My Lady' if titled) and Gentlemen' or 'Mrs (Lady) Blank, Gentlemen': never 'Madam and Gentlemen'.

General notes on Roman Catholic Archbishops and Bishops. A Cardinal Archbishop may be included in the form 'Your Eminence', placed by courtesy after 'Your Graces'. Other Archbishops and Bishops are by courtesy mentioned in the same way as those of the Anglican Church.

Clergy
Clergy, other than Archbishops and Bishops, should not be included. In particular the forms 'Reverend Sir' and 'Reverend Father' are archaic. Exceptionally, 'Mr Dean', 'Mr Provost' or 'Archdeacon' may be included.

Guest of Honour
When the guest of honour is not covered by one of the above terms, he is included in the Preamble by his office – for example, 'Mr President', 'Mr Chairman' etc. – immediately before 'Ladies and Gentlemen'. This specific mention also applies when a President, Vice-Chancellor etc. is providing the building in which the function takes place.

Aldermen and Sheriffs
Within the City of London it is customary to refer to these as 'Mr Alderman' or 'Aldermen' and 'Mr Sheriff' or 'Sheriffs' immediately before 'Ladies and Gentlemen'. Elsewhere, 'Councillors' may be included at civic functions immediately before 'Ladies and Gentlemen'.

The Ending
A speaker proposing a toast should make this clear at the end of his speech in some such form as, 'I give you the toast of . . .' or 'I ask you to rise and drink to the toast of your . . .'. This obviates any need for the Toastmaster to say, 'The toast is . . .'.

Toastmaster
The Toastmaster should be given the form in which he is to make all announcements in writing and not left to devise his own often exaggerated forms.

For the first speaker the announcement should have a Preamble, as for the speech, followed by, 'Pray silence for . . .'. For subsequent announcements the Preamble should be omitted.

A speaker is announced by his name, followed by his office where applicable: for example, 'the Right Honourable John Jones, Her Majesty's Secretary of State for . . .'. Suffixes such as 'Companion of the Distinguished Service Order', 'One of Her Majesty's Justices of the Peace' etc. should not be used.

DRESS CODES

It is with good reason that the arcana of correct dressing is referred to as 'code'. This is a language not spoken by all, and requiring considerable encryption and deciphering skills.

The area is a minefield, what with the encroachment of ever greater informality and the disappearance of the higher levels of formality from most people's lives. The result is confusion and, frequently, nervousness on the part of invitees, who are unsure as to what a particular formulation requires and terrified of turning up in inappropriate attire.

As a general rule it is better to be over- rather than under-dressed in order to avoid either looking out of place or giving offence. Common sense will usually dictate and ensure you're not wearing wellies while the others are wearing their best jewels. The good news is that most people are not such sticklers for form these days, but there are still many occasions when it is advisable to try to get it right. It is also worth remembering that the town/country divide is pronounced where fashion is concerned, and one should err even further on the side of conservatism at country functions.

For social events such as Ascot and Henley, tradition dictates in no uncertain terms what is expected (see the appropriate section under Social Occasions, below), and for most other functions it is the responsibility of the hosts to make this clear. The bad news is that it is the responsibility of the guest to figure out what the host is talking about.

The common coded formulations are: evening dress/white tie; dinner jackets/black tie; smart day/formal day dress; smart/casual; unchanged; come as you are – to which list one may add 'decorations' as an extra source of confusion.

Evening Dress/White Tie
The most formal and, nowadays, the least common. Immaculate smartness is demanded. For men it implies black evening tail coat with matching trousers, stiff boiled shirt with detachable stick-up or wing

302

collar, white bow tie and evening waistcoat, black 'whole cut' patent shoes with black ribbon laces, and black silk socks.

Women are expected to wear long formal evening dresses. Long evening gloves are traditional but are not an absolute necessity nowadays. Shoes should be in keeping with the dress, though comfort is important, particularly if the evening will involve dancing.

Decorations

Decorations should be worn only if the invitation indicates the necessity. This will commonly be the case only if a member of the Royal Family is to be present at social functions, although other occasions may arise where the host deems decorations appropriate.

Knights and Dames should wear the most senior chivalric orders to which they belong. The maximum is four stars, to be displayed on the left side of the evening coat or dress. Knights Grand Cross wear a broad sash as well as a badge. One neck badge on a miniature ribbon may be worn beneath the tie. Miniature orders and decorations are worn on a metal bar. On black tie occasions, miniatures dominate, worn on the left breast, with only one star and a neck badge customarily displayed.

Decorations are rarely worn with morning dress, except at special public functions, grand memorial services or religious services connected to the chivalric orders. Full-size orders and decorations are worn, with up to four stars, but with no sashes.

Occasionally, decorations may be worn with dark suits or overcoats, notably on Remembrance Sunday and at regimental gatherings. Medals should be full-size, worn on the left side. A neck riband is permissible, but stars and ribands are not worn.

Collars of the orders of knighthood are worn when specified, though never after sunset.

British decorations take precedence over foreign ones, except when the function is one associated with the relevant country.

'Decorations' is also the cue for women to wear their most important jewellery, including, where only married women are concerned, tiaras.

Black Tie (Dinner Jackets)

Men wear a black barathea dinner jacket, single- or double-breasted, preferably with ribbed silk lapels, tapered trousers, cut for braces, with one row of braid. Silk or cotton shirts should have a pleated or marcella front, with a soft turn-down collar. A black tie is preferable, whether silk barathea or faille. Evening waistcoats remain preferable to cummerbunds. Patent pumps and lace-ups are both permissible. Velvet smoking jackets are nowadays also deemed acceptable.

For women the issue is not so simple, particularly in view of the wide range of events for which black tie is requested in this day and age. Expected attire may range from verging on white tie formality to the trusted little black dress. The nature of the occasion should therefore be borne carefully in mind during the dress selection process. If possible, it may be wise to seek guidance from the hostess as to the level of formality desired.

The timing of the event may also hold a key to deciding. An invitation for early-evening drinks will clearly demand less of an effort than one for a big dinner or celebration of some kind.

The traditional view that long dresses are more formal than short ones is losing its force. However, should uncertainty or indecision set in, long remains the safe option on all occasions smarter than a cocktail party. (Perversely, long is less smart for day than knee length or thereabouts.)

Best jewels can be worn, but no tiaras.

Smart Day Formal Day Dress

This category encompasses weddings, smart race meetings and formal day events. There is a scale of formality descending, in the case of men, from morning coats to dark suits.

Morning dress implies a curve-fronted body coat, with black currently preferred to grey unless it happens to be Ladies' Day at Ascot. If in doubt, keep waistcoat colours traditional – white, grey or buff for racing, black for memorials and daytime city functions, and the appropriate point in the spectrum between colourful and con-servative for weddings, depending on the setting, the age of bride and groom and such like. Trousers can be striped or checked, should be cut for braces, and have one pleat. Ideally – but here, as so often, the ideal is stranger to the usual – the shirt should have a stiff white turned-down detachable collar. A heavy woven silk tie, or some equivalent – but definitely not a foulard – formal lace-up shoes, not loafers, and, traditionally, a top hat round off the look. The last is a must for the Ascot Royal Enclosure but is no longer requisite at weddings. It is most commonly worn for formal weddings, entry into the Royal Enclosure at Ascot, Garden Parties at Buckingham Palace and at formal funerals.

Women should dress formally but colourfully. Suits or dresses with jackets, topped with hats, are customary. Traditionally, neither white nor black should be worn at weddings. Beware events such as Ascot and Henley where codes are very strict and cannot be stretched, least of all avoided. On such occasions, hats without crowns and trousers are only for those who take perverse pleasure at being turned away by officials. White gloves have rather had their day, and all other accessories should be chosen with care so as not to let down the rest of the attire. Also think carefully about the practicality of shoe selection – very high heels and turf do not mix well.

Women's hats are a must for weddings and the smart racing enclosures, but are not essential any more at royal Garden Parties, christenings and the like.

Smart/Casual
Presentable but not overly formal. For men, blazer or other sports jacket, with either flannels, shirt and tie, or cotton trousers, polo shirt and sweater, depending on the occasion. Casual linen or cotton suits are also an option. Brown shoes, but no trainers, round off the look, with a Panama hat as a potential addition.

For women, it means a blazer-type jacket, worn with dress, long skirt or trousers, shirt or blouse or a trouser suit (almost smart casual uniform at some season events!).

Unchanged
A hangover from the days when most people dressed relatively smartly on a day-to-day basis, so it should not be taken too literally. Most effectively translated as 'not black tie', unless you know better, or the hosts have been more explicit. Men should wear suit or jacket and tie, with a formal shirt, and women presentable clothes.

Come as You Are
As with Unchanged, above, a metaphor, not a direct instruction. It means casual wear but is not intended to encourage scruffy attire.

Cords, cotton trousers, Bermuda shorts, casual shirts, sweaters, deck shoes and the like for men, depending on the season, and the equivalent for women, with trousers, shorts and skirts all equally acceptable.

THE SOCIAL SEASON

The main body of what is known as 'the season' stretches from April to August, encompassing everything from sporting and operatic festivals, through displays of pageantry, to a horticultural extravaganza.

The following are considered the highlights of this social whirligig – where to be, how to access the more exclusive enclosures, how to dress etc.

The Berkeley Dress Show

The charity dress show in aid of the NSPCC is usually held on the first Monday of April, as long as it does not coincide with Easter, in the early evening. The models are, to this day, the year's new debutantes, being seen for the first time in a formal public setting. Though in this era many of them find the whole thing somewhat embarrassing, the worth of the cause ensures the survival of the event.

Information and tickets are available from the NSPCC London Appeals Office, Yeoman House, 4th Floor, 168–172 Old Street, London EC1V 9BP.

Chelsea Flower Show

The English love only their pets more than their gardens. Recent attendances at the Chelsea Flower Show, held every May in the grounds of the Royal Hospital on the Embankment near the King's Road, have surpassed a quarter of a million.

Monday is royal private view day, with a gala charity preview in the evening. Tuesday and Wednesday are reserved for RHS members; Thursday and Friday are for the public.

A different charity benefits each year, and tickets for the gala are available from the relevant charity. Applications for tickets may have to be as much as two years in advance to stand a chance of success.

Ladies tend to wear summer dresses with hats, men suits. Sensible shoes are essential to cope with the walking. The preview night is smarter but still not formal.

307

For information, contact the Royal Horticultural Society, Vincent Square, London SW1P 2PE.

The Derby

Now run on the first Saturday of June, at Epsom, on the Downs, the Derby is known as the Blue Riband of the Turf. There was a time when the Stock Exchange used to close on Derby Day, and even Parliament adjourned for many years. Prior to TV, a quarter of a million spectators used to turn up.

Spectators can watch from the Downs or from one of the enclosures. Tickets for the grandstand can also be obtained by anyone, but the smartest and most sought-after viewing point is in Level Three of the Queen's Stand, which is in the Members' Enclosure.

Membership is relatively easy to come by, although members do have to be proposed and seconded. It is possible to join for the Derby meeting alone, but several other meetings are popular and worth attending. Book as early as possible, and certainly before the end of April.

Annual members receive two vouchers for guests when their new membership arrives. They can then pay to exchange these for badges, either through the Club Office until the end of May, or in person on the day. Accompanied children under sixteen are allowed in free, except to the Queen's Stand on Derby Day. Note that the Members' Dining Room is normally booked up by the end of January.

For members, on Derby Day, dress is top hat and tails for men, formal summer dress or suit with a hat for women. The rest of the time, smart dress is always required for the Members' Enclosure, and women must wear skirts or dresses rather than trousers. Be warned that it is often quite chilly, so the look is not as summery as at Ascot.

Details from the Racecourse, Epsom Downs, Surrey KT18 5LQ.

Trooping the Colour

The celebration of The Queen's official birthday takes place on the second Saturday in June at Horse Guards Parade, Whitehall, from 11 to 12.30 p.m. It is a rousing mix of ceremony, drill displays, marching bands and fainting soldiers in bearskins, performed by regiments of the Household Division.

The parade ground is surrounded by tiers of seats for spectators.

Tickets are allocated by ballot with a limit of two per person. There are also ballots for tickets for the rehearsals that take place on the two preceding Saturdays, the only missing ingredient being Her Majesty The Queen.

Applications for tickets must be made in writing, before 1 March, to the Brigade Major (Trooping the Colour), Headquarters, Household Division, Horse Guards, Whitehall, London SW1A 2AX.

For other information about the event, contact the Ticket Office, HQ Household Division, Chelsea Barracks, London SW1H 8RF.

Ascot

Aside from the racing, Royal Ascot is best known for the magnificence of its lady spectators' headwear. There is no need for a fancy hat, or a pass to the Royal Enclosure, in order to enjoy the racing, but for a full immersion in the Ascot experience both might well be considered essential.

Admittance to the Royal Enclosure, Ascot, lies within the jurisdiction of Her Majesty's Representative. The number of those to whom the privilege of receiving vouchers is accorded is not disclosed; nor are the reasons why vouchers have been given, or withheld, explained.

Applications are submitted to Her Majesty's Representative from January until the end of April. After that date, no further applications are considered. First-timers should apply by the end of March.

Visitors with overseas passports should apply for vouchers for the Royal Enclosure to their respective Ambassadors or High Commissioners and not to Her Majesty's Representative.

Applications may be made by either husband or wife. However, each application should include only members of a family; friends should make a separate application. Applications signed by proxy will not be accepted.

If vouchers are required by young people between the ages of sixteen and twenty-five inclusive at the date of the Royal Meeting, the age should be stated in brackets after the name, because their vouchers are issued at a reduced price. Children below the age of sixteen are not admitted to the Royal Enclosure, except on Friday of the Royal Meeting, when children between the ages of ten and fifteen are admitted, with a responsible adult, at a reduced rate. No prior application is required for young children.

New applicants are required to be sponsored by someone who has been present in the Royal Enclosure for at least eight years. Sponsors can sponsor only two people a year.

Vouchers are free and do not commit their recipients to attend. Payment is made only when the vouchers are exchanged for badges, valid either for individual days or for all four days. To avoid queuing on the day, this can be done in person at the Ascot Office during the preceding week. Badges must be worn for entrance to the enclosure.

In some years, to avoid overcrowding, restrictions are placed on which days new applicants may attend.

Morning suit with top hat, and formal day dress with hat, are required for the Royal Enclosure.

Information from the Secretary, Grandstand Office, Ascot Racecourse, Ascot, Berkshire SL5 7JN.

The application:
Colonel John Francis presents his compliments to Her Majesty's Representative and wishes to apply for vouchers to the Royal Enclosure for his wife, Mrs John Francis, his son, Mr William Francis (aged 22), his daughter, Miss Philippa Francis (aged 19), and himself.

Envelope:
>Her Majesty's Representative,
>Ascot Office,
>St James's Palace,
>London SW1A 1BP

Wimbledon

Despite being a relative newcomer, the event has become a pillar of the summer season.

From August to December, members of the public can write to the All England Tennis Club, enclosing an SAE with a request for a ballot form for the following year's tournament. The ballot form must then be returned by the end of January. Only one application for a pair of tickets per household is allowed.

It is possible for individuals or companies to purchase debentures, giving them a block of seats on Centre Court for every day of the tournament for five years. Debentures are traded on the London Stock Exchange. Debenture-holders have the added benefit of their own lounge for lunch and tea.

Members of the All England Club receive preferential treatment and can buy a pair of tickets for Centre Court for every day of the championships. The Members' Enclosure is set aside for the refreshment of members and their guests. Enquiries about membership should be sent to the All England Lawn Tennis and Croquet Club, Church Road, Wimbledon, London SW19 5AE.

It is notoriously difficult to obtain tickets for Centre Court, but quite possible to turn up and get a ticket for the grounds at short notice. Particularly during the early rounds, this may offer the opportunity to see some good games on the outside courts, and there will always be the chance to get hold of a show court ticket from someone who is leaving.

Public transport is recommended, as parking is very difficult (though local residents earn their summer holiday pocket money by renting out space in their driveways).

Henley Royal Regatta

Five days of serious rowing, and equally serious socialising, take place in early July in the serene setting of Henley-on-Thames. The towpath and Regatta Enclosure are open to all during the event, and hospitality tents also proliferate, catering for the corporate hordes. However, the most coveted area from which to spectate is, as ever, the Stewards' Enclosure.

Membership of the Stewards' Enclosure is limited to 6,000 and the waiting-list is lengthy. Would-be members must be proposed and seconded by existing members. Priority is given to past competitors, but even they face a long wait. Once accepted, there is a one-off membership fee and subsequent yearly subscription. Members can apply for badges to take guests into the Members' Enclosure, but numbers are restricted at the weekend.

Dress rules are legendarily strict: for men, lounge suits, jackets or blazers with flannels and a tie or cravat; for women, dresses or suits that must cover the knee, and absolutely no trousers or divided skirts.

The Leander Club, whose enclosure is next to the Stewards', also expects prospective members to be sponsored and has different levels of membership – full, ordinary and associate – depending on the applicant's services to rowing.

The Secretary, Henley Royal Regatta Headquarters, Henley-on-Thames, Oxfordshire RG9 2LY.

Goodwood

In a beautiful setting high on the Sussex Downs, the Goodwood Festival, aka Glorious Goodwood, takes place over five days at the end of July, signalling the traditional end of the London summer season. The days of week-long house parties are pretty much gone, but individual days are still very popular and well attended.

Entry to the Richmond Enclosure (after the Duke of Richmond, who started the event in 1801) is restricted to annual members and their guests. Full members must nevertheless apply for admission vouchers (supplied free) for each individual day during the festival. They may also order a guest badge for another adult and one junior badge (although no children under five are allowed), buy up to four daily badges a day during festival week, and reserve a parking space. Note that it is important to book these perks early, as they will sell out.

Applications for membership must be supported by an existing member or approved by the racecourse executive committee. It is advisable to apply at least three months ahead of time. The members' metal badge then allows free access to all racing at Goodwood, as well as entry to some other courses, Sussex County Cricket Club and Hickstead for certain events.

Membership is not necessary to enjoy the experience. Hospitality packages, private boxes, public enclosures and Trundle Hill all provide enjoyable alternatives.

There are no dress regulations. Most ladies wear summer dresses with simple straw hats, or light suits; men wear summer suits and straw hats. Nothing too dressy, but nothing too skimpy either. It is sensible to bring a coat.

Details from early spring onwards from the Goodwood Office, Goodwood Racecourse, Goodwood, Chichester, West Sussex PO18 0PX.

Glyndebourne

The festival runs from late May to the end of August. Aside from regularly outstanding opera, Glyndebourne is popular as a social and culinary occasion. The tradition of picnics on the grass is a delightful one and remains popular, but is somewhat dependent on weather, means of transport and such like. There are several good eating establishments on-site, but places should be booked in advance. Postal bookings can be made from April onwards, telephone ones from May. The popularity of the occasion makes bookings much in demand, but returns can also be come by relatively easily.

Evening dress is preferred but not insisted on.

Glyndebourne Festival Opera, Glyndebourne, Lewes, East Sussex BN8 5UU.

APPENDIX 1

ORDERS OF PRECEDENCE

The only person whose precedence is absolute is the Sovereign. The precedence of all others is the Sovereign's prerogative. Even the precedence of those who appear in the official tables of precedence below varies from time to time. There are many variations, depending on whether an event is national or local, and in the relationship between host and guests the requirements of courtesy and hospitality override any strict order of precedence.

General Table of Precedence in England and Wales

Gentlemen
The Queen
The Duke of Edinburgh
The Prince of Wales
The Sovereign's younger sons
The Sovereign's grandsons (according to the seniority of their
    fathers)
The Sovereign's cousins
Archbishop of Canterbury
Lord High Chancellor
Archbishop of York
The Prime Minister
Lord High Treasurer (no such office at the moment)
Lord President of the Council
Speaker of the House of Commons
Lord Privy Seal
Ambassadors and High Commissioners
Lord Great Chamberlain
Lord High Constable (when existing)
Earl Marshal
Lord Steward of the Household
Lord Chamberlain of the Household
Master of the Horse
Dukes of England

Dukes of Scotland (none created since 1707)
Dukes of Great Britain (1707–1801)
Dukes of Ireland (created before 1801)
Dukes of the United Kingdom (created since 1801)
Eldest sons of Dukes of the Blood Royal
Marquesses of England
Marquesses of Scotland
Marquesses of Great Britain
Marquesses of Ireland
Marquesses of the United Kingdom
Eldest sons of Dukes
Earls of England
Earls of Scotland
Earls of Great Britain
Earls of Ireland
Earls of the United Kingdom and Ireland since the Union
Younger sons of Dukes of the Blood Royal
Marquesses' eldest sons
Dukes' younger sons
Viscounts of England
Viscounts of Scotland
Viscounts of Great Britain
Viscounts of Ireland
Viscounts of the United Kingdom and Ireland
Earls' eldest sons
Marquesses' younger sons
Bishop of London
Bishop of Durham
Bishop of Winchester
English Diocesan Bishops according to date of consecration
Suffragan Bishops according to seniority of consecration
Secretaries of State, if Barons
Barons of England
Lords of Parliament of Scotland
Barons of Great Britain
Barons of Ireland
Barons of the United Kingdom
Lords of Appeal in Ordinary
Commissioners of the Great Seal (when existing)
Treasurer of the Household

Comptroller of the Household
Vice-Chamberlain of the Household
Secretaries of State (when not Barons)
Viscounts' eldest sons
Earls' younger sons
Barons' eldest sons
Knights of the Garter
Privy Counsellors
Chancellor of the Exchequer
Chancellor of the Duchy of Lancaster
Lord Chief Justice
Master of the Rolls
President of the Family Division
Vice Chancellor
Lord Justices of Appeal, according to date of appointment
Judges of the High Court of Justice
Viscounts' younger sons
Barons' younger sons
Sons of life peers and Lords of Appeal in Ordinary
Baronets, according to date of Patent
Knights of the Thistle
Knights Grand Cross of the Bath
Knights Grand Commanders of the Star of India
Knights Grand Cross of the Order of St Michael and St George
Knights Grand Commanders of the Indian Empire
Knights Grand Cross of the Royal Victorian Order
Knights Grand Cross of the Order of the British Empire
Knights Commanders of the Bath
Knights Commanders of the Star of India
Knights Commanders of St Michael and St George
Knights Commanders of the Indian Empire
Knights Commanders of the Royal Victorian Order
Knights Commanders of the Order of the British Empire
Knights Bachelor
Circuit Judges
Masters in Chancery
Master of Court of Protection
Companions of the Order of the Bath
Companions of the Order of the Star of India
Companions of the Order of St Michael and St George

Companions of the Order of the Indian Empire
Commanders of the Royal Victorian Order
Commanders of the Order of the British Empire
Companions of the Distinguished Service Order
Lieutenants of the Royal Victorian Order
Officers of the Order of the British Empire
Companions of the Imperial Service Order
Eldest sons of the younger sons of peers
Eldest sons of Baronets
Eldest sons of Knights, according to the precedence of their fathers
Members of the Royal Victorian Order
Members of the Order of the British Empire
Younger sons of Baronets
Younger sons of Knights
Esquires
Gentlemen

Ladies
The Queen
The Queen Mother
The Princess Royal
The Sovereign's sister
Granddaughters of the Sovereign
Wives of the Sovereign's uncles
Cousins of the Sovereign
The Prime Minister (if female)
Duchesses of England
Duchesses of Scotland
Duchesses of Great Britain
Duchesses of Ireland
Duchesses of the United Kingdom
Wives of the eldest sons of Dukes of the Blood Royal
Marchionesses (in the same order as Duchesses)
Wives of the eldest sons of Dukes
Daughters of Dukes
Countesses (in the same order as Duchesses)
Wives of the younger sons of Dukes of the Blood Royal
Wives of the eldest sons of Marquesses
Daughters of Marquesses

Wives of the younger sons of Dukes
Viscountesses (in the same order as Duchesses)
Wives of the eldest sons of Earls
Daughters of Earls
Wives of the younger sons of Marquesses
Baronesses (in the same order as Duchesses)
Wives of the eldest sons of Viscounts
Daughters of Viscounts
Wives of the younger sons of Earls
Wives of the eldest sons of Barons
Daughters of Barons
Wives of Knights of the Garter
Privy Counsellors (women)
Wives of the younger sons of Viscounts
Wives of the younger sons of Barons
Daughters of Lords of Appeal
Wives of sons of Legal Life Peers
Wives of Baronets
Wives of Knights of the Thistle
Dames Grand Cross of the Order of the Bath
Dames Grand Cross of the Order of the St Michael and St George
Dames Grand Cross of the Royal Victorian Order
Dames Grand Cross of the Order of the British Empire
Wives of Knights Grand Cross of the Bath
Wives of Knights Grand Commanders of the Star of India
Wives of Knights Grand Cross of St Michael and St George
Wives of Knights Grand Commanders of the Indian Empire
Wives of Knights Grand Cross of the Royal Victorian Order
Wives of Knights Grand Cross of the Order of the British Empire
Commanders of the Order of the Bath
Commanders of the Order of St Michael and St George
Commanders of the Royal Victorian Order
Commanders of the Order of the British Empire
Wives of Knights Commanders of the Bath
Wives of Knights Commanders of the Star of India
Wives of Knights Commanders of St Michael and St George
Wives of Knights Commanders of the Indian Empire
Wives of Knights Commanders of the Royal Victorian Order
Wives of Knights Commanders of the Order of the British Empire
Wives of Knights Bachelor

Commanders of St Michael and St George
Commanders of the Royal Victorian Order
Commanders of the Order of the British Empire
Wives of Commanders and Companions of the Orders of the Bath, the Star of India, St Michael and St George, Indian Empire, Royal Victorian Order and the British Empire
Wives of Companions of the Distinguished Service Order
Lieutenants of the Royal Victorian Order
Officers of the Order of the British Companions of the Imperial Service Order
Wives of Companions of the Imperial Service Order
Wives of the eldest sons of the younger sons of peers
Daughters of the younger sons of peers
Wives of the eldest sons of Baronets
Daughters of Baronets
Wives of the eldest sons of Knights of the Garter
Wives of the eldest sons of Knights
Daughters of Knights
Members of the Royal Victorian Order
Members of the Order of the British Empire
Wives of Members of the Royal Victorian Order
Wives of Members of the Order of the British Empire
Wives of the younger sons of Baronets
Wives of the younger sons of Knights
Wives of Esquires
Wives of Gentlemen

Precedence in Scotland
Gentlemen
The Queen
The Duke of Edinburgh
Lord High Commissioner to the General Assembly of the Church of Scotland (during sitting of General Assembly)
Duke of Rothesay (The Prince of Wales)
The Sovereign's younger sons
The Sovereign's grandsons
The Sovereign's cousins
Lord-Lieutenants of counties
Lord Provosts of cities who are ex officio Lord-Lieutenants

Sheriffs Principal
Lord Chancellor of Great Britain
Moderator of the General Assembly of the Church of Scotland
(during office)
The Prime Minister
Keeper of the Great Seal of Scotland (Secretary of State for
Scotland) (if a peer)
Keeper of the Privy Seal of Scotland (if a peer)
Hereditary High Constable of Scotland
Hereditary Master of the Household in Scotland
Dukes (as in English Table)
Eldest sons of Dukes of the Blood Royal
Marquesses (as in English Table)
Eldest sons of Dukes
Earls (as in English Table)
Younger sons of Dukes of the Blood Royal
Eldest sons of Marquesses
Younger sons of Dukes
Keeper of the Great Seal of Scotland (Secretary of State for
Scotland) (if not a peer)
Keeper of the Privy Seal of Scotland (if not a peer)
Lord Justice General
Lord Clerk Register
Lord Advocate
Lord Justice Clerk
Viscounts (as in English Table)
Eldest sons of Earls
Younger sons of Marquesses
Lords of Parliament of Scotland (as in English Table)
Eldest sons of Viscounts
Younger sons of Earls
Eldest sons of Lords of Parliament
Knights of the Garter
Knights of the Thistle
Privy Counsellors
Senators of the College of Justice (Lords of Session), including the
Chairman of the Scottish Land Court
Younger sons of Viscounts
Younger sons of Lords of Parliament
Baronets

Knights Grand Cross and Knights Grand Commanders of Orders (as in English Table)
Knights Commanders of Orders (as in English Table)
Solicitor-General for Scotland
Lyon King of Arms
Sheriffs Principal (when not within own county)
Knights Bachelor
Sheriffs
Companions of the Order of the Bath

Ladies
The Queen
The Queen Mother
The Princess Royal
The Sovereign's sister
Granddaughters of the Sovereign
Wives of the Sovereign's uncles
Wives of Dukes of the Blood Royal
Wives of Princes of the Blood Royal
Cousins of the Sovereign
The Prime Minister (if female)
Duchesses (as in English Table)
Wives of the eldest sons of Dukes of the Blood Royal
Marchionesses (as in English Table)
Wives of the eldest sons of Dukes
Daughters of Dukes
Wives of the younger sons of Dukes of the Blood Royal
Wives of eldest sons of Marquesses
Daughters of Marquesses
Wives of younger sons of Dukes
Countesses (as in English Table)
Viscountesses (as in English Table)
Wives of the eldest sons of Earls
Daughters of Earls
Wives of the younger sons of Marquesses
Ladies of Parliament
Wives of the eldest sons of Viscounts
Daughters of Viscounts

Wives of the younger sons of Earls
Wives of the eldest sons of Lords of Parliament
Daughters of Lords of Parliament
Wives of Knights of the Garter
Privy Counsellors (women)
Wives of the younger sons of Viscounts
Wives of the younger sons of Lords of Parliament
Wives of sons of life peers
Wives of Baronets
Wives of Knights of the Thistle
Dames Grand Cross of Orders (as in English Table)
Wives of Knights Grand Cross and Knights Grand Commanders of
    Orders (as in English Table)
Dames Commanders of Orders (as in English Table)
Wives of Knights Commanders of Orders (as in English Table)
Wives of Knights Bachelor and Wives of Senators of the College of
    Justice (Lords of Session) including the wife of the Chairman of
    the Scottish Land Court
Companions of the Order of the Bath

Ladies who hold appointments – for example, Secretaries of State or
High Court or Circuit Judges – should be assigned a corresponding
place as in the Gentlemen's Table.

APPENDIX 2

PRONUNCIATION OF TITLES AND SURNAMES

Correct pronunciation is quite rightly no longer restricted to what is called Received Pronunciation, but some guidance may be necessary for the pronunciation of placenames and names. The archaic pronunciations have not always developed at the same pace as our language and can cause confusion. These can belong to people, and not bothering to find out if a family traditionally uses an alternative pronunciation may cause offence.

Anomalies

'Ch' in Scottish, Welsh and Irish names is pronounced as in 'loch'. 'Mac' is not normally stressed so the 'a' is hardly pronounced at all. In Scottish the letter 'z' stood for a guttural 'y', which explains why 'Menzies' was originally 'Meyners'.

The Scottish 'l' in such prefixes as Col, Fal, Bal and Dal was usually not pronounced, and 'quh' was the Scottish way of writing 'wh' (for example, 'what' was spelt 'quhat'). This explains the pronunciation of 'Colquhoun'.

With names ending in intrusive forms for 's' (for example, 'ys', 'yss' and 'is'), the vowel should not be pronounced, such as in 'Wemyss', 'Inglis' and 'Spottiswoode'.

Some Difficult Pronunciations

Abercrombie	Aber-crum-by (but sometimes as spelled)
Abergavenny	Aber-genny (title) (hard 'g'); town as spelled
Abinger	Abin-jer
Acheson	Atchesson
Adye	Aydi
Aldous	All-dus
Alleyne	Alleen (but sometimes as spelled)
Alnwick	Annick
Althorp	All-trup
Altrincham	Altringham

329

Alvingham	All-ving-am
Aman	Amman
Ampthill	Ampt-hill
Annesley	Anns-li
Apethorpe	App-thorp
Arbuthnot (t)	A-buth-not
Ardee	A-dee
Arundel	Arun-del
Ashburnham	Ash-burn-am
Assheton	Ash-ton
Atholl	Uh-thol or Ah-thol
Auchinleck	Affleck or Ock-inleck
Audley	Awd-li
Ava	Ah-va
Ayscough	Askew
Babington	Babb-ington
Baden-Powell	Bayden-Poell
Bagot	Bag-ot
Balcarres	Bal-carris
Balogh	Balog ('Bal' as in 'Hal')
Bampfylde	Bam-field
Baring	Bear-ing
Barnardiston	Bar-nar-dis-ton
Barttelot	Bartlot
Basing	Bayzing
Bathurst	Bath-urst ('a' as in 'cat')
Bazalgette	Bazl-jet
Beauchamp	Beecham
Beauclerk	Bo-clare
Beaudesert	Bodezair
Beaufort	Bo-foot
Beaulieu	Bew-ly
Beaumont	Bo-mont
Becher	Beacher
Bechervaise	Besh-er-vayse
Bedingfeld	Beddingfield
Behrens	Barens
Belfast	Belfast
Bellew	Bell-ew

Bellingham	Bellingjam or Bellingum
Belvoir	Beevor
Bengough	Ben-goff
Beresford	Berris-fud
Berkeley	Barkli
Bertie	Barti
Betham	Bee-tham
Bethune	Beaton
Bicester	Bister
Blakiston	Blackiston
Bledisloe	Bledslow
Blenheim	Blen-im
Bligh	Bly
Blithfield	Bliffield
Blois	Bloyss
Blomefield	Bloomfield
Blount	Blunt
Blyth	Bly
Boevey	Boovey or Buvey (short 'u')
Boleyn	Bull-in
Bolingbroke	Bulling-brook
Boord	Board
Boreel	Borale
Borrowes	Burrows
Borwick	Borrick
Bosham	Bos-am
Bosanquet	Bozen-ket
Boscawen	Bos-cowen
Botetourt	Botti-tort
Boughey	Boey
Boughton	Bought-on (family), Bough-ton (Northamptonshire)
Bourchier	Bough-cher
Bourke	Burke
Bourne	Boorn
Bowden (Baron)	Bowden (as in 'no')
Bowes	Bose (to rhyme with 'rose')
Bowman	Boman
Bowyer	Bo-yer (as in 'no')
Brabazon	Brab-azon

331

Brabourne	Bray-burn
Breadalbane	Bread-auburn
Breitmeyer	Bright-mire
Brereton	Breer-ton
Brise	Brize
Brocas	Brockas
Broke	Brook (but HMS *Broke* as spelled)
Bromhead	Brumhead
Brougham	Broom or Brooham
Broughton	Brawton
Broun	Brune
Bruntisfield	Bruntsfield
Brynkir	Brinkeer
Buccleuch	Bu-cloo
Bulkeley	Buckley
Burgh	Borough
Burghersh	Burg-ish
Burghley	Ber-li
Bury	Berry (England), Bure-y (Ireland)
Caccia	Catch-a
Cadogan	Ka-dugan
Caius	Keys (College)
Caldecote	Call-di-cot
Calderon	Call-dron
Callaghan	Calla-han
Calver	Carver
Calverley	Car-verly or Calf-ley
Camoys	Cam-oyz
Capell	Cayple
Carew	As spelled – Cary has become archaic
Calthorpe	Call-thorpe – Cal-trop has become archaic
Carnegie	Car-neggie
Carteret	Carter-et
Cassilis	Cassels
Castlereagh	Castle-ray
Carthcart	Cath-cart
Cathie	Cay-thie
Cato	Kate-o
Cator	Cay-tor

Caulfield	Caw-field
Cavan	Cav-en ('a' as in 'cat')
Cavanagh	Cava-na
Cecil	Cicil
Chandos	Shandos
Charlemont	Shar-le-mont
Charteris	As spelled – Charters is archaic
Chattan	Hattan
Chenevix	Sheenivix
Chernocke	Char-nock
Chetwode	Chetwood
Chetwynd	Chetwind
Cheylesmore	Chyles-more
Cheyne	Chain, Chainy or Cheen
Chichele	Chich-ley
Chisholm	Chis-um
Cholmeley	Chum-li
Cholmondeley	Chum-li
Cilcennin	Kil-kennin
Cirencester	As spelled – Sisiter is becoming archaic
Claverhouse	Clayvers
Clerk	Clark
Cloete	Clootie
Clough	Cluff
Clowes	Clues
Clwyd	Cloo-id
Cochrane	Coch-ran
Cockburn	Co-bun
Coghlan	Co-lan
Coke	Cook (Earl of Leicester) and others, but sometimes as spelled
Coleraine	Cole-rain
Colquhoun	Ca-hoon
Colvile	Col-ville
Colville	Col-ville
Combe	Coom
Combermere	Cumber-mere
Compton	Cumpton (usually)
Conesford	Connis-ford
Conolly	Con-olly

Constable	Cunstable
Conyngham(e)	Cunningham
Cosham	As spelled
Cottenham	Cot-nam
Cottesloe	Cots-low
Couchman	Cowchman
Courthope	Cort-hope
Cowper	Cooper
Cozens	Cuzzens
Cracroft	Cray-croft
Craigavon	Craig-avv-on
Craster	Crarster
Creagh	Cray
Creighton	Cryton
Crespigny	See De Crespigny
Crichton	Cryton
Cromartie	Crum-aty
Crombie	Crumbie
Culme	Cullum (sometimes as spelled)
Cuming	Cumming
Cunynghame	Cunningham
D'Abrell	Dab-roo
Dacre	Dayker
Dalbiac	Dawl-biac
Dalhousie	Dal-howsi
Dalmeny	Dul-menny
Dalyell	Dee-el (sometimes Dayli-el)
Dalzell	Dee-el (sometimes Dayli-el)
Darcy de Knaith	Darcy de Nayth
Daresbury	Darsbury
Daubeney	Daub-ny
Daventry	As spelled – Daintry is archaic
Davies	Davis
De Blacquiere	De Black-yer
De Burgh	De Burg
Decies	Deeshies
De Courcy	De Koursey
De Crespigny	De Crepp-ni
De Freyne	De Frain

De Hoghton	De Hawton
De la Warr	Della-ware
Delamere	Della-mare
De la Poer	De la Poor
De la Rue	Della-rue
De L'Isle	De Lyle
De Lotbiniere	De Lobin-yare
De Moleyns	Demo-lins
Dering	Deer-ing
De Ros	De Roos
Derwent	Darwent
De Salis	De Saals or De Sal-is (according to branch of family)
Devereux	Dev-rooks (Viscount Hereford) or Dever-oo
De Vesci	De Vessy
De Villiers	De Villers
Diomede	Di-o-meed
Dilhorne	Dill'n
Dominguez	Dum-ing-ez
Doneraile	Dunnaral
Donoughmore	Duno-more
Doune	Doun
Douro	Dur-o
Drogheda	Droyi-da
Drumalbyn	Drum-albin
Duchesnes	Du Karn(s), but sometimes with French pronunciation Du-shayn
Ducie	Dew-si
Du Cros	Du Crow
Dukinfield	Duckin-field
Dumaresq	Du-merrick
Dunally	Dun-alley
Dundas	Dun-das
Dungarvan	Dun-gar-van
Dunglass	Dun-glass
Dunsany	Dun-saney
Duntze	Dunts
Du Plat	Du-Pla
Dupplin	Dupp-lin
Durand	Du-rand or Dur-rand

Dymoke	Dimmock
Dynevor	Dinny-yer
Dysart	Dy-z't
Ebury	Ee-bri
Echlin	Eck-lin
Edwardes	Edwards
Egan	Ee-gan
Egerton	Edger-ton
Elcho	Elco
Elgin	El-gin (hard 'g')
Elibank	Elli-bank
Elphinstone	Elfin-ston
Elveden	Elve-den (place Elden)
Elwes	El-wes
Erle	Earl
Ernle	Earnley
Erskine	Ers-kin
Eveleigh	Eve-ley
Eyre	Air
Every	As spelled
Eyton	I-tun
Falconer	Fawkner
Falkiner	Fawkner
Faringdon	Farringdon
Farquhar	Farkwar
Farquharson	Farkwerson
Fayrer	Fair-er
Featherstonhaugh	Fetherston-haugh or occasionally Fetherston
Feilding	Field-ing
Fenwick	Fenn-ick
Fergussen	Ferguson
Fermor	Farmer
Feversham	Fevver-sham (place Favversham)
ffolliott	Foll-y-ot
ffolkes	Foaks
Fiennes	Fines
Fingall	Fin-gawl
Fitzhardinge	Fitzharding

Foljambe	Full-jum
Forestier	Forest-tier
Fortuin	Fortayne
Foulis	Fowls
Fowke	Foke
Fremantle	Free-mantle
Freyberg	Fry-burg
Froude	Frood
Furneaux	Fur-no
Gairdner	Gardner
Galston	Gaul-ston
Galway	Gaulway
Garioch	Ghorric
Garvagh	Gar-va
Gathorne	Gaythorn
Geoghegan	Gay-gan
Gerrard	Jerrard
Gervis	Jervis
Giffard	Jiffard
Gill	As spelled (hard 'g')
Gillespie	Gill-es-py (hard 'g')
Gilmour	Gillmoor (hard 'g')
Glamis	Glahms
Glasgow	Glass-go
Glenavy	Glen-avy (as in 'day')
Glerawly	Gler-awly
Gorges	Gorjes
Gormanstown	Gor-mans-ton
Goschen	Go-shen
Gough	Goff
Goulding	Goolding
Gower	Gore (Gower Peninsula and Gower Street, London, as spelled)
Graeme	Grame (to rhyme with 'frame')
Grantham	Gran-tham
Greaves	Graves
Greig	Gregg
Grosvenor	Grove-nor
Guise	Gyze

337

Gwynedd	Gwinn-eth
Haden-Guest	Hayden-Gest (hard 'g')
Haldane	Hall-dane
Halsey	Hall-sey
Halsbury	Halls-bry
Hamond	Hammond
Harcourt	Har-cut
Hardinge	Harding
Harewood	Har-wood (title), Hare-wood (village)
Harington	Harrington
Harwich	Harrich
Hawarden	Hay-warden
Haworth	Hay-worth, Harden for the title has become archaic
Heathcoat	Heth-cut
Heathcote	Heth-cut
Heneage	Hennidge
Hepburn	Heb-b'n
Herschell	Her-shell
Hertford	Har-ford
Hervey	Harvey
Hever	Heaver
Heytesbury	Hetts-b'ry
Heywood	Haywood
Hindlip	Hynd-lip
Hippesley	Hips-ley
Hobart	Hubbard (but as spelled for the city)
Hogan	Ho-gan
Holbech	Hole-beech
Home	Hume
Honywood	Honeywood
Hopetoun	Hopeton
Horsbrugh	Horsbro
Hotham	Huth-am
Housman	House-man
Howick	Hoyck
Hugessen	Hu-ges-son (hard 'g')
Huth	Hooth
Hylton	Hilton

Iddesleigh	Idd-sli
Ikerrin	I-kerrin
Iliffe	I-liffe
Inchiquin	Inch-quin
Inchrye	Inch-rye
Inchyra	Inch-eye-ra
Inge	Ing
Ingestre	Ingustry (like 'industry')
Inglis	Ingles, or as spelled
Inigo	Inni-go
Innes	Inniss
Inveraray	Inver-air-a
Ionides	Ion-ee-diz
Isham	I-sham
Iveagh	I-va
Jervis	As spelt or Jarvis
Jervoise	Jervis
Jocelyn	Josslin
Joiliffe	Jroii-if
Kaberry	Kay-berry
Kavenagh	Kavan-a
Kekewich	Keck-which
Keighley	Keith-li
Kemeys	Kemmis
Kennard	Ken-ard
Kenyon	Ken-yon
Ker	Car or Cur (hard 'c')
Kerr	Car or Cur (hard 'c')
Keynes	Kaynes
Killanin	Kil-lah-nin
Kilmorey	Kil-murray
Kingsale	King-sale
Kinnoull	Kin-ool
Kirkcudbright	Cuck-coo-bri
Knollys	Nowles
Kylsant	Kill-sant
Knyvett	Nivett

Lacon	Lay-kon
Laffan	Laf-fan
Lamplugh	Lamp-loo
Lascelles	Lass-ells
Lathom	Lay-thom
LaTouche	La Toosh
Latymer	Latimer
Laurie	Lorry
Layard	Laird
Leacock	Laycock or Leccock
Lechmere	Letchmere
Le Fanu	Leff-new
Lefevre	Le-fever
Legard	Le-jard
Legh	Lee
Leighton	Layton
Leinster	Linster
Leitrim	Leetrim
Le Mesurier	Le Mezz-erer
Leominster	Lemster
Leven	Lee-ven
Leverhulme	Leaver-hume
Leveson-Gower	Loosun-Gore
Levinge	As spelled (hard 'g')
Levy	Levvy or Leevi
Ley	Lay or Lee
Leycester	Lester
Liardet	Lee-ardet
Liddell	Lid-el
Lisle	Lyle
Listowel	Lis-toe-ell
Lombe	Loam (sometimes Lumb)
Londesborough	Londs-bro'
Londonderry	Londond'ry (title), London-Derry (city)
Loudon	Loud-on
Loughborough	Luff-bro
Louth	(England) 'th' as in 'mouth', (Ireland) 'th' as in 'breathe'

Lovat	Luv-at
Lowson	Lo-son ('lo' as in 'go')
Lowther	Low-thr ('low' as in 'now')
Lycett	Lisset
Lygon	Liggon
Lyon	Lion
Lysaght	Ly-set
Lyveden	Live-den (as in 'give')
Macara	Mac-ara
Macbean	Mac-bain
McCorquodale	M'cork-o-dale
McCulloch	M'cull-och
McDonagh	Mac-Donna
McEvoy	Mac-evoy
McEwan	Mac-ewen
McFadzean	Mac fadd-yen
McGillycuddy	Mac-li-cuddy
Machell	May-chel
McIvor	Mac-Ivor
McKay	M'Kye (as in 'eye')
McKie	Mack-ie (though some branches pronounce their name 'M'Kye')
Maclean	Mac-layne
Macleay	Mac-lay
Macleod	Mac-loud
McLachlan	Mac-lochlan
Macnaghten	Mac-nawton
Macmahon	Mac-mahn
Maelor	Myla
Magdala	Mag-dahla
Magdalen	Maudlin
Magdalene	Maudlin
Magrath	Ma-grah
Mahon	Mahn or Ma-han
Mahony	Mah-ni
Mainwaring	Manner-ing
Mais	Mayz
Majendic	Ma-jendy
Makgill	Mc-gill (hard 'g')

Malpas	Mawl-pas
Malet	Mallet
Malmsbury	Marms-bri
Mandeville	Mande-ville (first 'e' slightly inflected)
Mander	Mahnder
Mansergh	Manser
Margesson	Mar-jesson
Marjoribanks	Marchbanks
Marlborough	Maul-bro
Marquand	Mark-wand
Martineau	Martinowe
Masham	Mass-ham
Masserene	Mazereen
Mathias	Math-ias
Maugham	Mawm
Mauchline	Mauch (as in 'loch')-lynn
Maunsell	Man-sel
Meath	Meeth ('th' as in 'breathe')
Meiklejohn	Mickel-john
Melhuish	Mell-ish
Menteth	Men-teeth
Menzies	Ming-iz (Scotland)
Merioneth	Merry-on-eth
Mereworth	Merry-worth
Metcalfe	Met-calf
Methuen	Meth-wen
Meux	Mews
Meynell	Men-el
Meyrick	Merr-ick
Michelham	Mitch-lam
Michie	Micky
Midleton	Middle-ton
Millais	Mill-ay
Mocatta	Mow-catta
Molyneux	Mully-neux (senior branches) or Mully-nu
Monaco	Mon-aco
Monck	Munk
Monckton	Munkton
Monro	Mun-roe

Monson	Mun-sun
Montagu	Mon-tagu
Montgomery	Mun-gum-eri
Montgomerie	Mun-gum-eri
Monzie	M'nee
Moran	Moor-an
Moray	Murray
Mordaunt	Mor-dant
Mosicy	Mozeley
Mostyn	Moss-tin
Mottistone	Mottiston
Moulton	Mole-ton
Mountmorres	Mount-morris
Mowbray	Mo-bray
Mowll	Mole
Moynihan	Moy ni han
Munro	Mun-roe
Myddelton	Middle-ton
Mytton	Mitton
Naas	Nace
Naesmyth	Nay-smith
Nall	Nawl
Napier	Nay-pier
Nathan	Naythan
Nepean	Ne-peen
Newburgh	New-bro'
Niven	Nivven
Northcote	North-cut
Nunburnholme	Nun-burnham
Ochterlony	Ochter-lony
Offaly	Off-aly
Ogilvie	Ogle-vi
Ogilvy	Ogle-vi
O'Hagan	O'Hay-gan
Olivier	O-livier
O'Loghlen	O'Loch-len
Ormonde	Or-mund
O'Rourke	O'Rork

343

Outram	Oot-ram
Pakington	Packington
Paget	Paj-it
Pakenham	Pack-en'um
Pasley	Pais-li
Paton	Payton
Paulet	Paul-et
Paunceforte	Pawns-fort
Pauncefote	Pawns-foot
Pechell	Peach-ell
Pennefather	Penn-ifither or Penny-feather
Pennycuick	Penny-cook
Pepys	Peppis (Peeps has become archaic, except for the diarist and the Pepys Cockerell family)
Perceval	Percival
Pery	Pairy
Peto	Peet-o
Petre	Peter
Petrie	Peet-rie
Peyton	Payton
Phayre	Fair
Pierpoint	Pierpont
Pleydell	Pleddel
Plowden	Ploughden
Plumtre	Plum-tri
Pole	Pole or Pool (see also Carew)
Poltimore	Pole-ti-more
Polwarth	Pol-worth
Pomeroy	Pom-roy
Pomfret	Pum-fret
Ponsonby	Punsunby
Poulett	Paul-et
Powell	Powell (as in 'now') usually, or Poell
Powerscourt	Poers-caut
Powis	Po-iss (Earl)
Powlett	Paul-et
Powys	Po-iss (name)
	Powiss (place) (as in 'now')
Praed	Praid

Prevost	Prev-o
Prideaux	Priddo
Puleston	Pill-ston
Purefuy	Pure-foy
Pytchley	Pietch-li
Quibell	Quy-bel (as in 'high')
Raleigh	Raw-li
Ranfurly	Ran-fully
Rankeillour	Rank-illour
Ratendone	Ratten-dun
Rathdonnell	Rath-donnell
Rea	Ree
Rearsby	Rears-hi
Reay	Ray
Redesdale	Reads-dale
Renwick	Renn-ick
Reresby	Rears-bi
Reuter	Roy-ter
Rhyl	Rill
Rhys	Rees (usually), or Rice
Riddell	Riddle
Rideau	Reed-owe
Roborough	Roe-bra'
Roche	Roach, or sometimes Rosh
Roden	Roe-den
Rolfe	Roaf (as in 'loaf')
Rolleston	Roll-ston
Romilly	Rum-illy
Romney	Rumney
Ronaldshay	Ron-alld-shay
Rotherwick	As spelled
Rothes	Roth-is
Rous	Rowse (as in 'grouse')
Rouse	Rowse (as in 'grouse')
Rowley	Roe-li
Roxburghe	Rox-bro
Ruabon	Ru-a-bon
Ruthin	Ruth-in (as the girl's name)

Ruthven	Rivven
Sacheverall	Sash-ever-al
Sacheverell	Sash-ev-rell
St Aubyn	S'nt Aw-bin
St Clair	Correctly Sinclair, but sometimes as spelled
St Cyres	S'nt Sires (to rhyme with 'fires')
St John	Sin-jun
St Leger	Correctly Sill-inger but often St Leger
St Levan	S'nt Leaven (as in 'leaven' for bread)
St Maur	S'nt More
Salisbury	Sawls-bri
Salkeld	Saul-keld
Saltoun	Salt-on
Salusbury	Sawls-bri
Sandbach	Sandbatch
Sandeman	Sandy-man
Sandys	Sands
Sanquhar	Sanker (Sanwer is historically correct)
Saumarez	Summer-ez or Saumer-ez
Sausmarez	Summer-ez or Saumer-ez
Savernake	Savver-nack
Savile	Saville
Saye and Sele	Say and Seal
Schilizzi	Skil-it-zy
Schuster	Shoo-ster
Sclater	Slater
Scone	Scoon
Scudamore	Scooda-more
Scrymgeour	Scrim-jer
Sedburgh	Sed-ber
Segal	Seagal
Segrave	Sea-grave
Sele	Seal
Sempill	Semple
Seton	Seaton
Seymour	Seamer but sometimes as spelled
Shakerley	As spelled
Shaughnessy	Shawnessy
Sherborne	Shirb'n

Shrewsbury	Shrows-b'ry (town has alternative pronunciation of Shrews-b'ry)
Shuckburgh	Shuck-bro'
Sieff	Seef
Simey	Symey
Skene	Skeen
Skrine	Screen
Smijth	Smyth
Smyth	Smith or Smythe
Smythe	Smythe
Sneyd	Sneed
Somers	Summers
Somerset	Summerset
Sotheby	Sutha-by
Soulbury	Sool-bri
Southwark	Suth-erk
Southwell	Suth-ell (surname and city)
Sowerby	Sour-by
Spottiswoode	Spotswood
Stanhope	Stannup
Staordale	Stav-erdale
Stonor	Stone-er
Stourton	Sturton
Strabane	Stra-bann
Strabolgi	Stra-bogie (hard 'g')
Strachan	Strawn
Straghan	Strawn
Strahan	Strawn
Strachi	Stray-chie
Stratheden	Strath-eden
Strathspey	Strath-spay
Streatfield	Stret-field
Stucley	Stewk-li
Suirdale	Sure-dale
Sysonby	Size-on-by
Synge	Sing
Talbot	Tall-bot
Tangye	Tang-y
Taverne	Tav-erne

347

Taylour	Taylor
Teignmouth	Tin-muth
Terregles	Terry-glaze
Teynham	Ten-'am
Thame	Tame
Thellusson	Tellus-son
Theobald	Tibbald some families, or as spelled
Thesiger	Thesi-jer
Thorold	Thurrald
Thynne	Thin
Tichbourne	Titch-bourne
Tighe	Tie
Tollemache	Tol-mash (Tall-mash has become archaic)
Torphichen	Tor-kken
Touchet	Touch-et
Tovey	Tuvvy
Trafalgar	Traffle-gar (title only)
Traquair	Tra-quare
Tredegar	Tre-deegar
Trefusis	Tre-fusis
Trevelyan	Tre-villian
Trimlestown	Trimmels-ton
Trowbridge	Troobridge
Tuchet	Touch-et
Tuite	Tute
Tullibardine	Tulli-bard-in
Turnour	Turner
Tuvey	Tuvvy
Twohy	Too-y
Twysden	Twis-den
Tynte	Tint
Tyrrell	Tirrell
Tyrwhitt	Tirrit
Tyzack	Tie-sack
Urquhart	Urk-ut
Uvedale	Youv-dale
Vachell	Vay-chell
Valentia	Val-en-shia

Valletort	Valley-tort
Van Straubenzee	Van Straw-ben-zie
Vaughan	Vawn
Vaux	Vokes
Vavasour	Vav-assur
Verschoyle	Ver-skoil
Vesey	Veezy
Vigor	Vygor
Villiers	Villers
Vyvyan	Vivian
Waechter	Vechter (guttural 'ch')
Wagner	As spelled (English families)
Waldegrave	Wall-grave
Waleran	Wall-ran
Walmer	Wall-mer
Walrond	Wall-rond
Walsingham	Wall-sing'm
Walwyn	Wall-wyn
Wathen	Wothen
Wauchope	Walk-up ('ch' as in 'loch')
Waugh	As spelled, to rhyme with 'flaw'
Wavell	Way-vell
Weighall	Wy-gall
Weighill	Wey-hill
Wellesley	Wells-li
Wemyss	Weems
Wernher	Werner
Westenra	Westen-ra
Westmeath	West-meath ('th' as in 'breathe')
Westmorland	West-morland
Wharton	Whor-ton
Wigoder	Wigg-oder
Wigram	Wigg-ram
Wilbraham	Will-bram
Willoughby de Eresby	Willow-bi deersby
Willoughby de Broke	Willow-bi de Brook
Winder	Winn-der
Woburn	Woo-burn
Wodehouse	Wood-house

Wollaston	Wool-aston
Wolley	Wooly
Wolmer	Wool-mer
Wolrige	Wool-ridge
Wolseley	Wool-sli
Wombwell	Woom-well
Wontner	Wantner
Worsley	Wers-li or Werz-li
Wortley	Wert-li
Wriothesley	Rottisli
Wrottesley	Rotts-li
Wykeham	Wick-am
Wyllie	Wy-lie
Wyndham	Wind-'am
Wynford	Win-fud
Wynyard	Win-yard
Wythenshaw	With-in-shaw
Yeatman	Yaytman
Yerburgh	Yar-bra'
Yonge	Young
Zouche	Zooch

Spelling of Peerage Titles

Note: The following spellings differ from those now adopted for placenames.

England	Ailesbury, Guilford, Scarbrough, Winchilsea
Wales	Carnarvon, Powis
Ireland	Donegall, Downe, Kingsale, Rosse.

APPENDIX 3

TITLES AND STYLES IN FOREIGN COUNTRIES

Austria
Titles are not recognised under the Constitution but are used socially.

Belgium
The Belgian nobility consists of Princes, Dukes, Counts, Viscounts, Barons, Knights and untitled nobles, the right to confer such titles being given to the King by the Constitution of 7 February 1831. Titles carry no special privileges and are purely for social use. The Belgian equivalent to *Debrett's Peerage* is *Annuaire de la Noblesse de Belgique*, first published in 1847.

Members of the Royal Family
Members of the Royal Family and their Households, whether or not they are titled, are officially addressed on the envelope:

A Monsieur	or	A Madame
Monsieur le Comte de Bruges		Madame la Comtesse de Bruges

Monsieur, Madame, Mademoiselle
Monsieur, Madame and Mademoiselle are not abbreviated in correspondence.

Monsieur is appended before appointments and names, as in France.

It is not usual to add 'Monsieur', 'Madame' or 'Mademoiselle' before the title.

Envelope
The envelope is normally addressed 'Comte de . . .' or 'Comtesse de . . .'.

Denmark

There was no titled nobility in Denmark until 1671, when King Christian v introduced the titles of Count and Baron. There was one creation of a Duke in 1818, the title still being extant, and two of a Marquis (Markgrever) in 1709 and 1710, but these are both extinct. Titles were never very liberally bestowed, and Danish nobles were deprived of all their privileges by the Constitution of 1849. However, the use of titles is retained socially, and the Danish equivalent to *Debrett's Peerage* is *Danmarks Adels Aarborg*, which is still published.

Finland

The Finnish nobility dates from the establishment of the Grand Duchy of Finland under Emperor Alexander I of Russia in 1809, and a Finnish College of Nobles was founded in 1816. The titles of Prince, Count and Baron were conferred as well as untitled nobility.

Titles are still used socially, and the Finnish equivalent to *Debrett's Peerage* is *Finlands Adels och Ridderskap Kalender*, published annually from 1858 and triennially from 1926.

France

The French nobility, whose titles are now of social significance only, consists of Dukes, Marquises, Counts, Viscounts and Barons created before the Revolution and during the Restoration (1814–30), Princes, Dukes, Counts, Barons and Knights of the Empire created by Napoleon I and Napoleon III, and Dukes, Marquises, Counts, Viscounts and Barons created by Louis Philippe (1830–48). There have been several publications similar to *Debrett's Peerage* the best known is the *Annuaire de la Noblesse de France*, first published in 1843.

Monsieur, Madame, Mademoiselle

Should be followed by the first name and surname and are used in place of the title, both in writing and in speech.

'Monsieur' is appended before all appointments and names, as in Monsieur le Président de la République, Monsieur le Docteur.

Monsieur is better not abbreviated to M, nor Madame to Mme, nor Mademoiselle to Mlle in correspondence. Mons is never used.

'Monsieur', 'Madame', 'Mademoiselle' are universally used in speech to everyone, whatever their status.

Duke, Duchess, Ambassador
A Duke or Duchess is addressed as 'Monsieur le Duc' or 'Madame la Duchesse', respectively. Ambassadors are addressed as 'Excellence'.

Officers of the Armed Forces
An officer is referred to by men as 'Mon Colonel' and by women as 'Colonel' or 'Général'.

A Marshal is referred to by all as 'Monsieur le Maréchal'.

The wife or widow of a Marshal of France is referred to for all purposes as 'Madame la Maréchale'.

The wife of those with high office is often colloquially referred to by her husband's rank, as in 'Madame la Générale'.

Germany

The Republican Constitution of 1920 did not abolish titles of nobility but stipulated that they were to be an integral part of the name. This was confirmed by the Federal Republic 1949. Thus, the forename is used before the title on the envelope.

Graf is often left untranslated, but sometimes Count is used. It is sometimes followed by the family name (for example, Wolf-Metternich), but more often by von, or very occasionally 'von' and 'zu' (for example, 'von und zu Bodman'). 'Zu' means that the family still owns their name place. 'von and Zu' is a nineteenth-century bit of nonsense which nevertheless exists. Schwarzenberg and Hohenlohe are 'zu' alone.

It is suggested that a handbook on the nobility be consulted for the exact wording, or the Protocol/Correspondence Office at the Embassy of the Federal Republic of Germany be contacted on 0171 824 1300.

Baron, in place of the older German title of Freiherr, is used extensively in south Germany and in the Baltic states from where some families had migrated. Both are normally translated in English to Baron.

The prefix 'zu' is only used in writing. A Baron with both designations would be announced either as 'Baron von . . .' or 'Herr von . . .', but would not introduce himself with either prefix.

For those with an appointment such as professor, doctor etc., it is customary to refer to them as Herr Professor or Frau Doktor.

Beginning of Letter
Dear Graf (von) Blank (feminine form: Gräfin)

Dear Baron (von) Blank (Baronin is translated Baroness)

Titles are also borne by sons and unmarried daughters before their forenames. They are not retained by daughters who have married outside the nobility.

Envelope

German		English
Moritz,	Graf/Freiherr/Baron (von) . . .	Graf (von) . . . (or appropriate title)
Anna,	Gräfin/Freifrau/Baronin (von) . . .	Grafin (von). . . (or appropriate title)

Sons and daughters are addressed, both in German and English, by their titles before their forenames – for example, Graf Luitpold von Blank and Gräfin Anna von Blank – though they sometimes are addressed Moritz, Graf von. . ., on the grounds that Graf von . . . is the surname. An unmarried daughter of a Freiherr is Freiin, of a Baron is Baronesse, and of a Graf is identical with his wife, viz. Gräfin.

Italy

Titles were abolished by the 1947 Constitution and no longer have official status or legal protection, the only trace of them remaining being a territorial designation which may continue to be recognised as an adjunct to the surname.

Titles are, however, used socially and are complicated in that they were conferred by a variety of states and cannot be treated as an entity.

Generally, Italian titles are restricted to the head of family, and all recent letters patent embody this system.

Some great families have several territorial titles (from fiefs held). Some are known by their title and surname (for example, Il Principe Colonna); others are styled formally by their title and fief (for example, Il Principe di Montesole) or less formally by their title, fief and surname (for example, Il Principe di Montesole Castagnaro), which is useful for purposes of identification.

Members of certain families of the nobility bear the styles of Don and Donna, which form four main groups, viz. in Lombardy, Rome, Naples and Sardinia.

Children of a noble without the styles of Don and Donna, and without a territorial title, are styled, for example, 'Nobile Antonio dei Conti Selvatichelli', and with a territorial title 'Nobile Antonio Selvatichelli dei Conti di Acquatorta' (dei = of the family).

Personal styles may be listed as under:

1. Cavaliere ereditario (hereditary knights, which are usual in Sardinia, Lombardy and Venice)

2. Nobile, Cavaliere, Don (Sardinia)

3. Nobile, as a title

4. Nobile, as a member of a noble family

Wives of those in group 1 are addressed, both in writing and speech, as Signora.

Latin America

Though the language of all countries is Spanish, except for Brazil, which is Portuguese-speaking, forms of address vary according to the country. In some countries accents have been abolished.

Señor, Señora, Señorita

Mr, Mrs and Miss are translated in Spanish-speaking countries as Señor, Señora, and Señorita, and in Brazil as Senhor, Senhora and Senhorita. Here, unmarried ladies who are senior in age are addressed as Senhora.

The prefixes of Excelentisimo and Excelentisima (ladies) (Excelentissimo and Excelentissima in Brazil) are given in some countries, often abbreviated to Exmo and Exma or Excmo and Excma. In Brazil, Illustrissimo and Ilustrissima are used, often abbreviated to Ilmo and Ilma.

Don, Dom, Doña

The use of Don (Dom in Brazil) and Doña (Dona in Brazil) varies according to the country. In Brazil, Dom is not used as a form of address, apart from special instances, such as to priests.

Dona is placed after Senhora, when writing formally. It is also used in speech to slight acquaintances (for example, Dona Maria . . .).

In Mexico, Don and Doña are less used than in Colombia but often formally in the provinces. In Peru, don (note small d) is used on envelopes – for example, Señor don Pablo Sanchez – but doña is used only in special instances. In Chile, Don and Doña are not generally used.

It is a general rule to include doctor, professor etc. between Señor and Don, or between Señor and the name.

Liechtenstein
The Prince of Liechtenstein occasionally confers the titles of Count and Baron, which are of social significance only.

Luxembourg
The titles of Count and Baron are conferred from time to time by the Grand Duke of Luxembourg and are of social significance only.

Monaco
The Prince of Monaco occasionally confers the title of Baron, which is of social significance only.

The Netherlands

Hereditary Titles
There are four hereditary titles: Graaf, Baron, Ridder and Jonkheer.

Graaf and Gravin are usually translated as Count and Countess, and Baron and Baronesse as Baron and Baroness.

Ridder is confined to one or two families only.

The word 'Jonkheer' is placed before the initials or first name. His wife has 'Mevrouw' and unmarried daughters have 'Jonkvrouwe' before the name.

Speech
Dutch titles are not used in speech. All are referred to as Mijnheer (Mr), Mevrouw (Mrs) and Freule (Miss) van Dam.

Norway
There is no titled nobility in Norway, and hereditary untitled nobility was abolished in 1821.

Papacy

The Holy See confers titles of Principe, Duca, Marchese and Conte, but not Barone, on Roman Catholics in countries all over the world: for example, Count John MacCormack.

Portugal

Titles

Those with titles are addressed formally as:

Excelentissimo Senhor

Conde de . . . (or appropriate title)

But envelopes are often addressed:

Dom Manuel de Braganca

'Dom' is restricted to a few families, but the feminine equivalent of 'Dona' is customarily used for all ladies, whether married or single. The abbreviation D is frequently used for both Dom and Dona.

Excelentissimo (or the feminine form Excelentissima) is written in full for a distinguished person, such as a Minister, Ambassador etc. For others, including wives of ministers etc., the abbreviations Exmo and Exma are used.

Appointments

It is customary for those with appointments to be addressed 'Senhor Professor . . .' ('Prof' is abbreviated for ordinary schoolmasters), 'Senhor Doutor (Doctor) . . .' etc. with their degrees and university appended after the name.

Those with degrees of Licenciado (Master) or Bacharel (Bachelor) are styled 'Dr'.

Portuguese men may add their mother's name *before* the surname. A married lady may retain her maiden before her married surname.

Russian, Polish and Hungarian Families

The ranks of Prince, Count and Baron all precede the family name, as in Prince Orlov, Count Potocki and Baron Orczy. In Magyar, 'Graf' comes after the surname, but not in translation of Hungarian names.

In Russia, unless a name has a foreign origin when it is indeclinable, the feminine form of -ski (meaning 'of') becomes -skaya; similarly

359

with -skoy: for example, Troubetskoy, Troubetskaya.

Names from the Ukraine which end with 'o' are also indeclinable. It is usual to add the father's name before the patronymic, viz. Count Ivan Ivanovich Tolstoy, Countess Anna Alexandrovna Tolstaya.

Many families who have settled outside Russia do not use the feminine ending.

In Poland, the usual ending is '-ski', with the feminine form '-ska'. If the ending of the name is -cki, the feminine form is -cka: for example, Count Potocki, Countess Potocka. Certain names, such as Dubis, have the feminine form 'owa' (pronounced 'ova'), as in Dubisowa. Others are indeclinable: Debiec for both sexes, for example.

Spain

Royal Family
The eldest son and heir of the Sovereign is Prince of the Asturias. Younger sons receive the title of Infante, and daughters that of Infanta. These titles may also be granted by the Sovereign to other members of the Royal Family.

Titles
All Duques, some Marqueses and Condes, and a few Viscondes are Grandees of Spain. All Grandees and their consorts are Excellencies. The form of address of Excellency is also given to holders of Grand Crosses of various Orders, Ambassadors, Generals, Bishops and eldest sons of Grandees of Spain and their wives.

An envelope to a person with the style of Excellency is addressed Excelentisimo Señor, usually abbreviated to Excmo Sr Duque de . . .

If he has no title, this is followed by Don, e.g. 'Excmo Sr General Don', followed by his forename and surname.

Married ladies are addressed similarly as 'Excelentisima Señora', usually abbreviated to Excma Sra.

Nobles who are not Grandees are addressed on the envelope 'El Visconde de . . .' or appropriate title.

Grades of various Orders below Excellency rank are addressed Illustrious, viz. Ilustrisimo (feminine Ilustrisima), of which the abbreviations are Ilmo and Ilma.

Don is a customary form of respect, rather equivalent to our Esquire. It is used in polite speech when referring to a person by his forename:

for example, Don Juan. An envelope is addressed Señor Don Juan before his surname. Doña, the feminine form, is used in the same way, both in speech and on the envelope.

Señor (Sr), Señora (Sra) and Señorita (Srta) are the usual forms of address for those without titles. 'Señora' is followed by the addition of 'de' before the surname on the envelope. A married lady may also be addressed by her maiden surname with her husband's appended: for example, Sra Doña Maria Luisa (then her maiden name) de (followed by her husband's surname). If a husband and wife are addressed jointly, his full name is given, before his wife's, as in Señor Don Juan Lopez and Señora de Lopez. An unmarried lady is called and addressed 'Señorita Doña Maria Luisa' (followed by her surname).

A man's surname is often followed by his mother's maiden name – for example, Señor Don Francisco Moreno y Garcia – both in corres-pondence and on visiting cards.

Sweden

Although an untitled nobility existed in Sweden from about 1290, titles were not introduced until the reign of King Eric xiv in 1561, when he created three Counts and nine Barons at his coronation. The title of Duke was reserved for members of the Royal Family. No titles are now created, but they are still used socially. The Swedish equivalent of *Debrett's Peerage* is *Sveriges Ridderskap och Adels Kalender*, first published in 1854 and now appearing at two-yearly intervals. Male-line descendants of Swedish Counts and Barons bear the title of Count/Countess, Baron/Baroness before their first names. Women do not retain the title on marriage.

INDEX

Beaverbrook, Lord 59
Bedford, Duke of 49–50
Bedford, Earl of 48
Belgium 353
Belhaven, Master of 60
Benedictine Order 88, 240–3; *see also* Dames
Berkeley Dress Show 307
Birmingham, University of 117–18
Bishops 80, 211, 213–15, 248
   retired 214
   Roman Catholic 234–6, 249, 300
   legal advisers to 167
   signatures of 224–5
Black Knight 99
Blues and Royals 132, 134
Borthwick, Henry 95
bowing 18, 21
Brassey of Apethorpe, Baron 32
Brazil 357
Brigadiers 130, 144
British Academy 89
British Empire, the, Order of 74, 78
'Brother', style of 220–1, 231, 239, 244
brothers of peers, whose fathers did not live to succeed 58
Browning, Lady 79
Brunei, Sultan of 102
Buddhism 247
Burdett-Coutts, Baroness 40
Burghersh, Lord 50
business cards 289–90

Cabinet Ministers 80, 207, 292
cadet branches of Scottish families 62–3
Cambridge, University of 108–11, 114, 116–18
Cameron, Donald 95
Canada 80, 101, 153–4
   Order of 83–4
Canons 112, 211, 216–18, 238, 249
Canterbury, Archbishop of 80–1, 211–13

Captains
   in the Army 131, 144
   in the Royal Navy 124, 144
   of aircraft 202
   of ships 200–1
   see also Clan Chattan; Clanranald; Corps of Gentlemen; Yeomen of the Guard
Cardigan, Earl of 50
Cardinals 232–3, 249, 300
Carrick, Earldoms of (Scottish and Irish) 33
casual dress 305
Catholic Church 231–41, 249
chairmen and chairwomen, differentiation between 179, 253
chairmen referred to in preamble to speeches 298
Chancellor of the Exchequer 209
Chancellors of universities 107–8
Chaplains
   to the Armed Forces 223–4
   to His Holiness the Pope 236
Chargés d'Affaires 147, 151, 293
Chelsea Flower Show 307–8
Chief Constables 205–6
Chief Rabbi 245–6, 250
chiefs, Scottish 93–6, 103
   daughters of 97–8, 103
   dormant chiefships 93
   eldest sons of 97, 103
   wives and widows of 96–7, 103
   women chiefs 96
   younger sons of 97, 103
children
   of Baronets 72
   of Dames 79
   of disclaimed peers 59–60
   of Knights 78
   of peers *see* Barons; Dukes; Earls; Marquesses; Viscounts
   of Scottish chiefs 97–8, 103
the Chisholm 94
Chisholm, Madam 96
Christmas cards 287–8

Church in Wales 213–14, 225
Church of England 211–25, 248–9
Church of Ireland 212, 215, 225
Church of Scotland 225–7
Churchill, Lady 78
Circuit Judges 165–6
cities as distinct from towns 190
City of London Police 203
civil service 208–9
Clan Chattan, Captain of 94
clan chiefs *see* chiefs, Scottish
Clanranald, Captain of 94
clergymen 73, 112, 211, 219, 227,
   229, 249, 264, 300
   wives of 77
   see also Archdeacons; Canons;
      Deans; Prebendaries; Provosts
   coats of arms 13
College of Arms 10, 13
Collier, William 60
Colonels 131, 144
Commanders
   Police Force 204
   Royal Navy 124–5, 144
Commissioners of Police 203, 206
Commodore Chief Engineers 200–1
Commodores
   Merchant Navy 200–1
   Royal Navy 124, 144
Companion of Literature award 89
Companions of Honour 82
Comptroller of the Royal Household
   23
Congregational Church 228
Consorts of lady Mayors and lady
   Lord Mayors 184, 186, 191
Consuls 152–3
Convenors of Scottish Councils 179–
   80, 188
 wives of 190
Cornets 132
Coroners 167
Corps of Gentlemen, Captain of 23
Council for National Academic
   Awards 119

Council of Engineering Institutions
   91
Councillors 187–8, 190–1
Countesses 5, 42, 60, 64; *see also*
   Earls: wives
Counts of Malta 101
County Councils, Chairmen of 179,
   292–3
County Court judges 87
Court of Appeal 161–3
Courtesy Lords *see* peers by courtesy
courtesy styles and titles 12, 30–1,
   45–50 *passim*, 55–6, 61–2
Crawford, Earl of 61
Crown Equerry 22–3
Cunliffe-Lister, John 49
curtsying 18, 21
Curzon of Kedleston, Lord 31

Dames 12, 70, 76, 78–9, 102, 303
   children of 79
Dames Grand Cross 78
Dames of Justice and of Grace 78
Dames of the Benedictine Order 88,
   222–3, 241
Davies, Lord Justice 162
Davies, Lord Justice Edmund 163
Deaconess of the Methodist Church
   228
Dean of the Chapel Royal 227
Dean of the Thistle 227
Deans 211, 215–16, 248
'Dear ...' 4–5, 7
debutantes 307
decorations, wearing of 260, 303
deed poll 10
degrees, academic 88, 115–19, 295
Denmark 354
dental practitioners 193, 199
Department of Health 198
Deputes 190
Deputy Lieutenants 87, 166
Deputy Prime Minister 209
Derby, the 308
Deskford, Master of 61